Conversations
with Maharishi

Conversations with Maharishi

Maharishi Mahesh Yogi
Speaks about the Full Development
of Human Consciousness

VOLUME I

Vernon Katz

Published by
Maharishi University of Management Press
Fairfield, Iowa, United States of America

ISBN 978-0-923569-36-5

PRINTED IN CHINA

To Maharishi
with deep gratitude

Author's Note

Written in 2011

Iwas fortunate to encounter Maharishi's teachings from near their beginnings. I marvel at their beauty — the way they opened up like a beautiful flower. He was not like other teachers, doling out a fixed corpus of knowledge. He was always exploring new avenues and new practical programmes, forever refining and expanding. His teaching was a living, growing organism.

Partly as a result of this constant expansion, work such as translation of the Brahma Sūtra — and publication of these conversations — did not always come to immediate fruition. It is hoped that the translation and commentary that Maharishi did over the years on the Brahma Sūtra will be published before too long, as they will be Maharishi's definitive statement whereas these conversations are supplementary. The conversations in this volume date from 1968 and 1969; a second volume is planned for conversations that took place in the early seventies. The introductory material dates from the time between 1968 and 1976. I have made only minimal changes, keeping the use of present tense, and have not tried to update the material. Consequently Maharishi's later teaching is not included except for a brief overview of the whole teaching in an appendix.

The basic message of knowledge of the inner Self and of

the unity of all things was always there but new details kept emerging and new areas of knowledge were covered. Each stage of Maharishi's teaching is complete, coherent, and consistent, able to stand on its own, and should be respected as such. Each phase has its beauty and its legitimacy. We cannot judge Beethoven just by his late quartets and leave out the piano concertos and violin sonatas and so on.

The earlier knowledge has its own integrity, which should be upheld — to do justice to the beautiful edifice of knowledge that Maharishi gave the world. By understanding the earlier knowledge one perceives the whole beauty of the development of Maharishi's teaching — how he builds on what has gone before. He has gone more deeply into each area of Vedic knowledge and at the same time has widened the scope of each area.

Maharishi has bestowed an extraordinary legacy of knowledge on all mankind, and we can only bow in gratitude when we review the treasury that he left us.

CONTENTS

INTRODUCTION

BACKGROUND TO THE CONVERSATIONS

GROWTH OF HIGHER STATES OF CONSCIOUSNESS

THE UNFOLDMENT OF MAHARISHI'S TEACHING

MAHARISHI AS COMMENTATOR AND TEACHER

THE CONVERSATIONS

I

ON THE NATURE AND PURPOSE
OF DISCUSSION — AN OVERALL PERSPECTIVE

II

LAKE TAHOE, CALIFORNIA: SUMMER 1968

CONTENTS

III

SRINAGAR, KASHMIR: SUMMER 1969

Acknowledgements

Most of all I would like to thank Sue Brown for editing the final manuscript. Her suggestions were always apt and to the point, her eagle eye spotted any mistakes and inconsistencies, and she lifted many a burden from my shoulders. It was she, not I, who kept the manuscript moving towards publication. I cannot thank her enough for enabling me just to focus on the text. I have been very fortunate in my editor. The commitment and expertise of Harry Bright, director of Maharishi University of Management (MUM) Press, have also been invaluable in the final stages of preparation for printing.

I would also like to thank my friend Tom Egenes for checking the Sanskrit and for the laborious task of putting all the diacritical marks into a text swimming with Sanskrit terms. To accommodate the numerous letters of the Sanskrit alphabet (more than double the number of our modern Latin alphabet), Tom has applied the simplified method of transliteration favoured by MUM, which makes the text easier to read.

Michael Dillbeck and Susan Dillbeck made valuable suggestions for improving the book. I am really grateful to them for taking time off from their many responsibilities to give their attention to this work.

Star designer Shepley Hansen has overseen the layout and design, including the cover. I am most grateful to him. My thanks also go to Nora Mylett and Susan Marcus for proof-reading the text, quite a major undertaking.

The conversations were assembled and transcribed in the early seventies and I would like to pay tribute to people who helped in those distant days. My gratitude goes to the late Jessica Ware for her help and encouragement. I learnt to appreciate her thoroughness and good sense, and her fine feeling for Maharishi's language, when we worked together on the manuscript of Maharishi's Bhagavad-Gītā commentary. Her suggestions for the present volume were most valuable.

I should also like to thank Judy Booth for helping me assemble my unruly manuscripts and for her preliminary editing of various sections of this book. Without her meticulous work, many more errors and ambiguities would have remained.

My special thanks to Joanne Napoli for reading through the manuscript and suggesting a number of important changes, and to Robert M. Oates Jr., for his expert suggestions, especially concerning the Introduction.

I was fortunate in being able to turn to Anne Chetwynd-Stapylton, Tom Murphy, Myron Feld, and Ingrid Hergstrom for highly intelligent transcribing and typing. I am also extremely grateful to Daphne Grace for all her patient editorial work and technical advice.

Lastly, I should like to thank my late business partner, Guido Bianchi, but for whose kindness and forbearance in enabling me to spend so much time with Maharishi over the years, this book would not have been possible.

About the Text

This book is a record of conversations that took place at Lake Tahoe, California, in the summer of 1968, and at Srinagar, Kashmir, during the following summer. On both occasions I was working with Maharishi on his translation of and commentary on the Brahma Sūtra, the basic text of the Vedānta philosophy. Some of the conversations are simply interludes between sessions of work on the Sūtra, while in others some question of translation or interpretation forms the starting point for a more general discussion. However, quite a number of the conversations are directly concerned either with the significance of the Brahma Sūtra as a whole, or with the translation and meaning of one or more of its 555 component sūtras. Where possible, the sūtra being discussed is identified. (The Brahma Sūtra has four chapters, known as adhyāya, each with four sections or pāda. Thus, for example, BS 2.2.18 means chapter 2, section 2, sūtra 18.)

In the Lake Tahoe material there are few general discussions; most of the conversations deal specifically with the Brahma Sūtra. In order to keep a continuity of theme I have followed on with similar Brahma Sūtra conversations in the first part of the Kashmir section. The earlier part of the book is perhaps, therefore, more technical and less easy of access than the later part. This may not seem a very logical order, but I thought it best to begin with the Tahoe conversations, which represent the first fruit of Maharishi's thinking on the Brahma Sūtra. The reader interested in general discussions about higher states of consciousness may prefer to start with the conversation in the Kashmir section entitled 'Ultimate Reality and Different States of Consciousness' and go on till the end of the book, before starting on the earlier conversations.

Except for keeping the Tahoe and Kashmir conversations separate, I have made no attempt to maintain the chronological order. Rather, I have tried to group together related themes wherever possible. Because the conversations are so varied and wide-ranging, it has not always been easy to maintain a continuity of argument, and the titles give only a very general idea of the subject matter.

During 1974 and 1975 I read Maharishi most of the conversations I had selected for the book, and from time to time he commented on one or another of them. I have embodied these additional explanations as footnotes or, where they turned into new conversations, as postscripts to the original conversations on which they comment.

At the beginning of the text, before the Tahoe section, I have reproduced two conversations which also date from the 1970s. They give Maharishi's views on the nature and purpose of discussion and should help to put all the other conversations into a proper perspective.

All the material in the conversations themselves has been transcribed from tapes. There are some omissions in the text, especially when the discussion is about Sanskrit words. Provided the sense is continuous I have not indicated such omissions, nor the inevitable tape breaks. A definite break in subject-matter is marked by * * * below the line. In the text of the conversations dots (...) indicate implied omissions where sentences trail off, are interrupted, or are otherwise left unfinished. For quotations given in the Introduction and footnotes, dots are used in the usual way to indicate omission of subject-matter. Additional explanations, which I have provided where the text does not seem clear, are in square brackets.

When quoting Maharishi in the introductory and footnote material, I occasionally drew on transcripts of conversations recorded as part of the work on this book, and from other talks during these same years. I also drew on my own notes, including those of unrecorded talks. Maharishi permitted me the privilege, at the time, of working in this way. It is rewarding to see that as Maharishi's knowledge has unfolded in subsequent years into a whole discipline of his Vedic Science℠, academic standards of referencing have been adopted for scholarly work in this area.

Because there are so many Sanskrit words, these are given in plain roman type with the English meaning in brackets wherever this seems called for. This enables me to use italics to show when words, Sanskrit as well as English, are being emphasized. As this book is not particularly intended for scholars, I have used a simple system of transliteration (that preferred by Maharishi University of Management Press, publishers of this volume).

For the Brahma Sūtra I have used Maharishi's translations. For the first six chapters of the Bhagavad-Gītā I have used the translations given in Maharishi's published commentary. Translations of other classical Sanskrit texts, including the later chapters of the Bhagavad-Gītā, are my own. Where no author is mentioned I am quoting from Maharishi.

Abbreviations

BS:	The Brahma Sūtra. (Translations are those of Maharishi at the time of the conversations.)
SBS:	Shankara's commentary on the Brahma Sūtra. See *The Brahma Sūtra Sankara Bhāsya, with commentaries of Bhamati, Kalpataru and Parimala, edited with notes, etc., by Anantkrisna Sastri*, re-edited by Bhargav Sastri Sastracarya.
BU:	The Bṛihadāraṇyaka Upanishad. (Translations of the Upanishads are those of the author.)
CU:	The Chhāndogya Upanishad.
MU:	The Muṇḍaka Upanishad.
BG:	The Bhagavad-Gītā.

SBG: Shankara's commentary on the Bhagavad-Gītā. See *The Bhagavad-Gītā with the Commentary of Sri Sankarācārya*, critically edited by Dinkar Vishnu Gokhale, second revised edition.

MBG: *Maharishi Mahesh Yogi on the Bhagavad-Gita. A New Translation and Commentary with Sanskrit Text, Chapters 1 to 6.*

YS: The Yoga Sūtra. See *Yoga Philosophy of Patanjali, containing his Yoga Aphorisms with the commentary of Vyāsa in original Sanskrit, and annotations thereon with copious hints on the practice of Yoga,* by Swami Hariharānanda Āraṇya, rendered into English by P. N. Mukerji.

*His Holiness Maharishi Mahesh Yogi and Vernon Katz
at Lake Tahoe, California, U.S.A., in the summer of 1968, working
on Maharishi's translation of and commentary on the Brahma Sūtra.
The conversations in this book took place that summer and
the following summer in Kashmir, India.*

INTRODUCTION

Written in 1976

BACKGROUND TO THE CONVERSATIONS

Meeting Maharishi

It was my privilege and joy on many occasions over a dozen or more years to sit in conversation with His Holiness Maharishi Mahesh Yogi. Maharishi is best known as the practical teacher who introduced the Transcendental Meditation® technique to the world. The present volume brings out the more philosophical side of his genius, which expresses the insights of deep inner silence. He is seen here primarily as a commentator on one of the great philosophical texts of India, speaking to someone with a background in Indian philosophy and an argumentative turn of mind. The phase in Maharishi's life where he could spend time in intimate conversation on philosophical topics came to an end soon after those years of working with him. It was a very precious period for me, and in this book I should like to share its happiness and its insights with others.

I first met Maharishi in the summer of 1960, in London. He was sitting in a small room on the first floor of number two Prince Albert Road, a house overlooking Regents Park. I was introduced to him as a former student of Dr. Sarvepalli

Radhakrishnan, the eminent Indian philosopher and states-
man. Almost his first words to me were something like this:
'Ah, I met Dr. Radhakrishnan some years ago. He was saying
that meditation and Self-realization were arduous and difficult, and I said, "But it is so easy to dive within — simple." '

I immediately began to object, stoutly defending the
Radhakrishnan position, and thus was set the pattern of our
interchanges. I do not recall the details of this first conversation, only the quality and frequency of Maharishi's laughter.
It seemed in those days as if the inner bliss would not be
contained. Only the slightest excuse was needed for it to spill
over into heartfelt laughter. As he laughed his whole frame
seemed to vibrate with life and with joy. It was as if he were
floating and yet had his feet firmly planted on the ground.

I was captivated but not convinced. The idea that meditation was easy — that one did not have to prepare for it by
long periods of concentration — ran counter to everything I
had heard, and I remember thinking: 'You are very charming
and I like you very much, but either you don't know what
you are saying or else you don't mean what you are saying.'
I opted for the latter alternative, accounting for Maharishi's
assertions by the need to give people some hope, just to make
them start on the path.

This encounter with Maharishi was not by any means my
first with Eastern men of wisdom. At Oxford University I
had helped run a small group whose purpose it was to en-
tice to the city of dreaming spires any such luminaries as

happened to touch upon our shores. A variety of swāmis, lamas, bhikkus, imams, and archimandrites would come to enlighten us, their advent sometimes preceded by a lengthy correspondence about the demands of their diet. And when I settled in London, my many Indian friends saw to it that I did not miss any visiting spiritual celebrities from their country. They took me on a number of pilgrimages to the outer suburbs where we would sit at the feet of these lights of Asia in the homes of Indian businessmen, crammed for the occasion with devotees and curiosity seekers. In the search for Eastern wisdom personified I met many good and even holy people, but once I had seen Maharishi I realized that none of them had possessed that quality of lively joy which he had in such full measure. It was this quality that attracted me to him — not what he said, but what he was.

By the time I met Maharishi I was no longer an active 'seeker'. All the Indian friends from my university days had gone home and I was absorbed in the world of business. It was during a dinner at Bianchi's Restaurant in Soho that I first heard about Maharishi. The relatives I was meeting brought along a friend of theirs, who happened to be one of Maharishi's 'meditation guides'. He told us about the guru who was setting up house in Regents Park and in the weeks that followed he telephoned two or three times, inviting me to meet this interesting addition to the London scene. Finally I went, more or less as a matter of courtesy, little knowing what influence that courtesy call was to have on my life.

Maharishi certainly revived my interest in Indian philosophy. From our first meeting I became an almost daily visitor to the house in Prince Albert Road. On the very next day he asked me to go to Oslo and arrange a meeting for him there. Being more of a talker than a doer, I politely but firmly declined the honour. But when it came to matters less strenuous and incommoding, like the preparation of booklets and other material, I put my talents, such as they were, at his disposal.

Most of those around Maharishi at that time were, like myself, seekers — people no longer very young, who had been shopping around for the wisdom of the soul. 'Scratched slates', Maharishi sometimes used to call us. We were very different from the young people who came to Maharishi later in the sixties and in the seventies. Each one of us was a prima donna, assuming our own right to Maharishi's full attention. In the evenings he met us either in the lecture room or in his own bedroom and, his face shining, answered our often naive questions with great patience and goodwill. On the days when he was initiating people into Transcendental Meditation there would be crowds waiting in the hall and lining the stairs, but on the whole it was an intimate, 'āshram' kind of existence. We were like a big family, and so far as I was concerned this cozy idyll could have gone on forever.

But Maharishi never meant to devote himself to just one small group of people, and soon after I met him he began his journeys to the Continent, which were a prelude to his world tours of the sixties. In one of the first booklets with which I helped, Maharishi said: 'My mission is to regenerate the world.' I did not take this statement very seriously. In the context of our small group it seemed more like an amiable idiosyncrasy, an oriental flourish. But Maharishi never doubted his own mission. If it were to survive, mankind needed to regain contact with its own inner core, and by the grace of his master he had a simple, universally applicable procedure which could bring about this spiritual regeneration.

I was fascinated by Maharishi and loved to hear him talk and to work, argue, and plan with him. But I looked on myself as an intellectual seeker, and Dr. Radhakrishnan had emphasized that meditation itself was difficult. It was preconceived ideas such as this that prevented me, at first, from understanding Maharishi's teaching. Whenever he said something, whether to give practical instruction or philosophical explanation, I did a quick double-think and interpreted his words in my own terms: he says this but he really means that. It took me some time before I would allow his teaching to exist in its own right.[1]

I remember when the change in my attitude began. I was attending Maharishi's first European residence course, in the Black Forest over Christmas 1960. The talk was of some experience in meditation. Maharishi linked this experience to one of the creation stories from the Upanishads,

---

1 I have noticed some others, especially Indians, doing the self-same thing — interpreting Maharishi's teaching in terms of their received ideas, rather than really listening to him.

the great Sanskrit writings that give the clearest description to be found in any language of the ultimate ground of all existence. He said that in Transcendental Meditation, as we go deep within, we traverse the whole process of creation backwards. As the mind settles down, we experience all the steps of creation right back to their source in a pure, absolute, transcendental field of unity, unbounded and without parts. Somehow this explanation opened a door. I suddenly realized that here was a man who could bring the Upanishads to life — and the Upanishads had been for me, ever since I first read them with Dr. Radhakrishnan, the most complete expression of wisdom extant.

During the rest of the course I asked Maharishi question after question, and in his replies wisdom seemed to pour over me like a cascade as one truth after another dawned upon my now receptive mind. I began to understand, too, what Maharishi meant when he said that meditation was simple and easy, and that the one-pointedness of the mind, the non-attachment, the surrender of the sense of 'I' and 'mine', which were generally regarded as means to Self-realization, were really its results. Maharishi must have noticed that something had changed, for when I said good-bye to him in Munich he smiled and said: 'Very good, very good, you have unlearnt a lot of things.' On the plane back to London it came to me with a feeling of very great gratitude that I had to seek no further: I had found what I had been looking for years ago when I made those pilgrimages.

Work on the Bhagavad-Gītā

In 1961 Maharishi went back to India for some months to give a Teacher Training Course. A friend, Ulla Goodman, who was attending the course, sent me a glowing account of how Maharishi had begun, on the banks of the Ganges, a translation of and commentary on the Bhagavad-Gītā. My curiosity was at once aroused, since that much-loved text had formed the subject of my doctoral thesis at Oxford. When Maharishi continued work on the Gītā after his return to Europe it seemed natural that I should be one of those principally involved, especially as I was then the only person around him who had a little Sanskrit. This work went on over the next four or five years whenever Maharishi could spare a few days from his endless round of lecturing and teaching, and I would be with him whenever I could take time off from business. The Gītā was translated and discussed on land, sea, and in the air, in town houses and country houses, by the Thames and by the Ganges, in the Alps, and on the canals of Venice.

I had never known such happiness as this work with Maharishi gave me. Each person finds in Maharishi what he seeks, according to his own level, and Maharishi treats each according to his needs. There are those to whom he says very little and who have little to say to him because speech is unnecessary. My way of approaching him was very much through speech — argumentative speech, to be precise. I love to argue, and fortunately Maharishi enjoyed the challenge. One had only to attend one of his courses to see the delight he took in a lively, questing mind. A discussion on the Gītā would usually begin with a particular point relating to a translation and commentary, but it often tended to continue for the sheer joy of argument, although Maharishi was obviously teaching and I learning as I argued.

I would uphold the traditional interpretations but at the same time was thrilled to find myself in the presence of a wholly original mind. In the very process of disputing his interpretations I would realize how fresh was Maharishi's approach. He is unbound by the past and unawed by experts. The clear light of his intellect lights up everything on which it falls, whether it concerns printing, building, organization, or Indian philosophy. Once I had begun to grasp his way of approaching the central themes of the Gītā I wondered why I had never drawn the same conclusions myself — they seemed so obvious and so just.[2]

Unfortunately none of the conversations relating to the Gītā were recorded. For this I can hardly forgive myself. When the idea of taping the sessions did fleetingly cross my mind it was quickly and selfishly crushed by the thought that a recording device would interpose an artificial element and

---

2 Maharishi's fresh insights into the Bhagavad-Gītā are too numerous to be summarized here. The reader is referred to *Maharishi Mahesh Yogi on the Bhagavad-Gita: A New Translation and Commentary with Sanskrit Text, Chapters 1 to 6* (Penguin Books, 1969), especially to pp. 135, 139, 157, and 433.

prevent the free flow of conversation. I realized how wrong that thought had been when, in 1968, I finally invested in a cassette tape recorder. One quickly became completely oblivious of the machine, so much so that the conversations used to run on long after the tape had run its course. The warning bleep of later models has put an end to this danger.

The Present Conversations

The present conversations start from the acquisition of that first tape recorder. I took the new toy with me when Maharishi called me to Lake Tahoe in northern California in the summer of 1968, and again to Kashmir in the following summer, to work with him on the translation of and commentary on the Brahma Sūtra, the basic text of the Vedānta philosophy. The conversations reproduced here relate to those two visits. I chanced upon them while listening to tapes in order to prepare summaries of Maharishi's commentaries. There, hidden among long discussions about Sanskrit words, were these precious talks. I began to transcribe them for my own pleasure and that of a few friends.

Only later did the thought of sharing them more generally arise. Eventually I asked Maharishi if they could be published and he allowed me to go ahead.

Culled as they are from different tapes recorded over a period of some two months each summer, the conversations have no continuity of theme, except in so far as the raising of human consciousness is the theme of all that Maharishi says, does, and is. Many of them might well be described as Maharishi's table-talk — quite literally, because the conversations often took place during meals. Maharishi being Maharishi, it is table-talk of a high order, but one should not expect the extended and considered expositions of his teaching that are to be found in his lectures and his books. The conversation form, while it makes for intimacy and liveliness, also interrupts the flow of teaching.

The Brahma Sūtra

The text around which the conversations centre, the Brahma Sūtra, came as quite a change after the poetic riches of the Bhagavad-Gītā. The sūtra is a favourite form in Indian classical literature. It consists of a string ('sūtra' literally means 'thread') of aphorisms — short, highly compact expressions with an infinitely expanded range of meaning: 'an ocean of knowledge contained within a drop'.[3] These terse phrases and sentences form a shorthand language designed to convey the essence of a teaching in a way that is easy to memorize and hand down to future generations. It is not always quite so easy for future generations to decipher the meaning. The true sūtra is elliptical, stripped of inessentials — there are very few verbs — and provides a happy hunting-ground for commentators, and commentators on commentators.

There are sūtras on every kind of topic from grammar to astrology. Each of the six classical systems of Indian philosophy

_____

3 Humboldt State College, California, 17 August 1971.

— Nyāya, Vaisheshika, Sāṁkhya, Yoga, Karma Mīmāṁsā, and Vedānta — is based on sūtras ascribed to the system's traditional founder and stating its principal tenets in a concise form.

Each such expression is also known as a sūtra, hence the use of the plural, Brahma Sūtras, Yoga Sūtras, etc., as well as Brahma Sūtra, Yoga Sūtra. In the text I use capitals when referring to the Brahma Sūtra, or Sūtras, as a whole, and lower case when referring to particular sūtras. The Brahma Sūtra, or Vedānta Sūtra as it is also called, is the fundamental text of the sixth of the six systems, the Vedānta, and its author, Bādarāyaṇa, is traditionally identified with the great Vyāsa, who gathered together the Veda and other ancient texts.[4] The six systems are known as 'darshaṇas', 'cognitions', or 'points of view', which indicates that they are regarded as complementary rather than mutually exclusive. Each has its own job to do and does it to perfection. Each gives us the criteria for understanding some aspect of the truth. Maharishi has said that for knowledge to be complete, correct, and useful, it must be verified by each of the six systems.[5]

According to Maharishi, as I understand him, the Nyāya Sūtra of Gautama investigates the correct approach to the object of enquiry. Nyāya (justice) is the science of just rea-

---

4 The Veda (the word means 'knowledge') comprises a whole corpus of texts, beginning with the four Vedas — Ṛig, Sāma, Yajur, and Atharva — and including the Upanishads, which are the source of the Brahma Sūtra (also known as Vedānta Sūtra — Vedānta literally means 'end of the Veda').

5 MBG Introduction, p. 21.

soning. The Vaisheshika Sūtra of Kaṇāda analyses the specific qualities (vishesha) that distinguish the object from other objects. The Sāṁkhya-pravacana Sūtra of Kapila digs more deeply into the object of enquiry in order to enumerate (Sāṁkhya) its ultimate constituents. Sāṁkhya is a dualistic system. It finds that the knowing subject, the life-principle (Purusha), is in reality quite separate from nature, the principle of objectivity (Prakṛiti), and from its twenty-three evolutes, even though the presence of Purusha is necessary for Prakṛiti to evolve. The Yoga Sūtra of Patanjali shows how the knowledge discovered by Sāṁkhya can be brought to direct experience — how the subject can know himself so clearly that he recognizes his complete singularity (kaivalya) and self-sufficiency, entirely independent of and isolated from the changing world of objects. The Mīmāṁsā Sūtra of Jaimini is an investigation (Mīmāṁsā) into the whole world of activity (karma), which has been excluded by Patanjali from the goal of life. Jaimini locates the source of activity within the structure of the subject himself as he is realized in his state of kaivalya. Finally, the Brahma Sūtra, or Vedānta Sūtra, of Bādarāyaṇa goes a step further than Jaimini and finds knowledge to be at the basis of every grain of action. Its 'higher investigation' (Uttara Mīmāṁsā)[6] is able to overcome the duality between the subject and the world of objects, between Purusha and Prakṛiti, by recognizing as their common

---

6 The Vedānta System is also known as 'Uttara Mīmāṁsā' to distinguish it from the 'Pūrva Mīmāṁsā', or 'earlier investigation', of Jaimini.

basis that knowledge of totality which is able to hold both of them together in a single wholeness of awareness.[7]

The Brahma Sūtra is the king of sūtras, for its subject, Brahman, is the wholeness of life. When, following some commentators, I tried to interpret a sūtra in terms of a particular aspect of life, without reference to its wholeness, Maharishi gently rebuked me: 'These are *Brahma* Sūtras (sūtras about Brahman), not *jagat* sūtras (sūtras about the world).'[8] To know Brahman one has to awaken to that wholeness of awareness which encompasses everything, which leaves out nothing.[9] And when one knows Brahman one *is* Brahman. Brahman is a state of consciousness. 'The reality of Brahman is only the reality of the knower. Brahman is not there without a knower, because it is just that level of awareness ... That is why it is said, "brahmavid brahmaiva bhavati"[10] ... The knower is nothing other than Brahman and therefore

---

7 When Maharishi speaks of Vedānta he always has in mind this interpretation of the Brahma Sūtra from the point of view of non-dualism (advaita). But there are other interpretations — see introduction to 'The Significance of Maharishi's Commentary for the Modern Age'.

8 Quote drawn from additional material in the recorded conversations transcribed for this book.

9 'That is the awakening about the Great, the Huge, enveloping everything, leaving off nothing. The entire course of action, the whole unboundedness of the field of non-action — all taken together in one awareness, and that awareness is ... the structure of Brahman, the knowledge of totality.' Seelisberg, Switzerland, July 1977. The nature of this wholeness of awareness should become clearer as the Introduction proceeds.

10 'The knower of Brahman is Brahman', MU 3.2.9. The Upanishad says: 'brahmaveda brahmaiva bhavati.'

Brahman is nothing other than the knower.'[11]

Maharishi likes to explain wholeness by way of an analogy. 'The whole is something more than the collection of parts. The house is more than the walls, floor, and ceiling put together, but without these components the house will not be found.'[12] We could say that the 'houseness' of the house is Brahman, and that its components are the experiences of higher states of consciousness. Brahman is built up out of these experiences but transcends them, not because it is an empty abstraction but because it is completely full — it excludes nothing.

The word 'Brahman' derives from the root 'brih', to grow great, and its present participle, 'brihat' — vast, abundant, huge, unbounded. The Brahma Sūtra traces the steps whereby Brahman waxes great in the awareness, until it becomes full-grown as that vast, unbounded whole which is more than the collection of the different states of awareness out of which it has grown. The story of Brahman, therefore, is the story of the growth of consciousness. I tell that story in some detail here because Brahman will, after all, remain an empty abstraction unless it is seen in the context of the states of consciousness out of which it has evolved, the parts that structure the whole. Maharishi sees the Brahma Sūtra mainly as the final pages of the story, but it is difficult to understand the climax of a tale without reading what has gone

---

11 Conversation, Vittel, France, 19 December, 1973.
12 Lake Tahoe, California, 30 November, 1972.

before. From one point of view, indeed, the Brahma Sūtra tells the whole story. The very first sūtra reads: 'Now from here the desire to know Brahman.' Commenting on it in Kashmir (1969), Maharishi said: ' "From here" means, having taken birth as man, having gained this beautiful nervous system. Anything that is born evolves; evolution is natural. Vyāsa wants everyone to evolve in such a manner that the course of evolution is known to himself, not just to drift on the path of evolution like a river which does not know where it is heading. He wants everyone to desire to know Brahman, and then to evolve to that value [Brahman] ... The sūtra exhorts us to desire for the knowledge of Brahman, not in the future but here and now. Begin from here, from this moment, from this level of consciousness, from this place ... start to desire now.'

GROWTH OF HIGHER STATES OF CONSCIOUSNESS

It is in any case difficult to understand the final pages of a book without reading what has gone before. With this in mind I propose to give an outline of the growth of consciousness, as explained by Maharishi, trusting that this will provide useful background knowledge even for those conversations not directly concerned with the nature of Brahman.

The beneficial effects of Transcendental Meditation on one's life are well known. Here I will concentrate on its capacity to bring about higher states of consciousness.

Maharishi discusses in depth how growth of higher states of consciousness takes place through regular practice of the Transcendental Meditation technique.[13] This growth is accompanied by physical and psychological changes that are of great benefit to the nervous system. Such improvements at a functional level, correlated as they are with the changes in consciousness, provide the empirical justification for calling the process one of growth of consciousness. They have been very well documented in recent years[14] and I propose here to concentrate on tracing the development of the subjective experience of higher states of consciousness.

Transcendental Consciousness

In the ordinary course of things we live, move, and have our being in the waking, dreaming, and sleeping states of consciousness. Or rather, we do not have our being, we are not aware of it, for it lies imprisoned in our thoughts and percepts. Our true subjectivity, our Self — that which cognizes rather than is cognized — is overshadowed by the thoughts we think and the objects we perceive, so that we are

---

13 This was written before Maharishi brought out the Transcendental Meditation-Sidhi® programme (see footnote 290 in the appendix).

14 For a comprehensive account see *Scientific Research on the Transcendental Meditation Program: Collected Papers, Volume One*, edited by David W. Orme-Johnson and John T. Farrow (West Germany, MERU Press, 1976). Five volumes of the *Collected Papers* are available at the time of publication of this book, with the sixth and seventh volumes in preparation.

aware, not of ourselves, but of our thoughts and percepts.[15] 'Whereby would one know him by means of whom one knows all this? Indeed, whereby would one know the knower?' asks the Upanishad,[16] and there seems to be no obvious solution to this conundrum. We could try to shut out sense objects by closing our eyes and shutting our ears, but the inner senses would continue to be active as thoughts and images. And if we tried to shut out the thoughts that constantly flood in upon us, we should be no more successful than was Dame Partington when she tried to sweep the ocean from her front door.[17]

How then to rid ourselves of the shadow cast by our experience? It seems that the first step is to habituate ourselves to a state where there is nothing that can cast a shadow. Those who try to shut out all thoughts are not wrong in their immediate aim; only their methods are faulty. It is quite impossible to jump from the intense activity of ordinary surface thought to a state of no thought. Transcendental Meditation

---

15 In deep sleep we do not appear to be aware at all. But Indian thought holds that awareness, or intelligence, is of our very essence and so must continue in some form during sleep, even though there is no determinate perception. This continuity is said to be vouched for by the continuity of experience and memory before and after sleep (see SBS 2.3.18; 3.2.9). It is certainly vouched for by the experience of many people who, after practising the Transcendental Meditation technique for some time, find that they are aware while asleep, witnessing their sleep, as it were.

16 BU 2.4.14.

17 *Editor's note:* Dame Partington is said to have tried to push back, with her mop, stormy Atlantic waves that reached her doorstep. Referring to her name became a taunt against those who try to withstand the inevitable.

is a technique, which, giving free rein to the proneness of the attention to move effortlessly towards greater satisfaction, permits thought activity to be reduced gradually, until the mind becomes completely still, yet remains alert. A specially chosen sound, or mantra, is allowed to become increasingly subtle, or refined, in the sense that a whisper is more refined than a shout. The technique is such that step by step and quite automatically, without any 'doing', the mantra becomes less concrete, less defined, more tenuous, until it reaches such a degree of refinement that the transition from thought to no thought happens easily, while one yet remains awake. Because one has gone beyond, or transcended, thought, this state of inner wakefulness, without thought, is known as Transcendental Consciousness.

Many other terms are used to describe this state, depending on one's viewpoint — physiological, psychological, ontological. It is known as pure awareness, pure consciousness, pure intelligence, in the sense that one is not aware of any object but purely and simply *aware*. Because all objective experience, everything extraneous to the knower, has disappeared and only 'knowingness', or pure subjectivity, remains, the terms 'Self-consciousness' and 'Self-awareness' are also used, though evidently in quite a different sense from ordinary usage. The transcendental state is also said to be one of 'pure being': in other states one is doing something, thinking something, perceiving something — in this state one simply *is*.[18] Since there is no division of subject and object, it is without relation, complete in itself, and therefore 'absolute'. Since the awareness is not circumscribed by any objects it is 'unbounded' or, to put it another way, since there are no boundaries one perceives nothing.

For those who consider this kind of language too high-flown there is the physiological dimension. It is a cardinal tenet of Maharishi's teaching that every state of consciousness is reflected in — is indeed a reflection of — a particular state of the physical system;[19] one might say that they are two sides

18 'When the subject is left without an object of experience, having transcended the subtlest state of the object, he steps out of the process of experiencing and arrives at the state of Being.' Maharishi, *Science of Being and Art of Living* (International SRM Publications, 1966), p. 52.

19 'Every experience has its level of physiology, and so unbounded awareness has its own level of physiology, which can be measured. Every aspect of life is integrated and connected with every other phase. These days, we have instruments and methods to measure brain waves, blood content and so on ... When we talk of scientific measurements, it does not take away from the spiritual experience. We are not responsible for those times when spiritual experience was thought of as metaphysical. Everything is physical. Consciousness is the product of the functioning of the brain. Talking of scientific measurements is no damage to that wholeness of life which is present everywhere, and which begins to be lived when the physiology is taking a particular form. This is our understanding about spirituality; it is not on the level of faith — it is on the level of blood and bone and flesh and activity. It is measurable.' National Leaders' Conference, Arosa, Switzerland, 28 June 1974.

Editor's note: Maharishi's later teaching brought to light the *primary* nature of pure consciousness in the relationship of consciousness and physiology. Understanding of the human physiology as the expression of consciousness is detailed in the book *Human Physiology: Expression of Veda and the Vedic Literature* (4th ed.), by Professor Tony Nader, M.D., Ph.D. (Holland, MVU Press, 1994) — presenting results of research conducted under Maharishi's guidance. Maharishi's comment above that 'Consciousness is the product of the functioning of the brain' has its own level of application in relation to individual experience of consciousness.

of the same coin. On the level of the body the reduced mental activity during Transcendental Meditation is translated into, among other things, a marked lowering of the metabolic rate, accompanied by increased orderliness in the higher associative areas of the central nervous system. Some physiologists have spoken of a 'wakeful hypometabolic state'.[20] But this term applies to Transcendental Meditation as a whole and is therefore more general than Maharishi's 'restful alertness', which refers specifically to the condition of the system in Transcendental Consciousness. Research on the physiological correlates of this and of other yet more evolved states of consciousness is ongoing but the essential point is that, according to Maharishi, the raising of human consciousness involves a real modification of 'this beautiful nervous system'; without such a change there are only flights of fancy — balloons floating in the air with no connection to the ground.

Cosmic Consciousness

Transcendental Consciousness, with its absence of objective experience, is clearly a proximate goal. One does not want to be rid of the objects of experience but merely of their overshadowing and limiting character.

---

20 See Robert Keith Wallace, et al., 'A Wakeful Hypometabolic State', *American Journal of Physiology*, 221:3 (1971), pp. 795–9. Keith Wallace's 1970 article, 'Physiological Effects of Transcendental Meditation', published in *Science*, was the first paper dealing with research on the Transcendental Meditation technique to be published in a major journal. These and other articles about the physiological correlates of the Transcendental Meditation technique are reproduced in the volumes of *Collected Papers*.

Through regular repetition of the process of transcending, the awareness becomes accustomed to maintaining itself in its 'pure' state as the subject, or Self, so that, even when confronted with the objects of experience, it is able to register them without being overshadowed and limited by them. The dignity of the knower is not overthrown by what he knows; the unbounded awareness of the perceiver is not lost in the boundaries of perception; silence is not lost in the midst of activity.

Generally, this development is first noticed during a most delicate phase of meditation when the inner wakefulness that marks Transcendental Consciousness no longer disappears as soon as thoughts float into the awareness. Thoughts are now appreciated as somehow independent of, or peripheral to, the awareness witnessing them. When Transcendental Consciousness penetrates other states of consciousness it takes on this character of what might be called 'witness consciousness'. One begins to experience the 'gap' between Self and non-Self, witness and witnessed, which is mentioned so often in the conversations in this volume. Gradually the state of being a witness penetrates sleep and dreams and also creeps into daily life until the momentum of even the most dynamic activity is powerless to overthrow it. When it becomes permanent and is never lost during waking, dreaming, or sleeping, it is known as Cosmic Consciousness.

Cosmic Consciousness is a state where inner silence, or non-activity, coexists with outer activity. One is in a sense both a spectator and a player in the game of life, acting but not involved. And yet life is more successful now that one stands at a distance from it, as it were. Perhaps this is not such a paradox as it seems, for one is merely rendering unto Caesar what was Caesar's all along. According to the Gītā: 'Actions are in every case performed by the guṇas of Nature. He whose mind is deluded by the sense of "I" holds "I am the doer". But he who knows the truth … knowing that it is the guṇas which act upon the guṇas, remains unattached.'[21]

In Cosmic Consciousness a process of sorting out has taken place whereby 'one lives quite naturally this state of pure existence separated from the field of activity, even while ego, intellect, mind, and senses are engaged in action.'[22] This holds advantages for both sides. The Self is no longer bound to the world of action ruled by cause and effect, for what is not part of one has no power to hold one. At the same time, effortless harmony reigns in the world of action, now that it is allowed to continue on its course without interference from the mistaken sense that one is a doer, identified with it. Thought and action, though they seem to proceed by themselves without the need for any 'doing', are more co-ordinated and effective than before. Their full potential is now available.

This state of separation is not a means but a result — a truth that has been tragically misunderstood by those in India and elsewhere who *practise* 'Self-awareness', 'Self-

---

21 3.27–8, see MBG, pp. 220–1. The guṇas are the basic impulses of nature. Their permutations and combinations make up relative existence.
22 MBG 3.28, p. 223.

22

remembering', non-attachment, or other ways of putting a distance between themselves and the world of experience. The sense of not being a doer but a witness, the absence of attachment, or involvement, so painfully sought through mental exercises and physical renunciation, come as they can only come if they are not to be mere moods — innocently, unexpectedly. Maharishi has shown that they are the outcome of a natural and automatic process whereby the Self, or subject, assumes its rightful place as central and intimate to one's existence, while all activity becomes peripheral. Even thought, the most intimate activity of all, is witnessed and in being witnessed returns where it belongs — to the relative universe of forms and phenomena that has nothing to do with the witness, or Self.

It is clear therefore that effort is no more needed to make Transcendental Consciousness permanent than it was needed to gain it in the first place. As I have shown elsewhere,[23] those who try to prolong it artificially are merely hindering the process whereby it seeps into daily life. Maharishi likes to point out that fullness will automatically flow into emptiness. As one comes back from Transcendental Consciousness to the ordinary waking state — alternating meditation with daily activity — it is not as if Transcendental Consciousness had never been. One takes something of its fullness with one. The fullness gets diluted or, as Maharishi

23 'Some Basic Insights of the Present Revival', *Creative Intelligence*, l, (SRM Foundation of Great Britain, 1972), pp. 12–15.

sometimes puts it, Being gets infused into the nature of the mind. It is like dipping a white cloth in dye and then exposing it to the sun. The cloth will lose some of its colour but it will not return to its former state. And if the dipping and bleaching are repeated often enough the dye will eventually become fast. Nothing else is required. 'Because it is such a beautiful, restful state, unbounded and fulfilling, very quickly the system starts to gain the habit of returning to that state.'[24] Alternating the restful, inward state of transcending with outer activity during the day enables the system gradually to accustom itself to those more 'refined' levels of functioning which form the necessary physiological basis for Cosmic Consciousness.[25]

Dissolution of Stress

The rigidities that set a limit to the refinement of the system, that is, to its ability to support higher states of consciousness, depend on the extent to which it has been accumulating stress. According to Maharishi, a stress is an impression left in the nervous system by undue pressure of experience. It is the residue of any experience which, when it occurred, overloaded the system and could not be fully absorbed and accommodated within its framework. Maharishi often gives the example of a sudden bright

---

24   Maharishi International University, SCI® Teacher Training Course, 1972, Lesson 23, 'The Seven States of Consciousness'.
25   See MBG 4.38, p. 314.

flash of light, but the possibilities are infinite — body, intellect, or emotions may be overtaxed, and this by pleasant as well as unpleasant experiences. Every such experience leaves a trace in the system, and it is reasonable to assume this to have a counterpart in terms of chemical and possibly morphological changes, which reduce the ability of the system to work in a balanced, efficient, and co-ordinated way.

Stress then, as Maharishi sees it, is physiological[26] and has to be distinguished from the mental impressions[27] with which it is associated. 'Now stress and deeply rooted impressions are two separate things, but they can be closely related for our understanding. Impressions are the lines of memory left by that experience, but over and above that the nervous system gets twisted.' But 'when, through meditation, these twists are taken away from the physical [nervous system] ... then the memory also loses its binding influence.'[28]

Accumulated stress is a permanent burden that the system carries. The Transcendental Meditation technique is designed to lighten and eventually eliminate this burden through deep rest.[29] The system likes to settle down but it

26 Compare Hans Selye: 'Stress is essentially the rate of wear and tear in the body.' *The Stress of Life* (New York, McGraw-Hill, 1956), p. 3.

27 These are known in Sanskrit as 'vāsanās', from the root 'vas', to dwell — that which is left dwelling in the mind.

28 Lecture, Rishikesh, India, January 30, 1969.

29 The decrease in plasma cortisol during the practice of the Transcendental Meditation technique found by R. Jevning, et. al., would seem to be a direct indicator of a reversal of anxiety and tension. See 'Plasma Prolactin and Cortisol During Transcendental Meditation', reprinted in the *Collected Papers*.

also likes to throw off stress, and it seems that these two tendencies are connected, rather as periods of restful deep sleep are followed by periods of the more active phase of dreaming. The rest given by Transcendental Meditation is a wakeful rest, different from the rest of sleep,[30] but the principle is the same: rest dissolves stress. The physical knots in the system get untwisted by greatly reducing its activity. The transcendental Self, no longer imprisoned in the depths, as it were, comes out into the daylight.

Because the technique is natural and effortless, each person experiences only what his system in a natural way allows him to experience and so he is able to integrate his experience with ease. The mechanism whereby Transcendental Meditation refines the system is completely self-regulating. The physical obstacles that obstruct the growth of higher states of consciousness are gradually removed, while the more normal functioning of the system makes it less subject to the overloading that causes stress.

Refinement of Perception

It may well seem that Cosmic Consciousness sets the limit to one's attainment, but Maharishi points out that 'The process of evolution does not end with Cosmic Consciousness.' Certainly, stresses 'have been released to an extent

---

30 It is interesting to note that the biochemical changes found by Jevning and his colleagues are quite different from those that accompany sleep.

sufficient for the Self to be forever maintained. But the system has not become foolproof … Foolproof means it has not become completely shielded from the possibility of gaining more stresses.' Maharishi continues by explaining that 'experiences in the world will not leave such deep impressions as could overshadow Being. But, sure enough, they will leave some impressions, some stresses, which will be eliminated during the night's rest.' Further, 'As evolution continues, the system becomes more and more cultured, more and more refined, and this greater refinement of the physical nervous system means that it will be gathering a smaller and smaller amount of stress to be neutralized during the night.'[31]

If there is refinement on the level of physiology, how is it reflected in our experience? There is no further room for growth on the subjective level: in Cosmic Consciousness the system is evolved enough for Self-awareness to be maintained — 'one is a witness to everything that is going on.'[32] So growth has to find an outlet on the objective level — by refining perception of what actually goes on. Witness consciousness can coexist with a relatively unrefined machinery of perception. To put it another way, unbounded inner awareness can coexist with an awareness of only rigid boundaries outside, so that the surface values, which distinguish one object from another, continue to dominate one's perception to the exclusion of the more deli-

---

31 See conversation, 'Purification of the Nervous System and the Growth of Consciousness'.
32 ibid.

cate, more universal aspects of the object.

We can therefore assume that in Cosmic Consciousness the physiological mechanisms dealing with the maintenance of inner awareness have been cultured to their fullest extent, while those dealing with the perception of outer objects have not. If we suddenly hear a loud bang it will be witnessed — it will not overshadow Self-awareness — but the system will yet receive something of a shock — 'some impressions, some stresses, which will be eliminated during the night's rest.' But suppose that the machinery of perception has been refined so that 'every perception is a joyful wave, then the chances of gaining stresses are naturally less'[33] — they still exist because not only unpleasant impressions such as loud noises, but also a surfeit of pleasant stimuli, can overload the system. And suppose that a further step of evolution has taken place whereby 'one perceives everything, not in terms of great waves of joyfulness, but in terms of one's Self, then the chance of accumulating stresses is eliminated forever.'[34] Experience loses once and for all that capacity to shock or frighten which causes stress. As the Upanishad says: 'Assuredly, fear arises from duality.'[35] One cannot be frightened by what is nothing but a wave of one's own Self.

It appears then that the windows of perception are cleansed in stages. Just as we cannot jump from ordinary sur-

---

33 ibid.
34 ibid.
35 BU 1.4.2; cf. 4.5.15.

face thought to Transcendental Consciousness, so we cannot jump from perceiving the world only in terms of its surface boundaries to perceiving it in terms of the unbounded Self. There is a sixth state of consciousness[36] where every perception has a joyful, even celestial character. It would seem that joy is the bridge on which we cross to Unity. Joy is a quality of the heart and Maharishi stresses the importance of the heart in that refinement of perception which converts separation into Unity.

While ignorance of one's own Self prevails, so does a kind of unity — Maharishi calls it a 'mirage of unity'[37] in the sense that the perceiver is wholly involved in the percept. With the growth of Cosmic Consciousness the knower begins to stand apart. There is a growing gap of non-involvement between witness and witnessed. When Cosmic Consciousness is complete, the gap[38] is complete. Certainly, this means freedom: the Self, once separated from the world of objects, is no longer in thrall to it. But the freedom is of a kind that involves some lack; where there is a hiatus complete fulfilment cannot be.

Any situation that involves separation must always be in-

---

36 The other five states are waking, dreaming, sleeping, Transcendental, and Cosmic Consciousness.

37 Humboldt, 12 August 1970.

38 *Editor's note:* The word 'gap' is used here in a context different from Maharishi's later discussion of the 'fourfold nature of the gap'. See, for example, Maharishi Mahesh Yogi, *Celebrating Perfection in Education: Dawn of Total Knowledge* (Holland, MVU Press, 1997), pp. 150-1, where the gap referred to is that between two syllables of the Vedic text.

herently unsatisfactory to the heart, because the heart longs for unity. And so evolution — as we may call the momentum of growth set up by the practice of Transcendental Meditation — using as its tool that tendency of the heart to unify, which is called love and which expresses itself in joy, proceeds to bridge the gap by uniting what Cosmic Consciousness has cast asunder. The stage of separation is essential, for without it there would be nothing for the heart to unite, but it is only a stage. 'It is this unifying factor of love that starts to function with great zeal and enthusiasm from the level of Cosmic Consciousness when the two aspects of life have been thrown apart — the Self and the non-Self. Because the instrument of unification can only show its efficiency of functioning when there are two things given and gradually the two are brought to one.'[39]

The neat differentiation into stages, where the refinement of perception follows upon the full growth of inner awareness, is of course somewhat artificial, because the one involves the other. From our very first meditation we begin to enliven hitherto unused phases of the machinery of perception because, in order to transcend thought, we have first to experience its finer, or subtler, phases. Thought, according to Maharishi, is a refined form of sense perception, and feeling is the most refined form of thought, so there is some 'warming-up' effect on the heart even at this early stage.

---

39 Humboldt, 12 August 1970.

Mere beginners sometimes report that when they are interrupted in the depths of meditation the experience is a joyful
one — the loud noise becomes a wave of joy. The flavour of
the inner experience has penetrated outward perception: it
has begun to spill over into daily life — which shows how
true is Maharishi's dictum that the world is as we are.

Every new state of consciousness expands from within,
outwards; so it takes some time for the machinery of perception sharpened during meditation to make any appreciable
difference in our perception of the external world. But as the
outward stroke becomes less outward and the inward stroke
less inward, the threshold from which one perceives the
world is gradually 'lowered', that is to say, one's perceptions
function from a more refined level, a level 'nearer' to Transcendental Consciousness. So long as accumulated stress has
not been dissolved, the refinement tends to be vitiated by
the power of the gross, surface aspect of the object, where
boundaries are rigid and well defined. One may have flashes
of more refined perception, but the refinement of the machinery of perception really gathers speed only when the system is free of the stresses pushing the awareness to the surface. Before that, 'the refinement is eaten up' by these stress
releases; but 'when the release of [deep] stress is over, then
the refinement is all added up quickly on to that celestial
vision.'[40] When those depths of stress which were keeping

---

40 Conversation, Cala Millor, Mallorca, 31 December 1970.

31

the Self bound to the world of objects have been dissolved, the long-constricted heart can expand. It 'begins to move, and this begins to draw everything together and eliminate the gulf of separation between the Self and activity.'[41]

Maharishi shows that the heart is far from blind. It can see where the mind cannot see. 'When the love is more, the crudeness is less. Greater love renders the tendency of perception to very great degrees of delicacy.' Maharishi continues, 'When perception is gross, the vision falls on the gross; when the perception is delicate, the vision, even though it falls on the gross, picks up the subtle. This growth of the ability of perception to perceive even the most delicate on this gross surface value of life, increases with increased ability to love.' Describing this expansion of the heart, Maharishi comments, 'When love is more, acceptance is more, and this acceptance increases the value of perception. Then the hidden value of the object begins to be obvious more and more because acceptance is increasing. When acceptance is increasing then much more hidden values show up; they begin to shine.' Later in the same talk Maharishi gives a beautiful example of this acceptance and appreciation: 'The mother doesn't mind what the child says, because deep within is the soul of the child, which is the soul of the mother — one together. Surface value of separation doesn't matter. It is the refined vision of love that doesn't mind the surface crude-

---

41 MBG 4.35, p. 307.

ness. It only appreciates, appreciates.'[42]

Such refined vision has nothing to do with changing the object. A son comes home. He is a college superintendent. The mother of a neighbouring family sees him as such. 'Now when the real mother sees him she doesn't see him as a superintendent, absolutely not. Nothing to do with that. It's a completely different vision... On the surface it's the same person but it has a completely different value. So the object of perception remains the same; what has changed is the level of consciousness on which it is evaluated.' Therefore, when we talk of experiencing the finer fields of an object, say a microphone, 'it does not mean that one goes deeper into the mike. It only means that the finest relative value, which is already on the surface of the mike, has so far been hidden from view. What is in view is only the shape of the mike.' Perception of its finest relative value has 'nothing to do with breaking the atoms of the mike. The awareness of the boundary on the surface becomes finer and finer and finer. The whole thing remains on the surface.'[43] That is to say, it is quite obvious for one who has eyes to see.

God Consciousness

What is the nature of this refined perception guided by love and accompanied by joy? 'Now the finest relative, as far as the awareness is

---

42 Humboldt, 12 August 1970.
43 Conversation, Arosa, Switzerland, 30 May 1974.

concerned, is a more and more diffused level of concentration. If we compare the awareness with air, just like air becoming thinner and thinner, so it is as if the awareness is becoming thinner and thinner, which means, more and more delicate.'[44] The vision is no longer dominated by the 'shape of the mike' — by those qualities which distinguish an object from the rest of the environment. These qualities are still there — more diffused does not mean out of focus;[45] it means seeing things in a more universal context and, therefore, seeing them more justly. Awareness of its molecular and atomic dimensions does not smudge our knowledge of the cell; on the contrary, our seeing the cell as an expression of molecules and atoms helps us to know it more clearly. The universal does not contradict the particular; it includes it. So the 'shape of the mike' does not disappear, only it no longer diverts the awareness from those more delicate, more fluid qualities which the mike shares with its environment. Those fortunate enough to be at home in this state of consciousness say that everything is more alive, everything glows. It is indeed as if the whole world were made of light.

This is the kind of experience that must have given rise to the saying that God is light, so it is perhaps not altogether surprising that Maharishi sometimes calls this state

---

44 ibid.

45 See Kenneth R. Pelletier, 'The Effects of the Transcendental Meditation Program on Perceptual Style: Increased Field Independence', and 'Influence of Transcendental Meditation upon Autokinetic Perception', both reprinted in the *Collected Papers*.

of refined perception God Consciousness. There is no question here of faith. Maharishi's approach is experiential; he is concerned with a fact of perception, a stage in the growth of consciousness. 'God Consciousness is one's own, it is on the level of one's own existence. The one who is in God Consciousness — he is like that, not because of the status of God or creation, but because of his own status ... Because it is the appreciation of that value of creation from where creation begins — the source of relative creation. That is why it gets a name: God Consciousness. Otherwise, it is his own consciousness.'[46]

So long as the machinery of perception has not been greatly refined, God Consciousness is not a meaningful term because the source of creation is not apparent. In Cosmic Consciousness silence and activity, Self and non-Self, Absolute and relative, stand facing each other across an unbridgeable gap. The gap, as I point out in one of the conversations, is unbridgeable in principle — the self-sufficient Absolute cannot be subject to any relationship. 'Yes,' replies Maharishi, 'but it then gets bridged.' Formerly so dark and impenetrable, the gap 'is filled by light'.[47]

If the gap were really unbridgeable we could not transcend. But in practice we find that there is a transcendental state — without relation, complete in itself, absolute — which is

---

46 See postscript to the conversation, 'The Transition from God-Consciousness to Unity'.
47 See conversation, 'The Gap'.

contiguous with relative subject–object states that precede and follow it. So there must be a point of transition where the unboundedness of the one gives way to the boundaries of the other, where pure awareness without any object gives way to the faintest vibration, or impulse, of objective awareness, or vice versa. For a long time this area of transition will remain obscure, apart from momentary glimpses in the depths of meditation. But from the time Cosmic Consciousness has been gained, the unbounded awareness of the conscious mind falls constantly upon the boundaries of our discrete perceptions, thus bringing more and more to the surface those finer, more delicate aspects of the object, which are closer to its own unboundedness. There comes a point where in broad daylight 'one recognizes the reality of how the Absolute expresses itself into the multiple relative … where one clearly sees the process of creation… And then what one finds is that the diversity of the relative is coming to a close and is coming to that one value of the faintest relative which is just the nature of the Absolute, the vibrant nature of the Absolute. And this is that level of awareness which starts to recognize very clearly, on one side unmanifest Absolute and on the other this faint, faintest relative impulse, which is the sprouting of creation — as a seed sprouts, the Absolute is sprouting — and that sprout as a reverberation of the entirety of the Absolute into the faintest relative impulse of existence… One cognizes absolute Being, completely like a still ocean, omnipresent, without an activity, as the finest spur of action — that is, the basis of all relative diversity.'[48]

It is at this point of transition that God is 'situated' in the awareness. God is the face of the Absolute turned towards the world. The Absolute, by definition, never changes; it remains 'completely like a still ocean, omnipresent, without an activity.' In so far as it is seen as giving rise to creation, it is no longer the relationless Absolute. It has, so to speak, to take form and 'become' the Creator. We could therefore say that God relates what in Cosmic Consciousness seemed unrelatable — the phenomenal world of activity, and the still, self-sufficient, limitless world of the Absolute. He can do so because he sits on the fence, as it were, with a foot in each camp. And if we are awake on this borderline of the relative and the Absolute where God resides, we will appreciate the Absolute and the relative as 'the two aspects of the nature of God. One is silent nature, the other vibrant nature. Silent nature progresses into vibrant nature.'[49]

If God himself is situated at this point of transition, his light yet spreads far and wide and is appreciated long before we can fully discern his nature. God Consciousness comprises a whole series of states[50] in which, on the firm basis of Cosmic Consciousness, the machinery of perception

---

48 Lecture, Seelisberg, Switzerland, 15 September 1973. (Maharishi, in the lecture hall, is answering by telephone a question from a Dutch priest attending a Science of Creative Intelligence course in Bergen, Holland.)

49 ibid.

50 See MBG commentary, p. 307, for one example of Maharishi's discussion of God Consciousness.

is gradually and progressively refined so that it can become aware of those finer levels of creation which Maharishi calls 'celestial', and on which, because of their 'nearness' to him, the radiance of God falls most strongly. The more general term 'refined Cosmic Consciousness', which is often used in place of 'God Consciousness', is perhaps more appropriate, because it seems that only near its climax does this state actually yield a cognition of the full display of God's nature.

Unity Consciousness

Once God is known, love starts to take on the character of devotion. 'Devotion is the result of the cognition of God.'[51] It is 'that intensified state of love, which unites in a very intimate manner the devotee and his God. When the uniting quality of love reaches a level where disunion is just not possible, then love gains the value of devotion. One is devoted to the other, and this is beyond the possibility of separation.'[52]

When 'the object of cognition is beyond the possibility of separation, then the object is cognized in terms of the subject;[53] the non-Being — what was hitherto non-Being — objective value of the object is now transformed into the subjective value of Being. Maharishi concludes that 'This is

---

51 See conversation, 'The Transition from God Consciousness to Unity'.
52 Humboldt, 12 August 1970.
53 Maharishi has said that the purer the level of consciousness, the more intimate the contact with the object of perception, and that ' "Absolute" means absolutely intimate.'

the fulfilment of devotion. The subject is so devoted to the object that the object is evaluated in terms of the subject. The eternal unity of the so-called two is transformed into the reality of one. And this brought about on the increasing degrees of love. Culture of the heart is at the basis of this laudable growth of perception.'[54]

At its apex, where the value of the object merges into that of the subject, the sixth state of consciousness dissolves of its own accord. It is the bridge between Cosmic Consciousness and Unity Consciousness, between seeing things in terms of themselves and seeing them in terms of one's own Self, between seeing them only in terms of their surface boundaries and seeing them in terms of their unboundedness, between seeing them *sub specie temporis* and seeing them *sub specie aeternitatis.* But when one has reached the other shore, the bridge has served its purpose.

Maharishi is fond of quoting these words from the Bhagavad-Gītā: 'kālenātmani vindati' — 'in time finds this within himself.'[55] He wants to show thereby that no doing, no contriving, is involved in the growth of higher states of consciousness. Transcendental Meditation itself is a process of less and less doing, and all its blessings arise spontaneously, unexpectedly — they come almost as a surprise. This was true of the growth of Transcendental and Cosmic

54 Humboldt, 12 August 1970.
55 MBG 4.38, p. 311. The verse is translated: 'Truly there is in this world nothing so purifying as knowledge; he who is perfected in Yoga, of himself in time finds this within himself.'

Consciousness and it is equally true of God Consciousness and Unity. It is not that sympathy, love, devotion have to be *cultivated* in order to overcome what Maslow has called 'the alienation of the knower from his known'[56] — they grow quite naturally once the fetters of stress which constrict the heart have been broken on attaining Cosmic Consciousness. The expansion of the heart in turn brings about that refined, or expanded, vision — the 'more diffused level of concentration'[57] — which alone can locate God. Cognition of God leads to devotion, which results in union. This is perhaps being rather schematic about what is after all a living process of growth, but it is important to emphasize that one state of consciousness leads quite naturally to another. It is no use trying to run before one can walk.[58]

---

56 A. Maslow, *The Psychology of Science* (Chicago, Gateway Edition, 1969), p. 52.

57 See full quote on p. 34.

58 A lecture given at Poland Springs, Maine, 13 July 1970, beautifully illustrates this point with reference to the growth of God Consciousness. I cannot resist quoting Maharishi at length: 'If we want to reach someone great, we must have some status of greatness', and, 'If the awareness is not broadened so as to be able to encompass that enormously great creation, how can the Creator be comprehensible?' After elaborating this idea, Maharishi gives an example: 'If a man wants to comprehend the field of the artist he should be able to appreciate all the pieces of art that he has created and then try to locate him.' In the same way, 'In order to realize God, creation has to be realized. In order to realize creation, the man who is going to realize should be established. When the situation is such that I say, "I see the mike but I don't know who I am" — when the knower is in darkness — how can the object of knowledge be in light?' Later in the talk, Maharishi comments: 'When I can't maintain [myself] against the small reality bound in time and space' then 'how can the unlimited creation be comprehended?' When 'I am so weak that looking at a flower I lose myself, so weak that even the sight of a small sand particle

Knowledge of Unity

We can take the sequence a step further: from union comes the recognition of Unity. Devotion is necessary to take the attention to the point where 'the object of cognition is beyond the possibility of separation.' Thereafter knowledge takes over. 'The level which is the highest in the relative is one with the Absolute… Faintest pink of the petal and colourless sap are two sides of the same coin. The supreme relative doesn't have to transcend — the transcendental is along with it. That is why the transformation from God Consciousness to Unity is not a phenomenon. It is only the knowledge that was hidden and is now unfolded. In God Consciousness, when the supreme relative is a normal reality of everyday life, the Unity becomes exposed. Exposed to whom? To itself. By whom? By itself. For whom? For itself. Nothing participates in the transformation from God Consciousness to Unity other than Unity itself. The highest attainment of life is brought about by nothing other than what life itself is. A phenomenon is only possible in the relative.'[59] 'The relative does not drop

---

on the ground overthrows my validity' then 'how can [I] withstand that impact of the vision of the Almighty of infinite value, the Creator of such a vast universe?' In conclusion: 'Self-realization is the prerequisite to realization of even a sand particle on the ground. Self-realization is the basis for the validity of any realization.'

Compare Eckhart: 'To get at the core of God at his greatest, one must first get into the core of himself at his least, for no one can know God who has not first known himself.' Raymond Blakney, trans. *Meister Eckhart* (New York, Harper and Row, 1941), p. 246.

59 Lecture, Rishikesh, India, Spring 1970.

off, rather every little bit of the relative becomes lively in its essential constituent, which is eternal, infinite Absolute. Every phase of relative existence is nothing other than the expressed value of the unmanifest Absolute. This situation is always there, only our awareness is not able to cognize it until, in the sixth state of consciousness, it becomes capable of organizing itself to meet that value. The sixth state of consciousness then glides into the seventh state.[60]

I think we must distinguish here the non-phenomenal from the phenomenal, the knowledge of an ever-existent reality from the actual mechanics by which that knowledge comes about, namely, the gliding of one state of consciousness into the other. When the supreme, the most refined, level of the relative becomes a normal feature of everyday life and one is no longer dazzled by its light, there comes a point — that point of transition, of merging and emergence[61] — where one finds the supreme relative to be continuous with one's own Self, or Being.[62]

---

60 Maharishi International University, SCI Teacher Training Course, 1972, Lesson 23, 'The Seven States of Consciousness'.

61 'At the point of merging is the story of emergence. When the awareness of the dual existence of the Self and non-Self merges into the oneness of eternity, at this point of merging, the emergence of creation from the unmanifest area of eternal existence is cognized. The story of the birth of creation is a direct cognition when one's vision is being transformed from God Consciousness to Unity.' Lecture, Rishikesh, India, Spring 1970.

62 Compare BG 18.55: 'Through devotion he knows Me intimately, [knows] My extent and who I am in truth; then, having known Me in truth, he at once enters Me.' Commenting on this verse Shankara says that immediately on knowing the Lord as He truly is, the understanding

Just as the faintest pink of the petal shades over into the colourless sap, so the almost unbounded shades over into boundlessness, the almost infinite into infinity. The experience is continuous, but the realization of what is happening brings about a kind of quantum leap — and that is knowledge. Maharishi talks about 'that awe-inspiring awareness which arises when celestial, finest celestial, and the Absolute [are experienced alongside each other], because then one knows, "Oh, this is the same"; the Absolute and this supreme celestial — one knows, "Oh, it's the same." '[63] The brightest but still 'concrete' celestial light is the same as the abstract light of one's own awareness that has been constantly shining since Cosmic Consciousness was attained. Once one has recognized the identity between the unboundedness perceived in the object and the unboundedness that is my Self, non-Self and Self lose their separate identity. They become one, become 'That'.[64]

When we look at the development of higher states of consciousness as outlined by Maharishi we realize that the whole process is one of strengthening the hold that the transcendental, unbounded Absolute has on our lives. We first locate it in the depths of meditation. Then we find it persisting even during daily life. Finally we see it as daily life.

---

that there is a difference between the Lord and the knower (īshvara-kshetrāgya-bheda-buddhi) vanishes without trace.

63 Vittel, France, 19 December 1973.

64 See conversation, 'The Transition from God Consciousness to Unity', where this is beautifully described.

Once contacted it cannot be contained; it spills over into more and more areas of life until every object reflects it. And at each stage, when we realize what is happening, there is the quantum leap of knowledge: First, 'Oh, I have found myself'; then, 'Oh, I am separate from all this around me'; and finally, 'Oh, I am one with what I am perceiving.'[65]

Evaluation of External Reality

The cognition, 'I am one with what I am perceiving', perhaps raises philosophical problems more awkward than those raised by the earlier cognitions. It can be argued that so long as we are content merely to speak about the inner Self, which witnesses but is not involved, we do not touch the sacred integrity of the external world. We may have to watch our language so that it does not stray too far from the actual experiences that it is purporting to explain, but the use of a term such as 'Self' can be justified by the centrality and continuity of witness consciousness. However, when we start talking about perceiving finer levels

---

65 The last two cognitions may be said to correspond in turn to the discriminative knowledge of the Sāṁkhya system of philosophy and the unitive knowledge of Shankara's system of Vedānta. Maharishi regards Cosmic Consciousness as the pre-condition of Unity. Similarly Shankara in his commentary on the Gītā holds that the discriminative knowledge of Self and non-Self (ātmānātma-viveka-vigyāna, see commentary, SBG 18.10), which he associates with the Sāṁkhya point of view (see SBG 3.3), is a prerequisite for the knowledge of the oneness of the knower and the supreme Self (kshetrāgya-paramātmaikatva-gyāna, see commentary, SBG 18.55). The knower here stands for the subjective, the supreme Self for the objective side of the unitive equation.

of an object and then pile Pelion upon Ossa[66] by stating that the subject is in reality one with the object, we are taking a big ontological jump. We are saying something about the external world as a result of our experience in meditation, perhaps even projecting that experience on the world around us. We are letting what happens when our eyes are closed affect what we perceive when they are open.

In answering this line of argument one can point out that Transcendental Meditation influences our experience of the external world, not by adding some imaginary element but by gradually reducing the obfuscation of the senses that prevents us from perceiving fully what is already there. Not that what we saw before was wrong — it was just incomplete. There is a theory that the senses have evolved primarily as filters, or selectors: they not only give information, but also withhold it so as to protect the system from being overloaded by the multiplicity of impulses that converge upon it from all sides. It may well be that this habit of the senses to focus on a very narrow range blocks the perception of other more abstract and universal levels of the object, much as someone long absorbed in his special subject tends to lose sight of the larger background against which he works. The localized perception — the 'shape of the mike'[67] — completely

---

66 *Editor's note:* Add difficulty to difficulty — this expression is derived from an account in classical Greek literature of giants attempting to scale Mount Olympus, home of the gods, by piling Mount Pelion upon Mount Ossa.

67 See full quote on p. 33.

dominates the vision. As a 'more and more diffused level of concentration'[68] develops, the blocks are gradually removed, the filters are reset. Awareness of the boundaries of the object — its shape, colour, sound, and so on — becomes delicate enough not to disturb awareness of its less bounded, more universal aspects, until finally the very boundaries are appreciated as the concrete expressions of unboundedness.

Maharishi has also described this process in terms of the senses gaining 'boldness', of their becoming so strong that they can operate in the realm of boundaries and in the unbounded at the same time. In the beginning they cannot function at all in the presence of unbounded awareness, but as Cosmic Consciousness develops, they learn to maintain their ability to recognize the outer world even while unbounded inner awareness is maintained on the level of the ego.[69] However, they are not as yet able to give expression to unbounded awareness in their own terms. Only in Unity Consciousness do they gain such 'strength within themselves that the wholeness of life could be lived within their boundaries', that it could 'dance in the waves of perception and action in the field of the senses', which is on the very surface of life. And in this way Unity becomes 'a living reality'.[70]

So in Unity Consciousness the senses do not lose that ca-

---

68 See full quote on p. 34.

69 I am using 'ego' in the Indian sense of the principle of personal identity (ahaṁkāra).

70 Lecture, Maharishi's residence, Humboldt County, California, 6 August 1972.

pacity to perceive boundaries which is of their very essence; only, the localized perception of sense objects no longer poses any obstacle to the penetration of unbounded awareness into all areas of life. It becomes, on the contrary, a means of renewing the awareness of Unity, as one object after another is appreciated in terms of one's own Self. The boundaries do not disappear — as we have seen, the 'shape of the mike' is still there — only they cease to dominate. Where before they were opaque or at best, as in God Consciousness, translucent, they are now fully transparent; where before they served to hide the boundless, they now become a means of reflecting and radiating one's own unboundedness.[71]

The ability to function in the world is not only unimpaired by the awe-inspiring realization of oneness, but greatly enhanced. It is not that one passes in one fell swoop from perception of everything as discrete to perception of everything as one. The experience and knowledge of Unity come as the climax of a gradual and orderly process of physiological[72] and psychological transformation.

As to the perennial problem of what is actually 'out there', the most elegant answer will be that in essence it is nothing other than what is 'in here'. Not so very long ago it seemed

---

71 See postscript to conversation, 'Superimposition'.

72 Maslow, *The Psychology of Science*, p. 35, says that 'in the fullest experiencing a kind of melting of the person experiencing with that which is experienced occurs.' But he does not seem to be aware that this must have a firm physiological basis if it is to be a permanent feature of one's life.

that the world could be described in purely objective terms; the role of the observer was merely to survey its majestic and inexorable progress through time and space. Things are no longer so clear-cut. The extension of physics into the domain of the very fast and the very small has forced on us totally un-expected world pictures. In their different ways both relativity and quantum mechanics have drawn attention to the fact that physics cannot leave the observer out of its calculations. Fur-ther, the process of perception itself is coming more and more to be regarded as an active phenomenon, imposing its own patterns rather than passively registering what is 'out there'.

To say that the relationship between observer and ob-served is closer than was realized, is not to say that they are one and the same. But there are surprising similarities be-tween the most fundamental of all of physical states and the most fundamental of all states of awareness, pure conscious-ness. We can speak about both in the same kind of language as states of least excitation, containing all potentialities in a virtual but not expressed state.[73] Neither state readily yields

---

73 Understanding of the unity of the laws of nature has culminated in recent years with advances in unified field theories. To quote quantum physicist John Hagelin: 'The essential characteristics of the unified field, and the qualities that characterize the deepest levels of nature, can be systematically derived from the mathematical structure of these theories. These qualities, including orderliness, simplicity, creativity, dynamism, self-referral, and unboundedness, correspond precisely to the properties of human intelligence expressed at deeper levels of consciousness.' *Manual for a Perfect Government* (Fairfield, Iowa, MUM Press, 1998), p. 56.

This underlying unity of nature means higher states of consciousness have profound implications for physical theory. For example, Heisen-berg's uncertainty principle recognized the quantum wave function as

its secrets to a mere surface consideration or to intellectual analysis, but it may be that someone who is fully at home with the state of least excitation on the level of awareness will have sensibilities delicate enough to appreciate its oneness with that which underlies the states of excitation in the world around him.

In the last resort the unity of the 'in here' and the 'out there' is a matter of personal experience. It is a reality only for someone whose nervous system permits him to have that experience at the point of transition, where he realizes, 'Oh, it's the same.' Perhaps it will not be long now before not merely the fact of observation, but also the state of the observer — the state of his nervous system rather than just his position in space, or his speed, or the scale of his observations — will be considered relevant to our knowledge of what we like to call the external world. Further research about how changes in the physical system affect our perceptions may give added cogency to Maharishi's dictum that the world is as we are. In the conversations that follow, Maharishi again and again emphasizes the autonomy of different states of consciousness. What we see depends on what glasses we are wearing — green, gold, transparent, or whatever. He will not

representing, not the objective system in itself, but rather our knowledge of that system. Literature of quantum theory contains a good deal of discussion of the role of consciousness in physical measurement. A knower in Unity Consciousness, compared to an ordinary observer, may experience an entirely different relationship to the quantum wave function — perhaps perceiving it directly as an expression of potentialities rather than forcing a particular experimental outcome.

even have it that the state of Unity is a better state than those which preceded it. 'It is a different state. It is worth living.'[74]

Brahman Consciousness

In later years Maharishi brought out more implications of the state of Unity and showed that even what is already unbounded can extend its territory of influence. At first, as I appreciate something in terms of my Self I am implicitly excluding something else. But this state of affairs does not last. 'Now, in the beginning days of Unity the object of the main focus of attention is appreciated in terms of the Self. This object is seen — the eyes fall on it — this object is appreciated in terms of the subject. But the eyes not only fall on this; there is the whole paraphernalia in the background. But that is in the background. The main focus is on this carnation, the secondary focus is on the table, the third-grade focus is on the floor, the fourth-grade is on this side. So, there are degrees of focus. In the beginning days of Unity only the first focus — the object of first attention — is in terms of the Self, and when this state is lived for a while the object of the second focus also participates in the same value. A little more practice, a little more living of Unity, and even the objects of the third-grade focus and then the fourth-grade focus [are in terms of the Self]. Like that, as we start to live the near environment in terms of the Self, so the

---

74 See conversation, 'Ultimate Reality and Different States of Consciousness'.

ability to appreciate the farther values of the environment in terms of the Self keeps increasing. And the time comes when all the galactic universe, which we can't even see — the whole thing becomes concretely cognized, and appreciated in terms of the Self. And that is the last [furthest] range of Unity Consciousness which, due to its different characteristic, has been given a name: Brahman Consciousness. It's Unity Consciousness; only, it's the expansion of Unity.'[75] 'From Unity is born that wholeness which is Brahman, in comparison to which, Unity becomes a part, has the value of a part.'[76] Even though, in a wider sense, Brahman Consciousness results from the whole process of development from Transcendental Consciousness onwards, it is out of the many separate cognitions of Unity, each already full — multiple infinities, as Maharishi has called them — that Brahman is directly structured. 'They say, "pūrṇāt-pūrṇam-udachyate"[77] — it is from fullness that fullness comes.'[78] One infinity is piled upon another until it comes as a revelatory flash: 'Truly, *all* this is Brahman'[79] — not just this and this and this. Here is another and even greater 'awe-inspiring value of awareness' than that which comes with the dawn of Unity. 'Some near objects in terms of myself, then some farther objects in terms

---

75 Lecture, Seelisberg, Switzerland, 4 October 1973. For a definition of Brahman, see above section, 'Brahma Sūtra'.
76 Vittel, France, 19 September 1973.
77 BU Introductory verse.
78 Vittel, France, 19 September 1973.
79 'Sarvaṁ khalvidaṁ brahma', CU 3.14.1. See footnote 86.

of myself, and then the farthest visible object, and then be-yond visibility. The range, the transcendental range of vision — that in terms of myself. That is the last, most refined level of unfoldment of Brahman awareness. So, when some faint-est remains of difference dissolve into the value of the Self, unboundedness, then that junction point, that awe-inspiring value of awareness — that is Brahman.'[80]

'Some faintest remains of difference' here refers to the re-maining cognitions of 'this in terms of myself' and 'this in terms of myself.'[81] The wholeness that grows out of these cognitions is not just more than the collection of these dif-ferent 'awarenesses'; in reality it has nothing to do with them. 'Like that skin which the snake leaves behind — it's born of the snake but it's left behind — nothing to do with the snake, [even though] it's born of it. So, Brahman is born of the appreciation of Unity Consciousness, but in its character is completely attributeless.'[82] The dissolution of the faintest remains of difference results in complete transformation. There is again that quantum leap of knowledge which, once it is taken, nothing can erase. As I perceive the part I know the whole. And even what I do not perceive and what, ow-ing to the limitations of my human nervous system, I can-

---

80 Vittel, France, 19 September 1973.

81 The theme here is the universalization of particular experiences: 'this' and 'this' in terms of myself dissolving into the experience that *everything* is in terms of myself. Leshāvidyā (the faint remainder of ig-norance — see conversation 'The Gap') does not dissolve; it is due to leshāvidyā that 'this' and 'this' continue to be experienced.

82 Vittel, France, 19 September 1973.

not perceive, I know to be the whole. There is 'acceptance of everything as the wholeness of my own unboundedness'.[83]

Experience and Understanding

After he had given the description of the growth of Brahman Consciousness quoted earlier, Maharishi immediately added, as if to bring us back to the reality of our practice: 'It's a very practical phase of experience. In one word, it's just the growth of the ability of perception, and this starts by experiencing the finer state of the mantra. We experience the finer state of the mantra and the result is that the ability of perception becomes sharper and sharper and sharper. This ability of perception to become more and more refined results in the appreciation of harmony in the midst of diversity, because the narrow boundaries expand — nothing remains narrow, everything becomes wide open to unboundedness. This is how, on the basis of experience, consciousness grows ... Growth of consciousness is a very concrete phenomenon, which one knows on the basis of one's own experience, and this experience is then understood intellectually to be so.'[84]

Experience first and then understanding would seem to be the right sequence. Experience matures slowly, for one has to lose in order to gain. Just as the cloth is repeatedly

---

83 Quote drawn from additional material in the conversations transcribed for this book.
84 Seelisberg, Switzerland, 4 October 1973.

dipped in dye and exposed to the sun many times before the colour becomes fast, so each higher state of consciousness, before it becomes permanent, is repeatedly gained and then lost as it is exposed to daily activity. The whole process is automatic. But, as often emphasized in these conversations, there is also a need for the teacher or study of the traditional texts, preferably both, to set the seal on the student's experience by enlivening understanding of it. In India the master usually gives the student one of the 'Mahāvākyas', or 'great sayings', of the Upanishads, at the appropriate moment to bring about enlightenment. During the conversation on 'The Mahāvākyas' printed in this volume, I asked Maharishi what difference the bestowal of these sayings could possibly make for Indians, who must have been familiar with them from childhood.

Maharishi replied: 'But when the experience is *ripe* … it's a *revelation.*' When there is no basis of experience the Mahāvākyas remain just phrases but when the experience is ripe, to be told 'That thou art'[85] — or 'Truly, all this is Brahman',[86] is awe-inspiring.

---

85 'Tat tvam asi', CU 6.8.7. This Mahāvākya would seem to be appropriate for Unity Consciousness; see conversation, 'The Transition from God Consciousness to Unity'. But see also the postscript to 'The Mahāvākyas'.

86 'Sarvaṁ khalvidaṁ brahma', CU 3.14.1. This saying is not generally included among the Mahāvākyas, although the Nirālamba Upanishad lists it as one. It seems most appropriately to express Brahman Consciousness, but see also the section, 'Maharishi's Approach to the Brahma Sūtra' later in this Introduction.

THE UNFOLDMENT OF MAHARISHI'S TEACHING
The States of Consciousness

I remember once telling Maharishi in my usual vein, apropos his description of the different states of consciousness: 'I cannot know if what you are saying is true; I only know that it's beautiful.' His account of the growth of consciousness has a grandeur, a sweep, a clarity, and a depth of psychological insight that has never, to the best of my knowledge, been equalled, let alone surpassed. Others may have had insight into this or that facet of the path but where they see the part he seems to see the whole. Not only is everything there, but it is there in the correct order, with all the mechanics laid out. Each detail fits perfectly into a design that is more than the sum of its parts. The whole scheme has a rightness, an inevitability reminiscent of a great work of art. Though perfect in every detail, however, it did not take shape all at once. Over the years I have watched with fascination how, like a flower that opens, Maharishi's teaching has gradually unfolded.

When I first met him, Maharishi was speaking mainly of Transcendental Consciousness. Cosmic Consciousness was there in the background hinted at as the ultimate goal, but its complete character as a state of separation was only gradually made clear. Then I well remember the lecture during the 1964/65 winter course at Bad Mergentheim in Germany, when, just before the new year began, Maharishi spoke of the possibility of refining Cosmic Consciousness into a sixth state of consciousness — God Consciousness. And there was the other memorable occasion during the course at Lago di Braies in the Dolomites, in the summer of 1967, when Maharishi said to us: 'Don't take notes, listen to me properly', and then proceeded to give out the teaching about Unity and supreme knowledge in what seemed a single breath. The distinction between Unity and its apex, Brahman Consciousness, was first made clear at Lake Tahoe in the autumn of 1972, when I again had the good luck to be working with Maharishi on the Brahma Sūtra. The thoughts that came were so fascinating that Maharishi did not find it in him to break their continuity, even when the time had come to leave Lake Tahoe. He went on with his commentary as we drove to Reno airport in a snowstorm, and then during the stormy flight to Los Angeles, and, rather more comfortably, at the special conference table made available to him on the jumbo jet from Los Angeles to Panama, and finally on the flight by ordinary jet from Panama to Rio de Janeiro. Nothing could stop the brilliant flow of his thought. On that memorable journey Brahman Consciousness seemed to stand revealed in its full clarity. But by the time the Teacher Training Course at La Antilla, Spain, had ended in the spring of 1973, many further refinements had emerged.

The Science of Creative Intelligence

I was not so intimately involved with the inception and early growth of another branch of Maharishi's teaching. In 1970, inspired by the successful results of the first scientific experiments on the effects of the Transcendental Meditation technique, Maharishi began to develop the Science of Creative Intelligence, which studies 'the nature and growth of orderliness in man and, through him, in the world at large. The main finding of this study is that there exists a source from which creative intelligence issues and a goal towards which it progresses as the process of evolution unfolds. Further, this source and this goal are identical and can be identified as the innermost area of one's own life on the level of the source of the thinking process.'[87]

The new science filled a gap. It not only gave Maharishi's teaching a systematic formulation but also extended its scope. By putting the teaching about the growth of consciousness in a much broader context, the Science of Creative Intelligence provides a unifying principle that integrates the knowledge given by other sciences. It finds that the laws governing the life of the individual also govern the life of the universe, or, to put it more generally, that nature repeats itself at different levels of organization.[88] In this way, understanding how na-

---

87 Maharishi International University Catalogue, 1974/75, pp. 132–3.

88 Maharishi's unifying principles of knowledge in the Science of Creative Intelligence deepen understanding of all branches of knowledge. For an early discussion of the principle mentioned here, see physicist Lawrence H. Domash in *Inauguration of the Dawn of the Age of En-*

ture works at the individual level will help us to understand better its working in the universe at large.

Individual and Collective Consciousness

Just recently, in the mid-seventies, the sociological or environmental dimension of Maharishi's teaching has become prominent. The impetus for this was a striking new indication that the practice of the Transcendental Meditation technique does indeed encourage that growth of orderliness in man, and through him the world at large, which the Science of Creative Intelligence examines. A preliminary study at the end of 1974 found in twelve American cities 'that when the number of meditators reached one per cent of the total population, the crime rate decreased in the following year by an average of eight per cent ... Control cities matched for resident population, college population, geographic location, and initial crime rate with the meditating cities showed a nine per cent increase in crime for the same year.'[89] Surprising parallels with the behaviour of physical systems have been pointed out. If orderliness is produced in a very small portion of the system it spreads of its own accord to the whole system if the conditions are right.[90]

Extensive studies of what has been called the 'Maharishi

---

lightenment (West Germany, MIU Press, 1975), p. 39–41. A more recent discussion of levels of organization in nature can be found in John Hagelin's *Manual for a Perfect Government*.

89 David Orme-Johnson in *Inauguration of the Dawn of the Age of Enlightenment*, p. 34.

90 ibid., Geoffrey Clements, p. 42.

Effect' are now under way. Seventy variables on crime, economics, and health are being examined, but even the evidence produced so far has sufficed for Maharishi to discern the dawning of a new age.[91] He shared this vision with us the night he came out of his seven days' silence at the beginning of 1975. At a celebration on Lake Lucerne on 12 January of that year he formally inaugurated the Dawn of the Age of Enlightenment for the world, and he followed this by separate inaugurations on five continents. A more cautious man might have waited until more evidence had been assembled before heralding a trend that seemed to contradict most of the available portents. But we are apt to forget that Maharishi is a seer[92] — we may call him the seer of the scientific age. He speaks out what he sees, when he sees it — when the signs are there. From the conversations on 'Shruti and Smṛiti' and 'Truth in Kali Yuga', it is obvious that he did not as yet see such definite signs of the new age in 1969. He sees them now, but if they were obvious to all and sundry there would have been no need for him to draw attention to them.

---

91 *Editor's note:* By the time of publication in 2011, more than 50 studies of the Maharishi Effect have been performed worldwide, with a number of studies published in leading academic journals or conference proceedings. These studies provide evidence that when one per cent of the population of a city or larger society learns the Transcendental Meditation technique, or when the square root of one per cent of the population of a city, state, nation, or even the world practise the advanced Transcendental Meditation-Sidhi programme together in a group, there is a measurable improvement in the quality of life of the whole society. Please refer to the *Collected Papers* for the details of these studies in reprinted form.

92 'Maharishi' means 'great seer'.

A seer, or knower, of reality naturally 'sees' more of the nature of existence than those around him.

Maharishi is very much in advance. Even when I first knew him in 1960 he was saying that great changes would take place in society if just a small percentage of the world's population began to meditate.[93] He also stated that scientists would be astounded once they started to investigate the effects of Transcendental Meditation, which they did nearly a decade later. And although surrounded at that time by the middle-aged and the elderly, with hardly a young face in sight, he repeated over and over again that the students should begin to meditate quickly, and his conviction that they would was not shaken by my most careful and, to me, conclusive demonstrations of their total lack of interest. It seems as if the later developments were already foreseen even though the statements were couched in conditional, optative, or hortatory terms. Likewise, if one studies Maharishi's early lectures, one can discern the seeds of all the states of consciousness that he was later to clarify.

The Need of the Time

One might be tempted to think that the unfoldment of Maharishi's teaching was all part of some detailed master plan, but one would be wrong. Whenever I have suggested something of the sort Maha-

---

93 Maharishi is on record in an Innsbruck, Austria, newspaper, the *Tiroler Tageszeitung*, 23 July 1962, as saying that while ten per cent would be ideal, even if only one per cent of the world's population meditated it would be sufficient to do away with the hatred that causes war.

rishi has emphasized that his teaching is a natural growth, that it comes out innocently, as the need for it arises — the environment draws it out. Of course he wanted right from the beginning to regenerate mankind, or he would not have called his movement the Spiritual Regeneration Movement. Of course he wanted to systematize and perfect his teaching, but I do not think he knew exactly how this would come about. He just let it evolve naturally. As the petals are all there in the bud, so the later developments are inherent in the earlier. But just as the petals open out in response to sunlight, so the teaching opens out in response to the need of the time.

Mere intellectual curiosity obviously does not constitute such a need. During the summer courses of the mid-sixties, I put question after question to Maharishi about the Vedānta, implying that its teaching went beyond the fifth and even the sixth state of consciousness, but Maharishi did not choose to take the point. He may enjoy discussion but he does not give out new knowledge in response to mere speculation based on a reading of Indian philosophy. There has to be experience. 'Some people brought some experiences and we had to come out with it'[94] — that is, to come out with the knowledge to

---

94 See conversation, 'On Inspiration III'. Speaking to the National Leaders' Conference at Arosa, Switzerland, on 27 June 1974, Maharishi said: 'For three, four, five years we talked about pure consciousness, Transcendental Consciousness, but when people started to express their experiences, then it was necessary to cross the boundaries of Transcendental Consciousness. Some experiences came along that gave expression to Cosmic Consciousness, and what glowed along from there for six years

explain the experiences. Other 'experiences' were brought by the physiologists and the statisticians. In every case some outside stimulus, indicating genuine need, some sign of the time, is necessary for Maharishi to put his attention on a particular area of experience so that the teaching relevant to it can blossom forth. 'Time does it. It's spontaneous, absolutely spontaneous ... Whenever we start to talk about it [the area of experience], to think about it, it becomes clear [to the understanding]. As long as we don't think about it, it does not become clear ... one just spontaneously lives it.'[95]

Maharishi continued to unfold his teaching at an increasingly rapid rate. As if to confirm the dawning of the new age, the experiences being brought to his attention as time passes are becoming much clearer, fuller, more profound. *Pari passu* with the growth in the *number* of meditators there has been an equally rapid inner growth. Maharishi has channelled this trend into 'Age of Enlightenment Courses', in which he is teaching an advanced programme, known as the Transcendental Meditation-Sidhi programme,[96] derived from the Yoga Sūtra of Patanjali. These courses have justified their name. Course participants have showered Maharishi with sublime experiences and he, in turn, has been moved

---

was God Consciousness. Then, very suddenly, experiences brought out the expression of Unity. Then someone said something and I couldn't resist — Brahman Consciousness. Such delightful upsurge of knowledge, growth of wholeness ... Experiences come on the basis of the naturalness of life itself.'

95 Conversation, Hertenstein, Switzerland, 25 February 1975.
96 See footnote 290 in the appendix.

to illuminate their experiences with great beams of knowl-edge.[97] It would need a new introduction to convey all the developments that have been crammed into even the last ten months,[98] and in any case their impact is still too fresh for adequate assessment. As so often with Maharishi, the 'new' developments are not completely new. I remember some asides many years ago when Maharishi first foreshadowed them. But he puts his full attention on something only when the time is ripe.[99]

MAHARISHI AS COMMENTATOR AND TEACHER

Maharishi's Approach to the Brahma Sūtra

Significantly it was to an Age of Enlightenment Course that Maharishi gave what is perhaps his clearest exposi-tion to date of the nature of Brahman Consciousness

---

97 *Editor's note:* Experiences have continued to grow, including those of participants in the on-going Invincible America Assembly at Maha-rishi University of Management (inaugurated by Maharishi in 2006), which in their depth and scope rival those of earlier years. Maharishi commented on these experiences regularly, and a book recording them is in publication.

98 I am writing this section in April 1976.

99 An important feature of the Age of Enlightenment Courses is the theoretical and practical study of the special faculties latent in human life. The examination of other scientific disciplines in the light of the Science of Creative Intelligence had already drawn attention to the fact that pure consciousness, like the quantum vacuum state, is a field of all possibilities. However, the idea of starting the new programme came to Maharishi only when he felt that there was a sufficient number of people so much at home in the state of pure consciousness that they could take advantage of the possibilities which it opened to them.

and the role of the Brahma Sūtra in kindling it. 'Brahman Consciousness is more than the sum total of the experiences of Unity. All such experiences are described in the expressions of the Upanishads. All these expressions together create that whole which is more than the collection of parts ... they create an awakening, they create a knowledge, and this knowledge stimulates consciousness to a value which is known as "the Great" — Brahman. So Brahman is the state of knowledge stimulated by the pieces of knowledge contained in the Upanishads, but taken on a holistic value ... These descriptions of the Absolute become the parts, and when they are put together some wholeness is produced. And in order to clarify what that wholeness is, Vyāsa had to structure expressions, and those are the Brahma Sūtras: sūtras of Brahman, the strings that weave the cloth of Brahman from the threads of the Upanishads put together ... The collected value of knowledge from the Upanishads, on the level of understanding, and the collected value of the experiences of Unity in daily life, on the experiential level — both these together are the subject matter of the Brahma Sūtra.'

Maharishi then makes a surprising statement. 'So the Brahma Sūtras stand as the expressions of supreme knowledge. Had they not been there, the collectedness of experiences of Unity would have remained just the collectedness of experiences of Unity in their segments — thousands of experiences, one after the other ... That kind of experience is like experiencing this pillar here, this pillar here, that pillar there, that pillar there — there is no chance of all the pillars being experienced in one vision and giving rise to the experience of the house as a whole. Experiences of Unity are very profound, very beautiful, one after the other, but there is no chance for that wholeness of experience — that tremendously unbounded, infinite value of experience — to rise up, which is more than the collection of the parts of these experiences. Vyāsa made it possible because of that knowledge which he forwarded [gave out] ... This awakening would have been left to some very, very fortunate people had not Vyāsa come along with his Sūtras ... But when experiences are growing — things [experienced one after the other] in terms of my Self — and then the Brahma Sūtra is available, immediately one begins to smile [and think], "Oh yes" — just because that awakening is on the level of intellect ... supreme knowledge ...

'This awakening is not possible by experiencing one thing after another in terms of the Self, or by understanding this in terms of the Absolute and this in terms of the Absolute ... Vyāsa, whose wisdom was so superb, gave us that supreme knowledge, those thrills of sūtras, those thrills, those impulses of knowledge, which would make us live in daily life that whole which is more than the collection of the parts of Unity experience.'[100]

In the present conversations the distinction between ex-

---

100 Lecture, Biarritz, France, 14 December 1975.

periences of Unity and supreme knowledge, or Brahman Consciousness, is not yet so clearly drawn. Dating as they do from 1968 and 1969, these conversations express only the first fruits of Maharishi's thinking about Brahman and Brahma Sūtras. Unity experiences had to become more common to provide that stimulus which made him give his thought a systematic form. But one has only to read the conversation on 'The Aggregate' to realize that the later teaching about Brahman Consciousness is already there in embryo.[101]

From the moment he started his commentary it became apparent that Maharishi's whole approach to the Brahma Sūtra was unique. The classical commentators, however they differ from one another, all treat the Sūtra largely in terms of logic and scriptural exegesis. They are content to emphasize the understanding of ultimate reality and take the experiences, which must form the raw material of true enlightenment, more or less for granted. Maharishi feels that this is no longer possible in the world today. His commentary, like everything he does, is a response to need. He wants to give a world thirsting for deeper experience a glimpse of the goal, and even more important, he wants to supply a guide whereby those who are reaching or have reached Unity Consciousness can verify and clarify their experiences. When Maharishi began work on the Brahma Sūtra in 1968 the need for

---

101 See also the conversation 'The Situation that Exists Between Relative and Absolute: The Snake and the String', where the point is made that Brahman is a state of supreme knowledge.

such guidance did not seem so pressing as it is now, when so many more people are experiencing Unity. It was, after all, especially for those who stand on the threshold of enlightenment that Vyāsa distilled into the terse phrases of the Brahma Sūtra the collected wisdom of the Upanishads so that it might enliven their understanding of what they were experiencing, and in due time generate the great awakening that is Brahman Consciousness. Maharishi is spelling out in great detail for the present age Vyāsa's age-old message of fulfillment.

Other present-day interpreters of the Sūtra (not having Maharishi's rapport with the pulse of the world) have been content to follow the older commentaries, particularly that of Shankara. Perhaps this is not altogether surprising because in Shankara's commentary, the Brahma Sūtra has elicited the greatest work of the greatest of Indian philosophers. Shankara foresaw and forestalled every possible objection to his arguments with such completeness and precision as to make any further debate along his lines almost impossible. With the dead weight of such perfection heavy upon them, the paṇḍits of recent centuries never thought of looking at the Sūtra from a different, more practical angle. Maharishi does not share this complacency. While honouring Shankara and emphasizing again and again that if he differs from him it is in approach rather than in substance, Maharishi is yet the first commentator for many hundreds of years to look at the Brahma Sūtra with new eyes, eyes that are suited to the time in which he lives.

During one of our talks at Lake Tahoe in 1968 I suggested to Maharishi that his vision was so fresh and pure because he had been too busy serving his master to read much philosophy. Maharishi then revealed a surprising fact: 'I am reading the Brahma Sūtra for the first time, absolutely for the first time. While I was with Guru Dev [Maharishi's master] there was a pandit who was interested in the Brahma Sūtra and he used to take a class of brahmachārīs. Sometimes I used to take off a few minutes to listen to him. He went on for two or three months, but he spoke only on those first four sūtras of the first chapter. From there I had a glimpse of the Brahma Sūtra and that was enough. And now I am reading it for the first time.' I said that this freshness was very fortunate. Maharishi agreed. 'It's very fortunate. The glamour of Guru Dev was so great, I didn't have a moment, day or night.'

Maharishi's Work and Status

In the present conversations I take up more or less the same position as during the work on the Bhagavad-Gītā, upholding the traditional interpretations while at the same time admiring Maharishi's originality. But when we worked on the Sūtra again in 1972 a subtle change began to take place in my point of view. It may have been the growth of a little wisdom on my part, or it may simply have been that the sūtra form gave Maharishi a greater freedom of interpretation than was possible with the Bhagavad-Gītā.

Whatever the reason, I began to glimpse something of the universality of the vision that lay behind and inspired the brilliant originality on the surface.

Although I continued in my old argumentative stance, more or less from force of habit, there was now a small voice at the back of my mind whispering that Maharishi could see what I could not. I began to recognize the true nature of that inconsistency with which I on occasion charge Maharishi in these conversations. One who knows the whole sees it in every part — every part becomes an expression of the whole. For Maharishi all roads lead to Brahman. He travels sometimes along one road, sometimes along another, with complete freedom because all the signposts point in one direction. 'Wherever you go, Brahman is there.'[102] And the Brahma Sūtra is so pregnant with possibilities that it provides him with many roads along which to travel. Imprisoned as we are in the narrow confines of 'either … or', it is difficult for most of us to share Maharishi's vision. Knowledge is structured in consciousness. I could no more help seeing through my narrow lens than Maharishi can help seeing through his wide-angle one. And even the intellectual recognition that there is a wide-angle lens, while a step forward, is utterly different from actually looking through one, as recognition of the validity of Maharishi's vision is quite different from actually sharing it.

---

102 See conversation, 'Defect as the Basis of the Realization of Brahman'.

Maharishi is 'inconsistent' because he does not work on the level of memory in the same way that we do. Every interpretation seems new because it *is* new. Each time, he goes to the source of things and comes out with a new creation. That is why what he says is always fresh, that is why his enthusiasm never wanes. During our stay in Kashmir he spoke to members of the United Nations Boundary Commission stationed there. They came to the house where we were staying and he gave them what was, in effect, an introductory talk on Transcendental Meditation. It was only after listening spellbound for about an hour that I asked myself why I was so interested when I must have heard it all hundreds of times before. Then I realized that Maharishi does not recall: he re-creates.

This may provide some clue to Maharishi's way of translating, which is under such frequent, if light-hearted, attack in these conversations. Generally speaking, he seems first to gauge the overall meaning of a sūtra, in the sense of grasping it as a whole and relating it to what has gone before. Only then does he go into details of syntax and semantics, and if these fail to fit his first meaning, he is not afraid to change it for another while still upholding the tenor of his teaching. Whatever the meaning of a particular sūtra, from his level of consciousness he can only see it as making some statement about the nature of Brahman and how Brahman is to be known.

This combination of great firmness of principle with extreme flexibility of method, complete openness to the lessons of experience, is one of the secrets of Maharishi's strength. It is to be found in all his work, teaching, and organization as well as translation and commentary. In his response to ever-changing circumstances, he can afford, from his basis of absolute stability, to leave all options open. He is never bound by what has gone before, sometimes to the discomposure of hidebound creatures around him.

Perhaps such flexibility contradicts our preconceived ideas of a realized man delivering fixed pronouncements *ex cathedra* on all subjects, never changing his mind. I believe these preconceptions to be mistaken. If we are to judge by his creation, is not the Creator the greatest experimenter of all? Does he not show an infinite willingness to learn from experience and to start again? The most we can say for him is that his fullness must be such as to overflow into infinite creativeness in all directions. Sometimes he succeeds, sometimes he seems to fail, but he goes on creating — and experimenting. Maharishi is a brilliant example of creative intelligence in action — or at play — and I see his work in much the same light. It is wrong, if very human, to seek the unchanging values of the Absolute in the flux of the relative. I may not yet be secure in the absoluteness of the Absolute, but Maharishi has certainly taught me the relativity of things relative.

I have sometimes wondered of late how any interchange is possible at all between such a mind as his and a mere ignorant seeker. Perhaps it is because Maharishi is so good at observing the conventions of relative life. He has often pointed out that Unity has to be kept in its place, which is on the level of awareness. It should not spill over into activity. Maharishi does not even let it spill over into his speech. His achievements may be larger than life but he does not act as if he himself were, nor does he talk in terms of his own universality or omnipresence, in the way that the sages of India so often do.[103] He likes to tell the story of the meal he was having with some wise men when one of them asked him: 'What are you eating?' Without waiting for his answer another of the company replied: 'I am eating Brahman.' They looked at Maharishi, who said: 'I am eating rice.' He continued that if he had to be associated with eating, then it should be rice, and if he was not to be associated with eating then he was not eating.

The clue to what, for want of a better phrase, I would call Maharishi's sense of proportion may lie in his devotion to his master. He frequently emphasizes the need to continue such devotion even after Unity has been reached and thus to keep alive a remnant of duality. His own devotion was by all accounts exceptional,[104] but then, so was its object, Swami Brah-

---

103 I remember one such instance when a famous sage was confronted with a German television crew during the 1966 Kumbha Melā, the great spiritual gathering, at Allahabad. 'I know Germany well', quoth he, never having set foot outside India. He added, 'Germany is my Self.' After Maharishi's simplicity I found such talk grating, but it is common usage in India, both among those who are realized and among those who think they are.

104 Some of us had a chance confirmation of this, again at the 1966 Kumbha Melā. While visiting Anandamoyi Ma, we fell to talking with an Indian High Court judge who happened to have known Guru Dev.

mananda Saraswati, who for the last twelve years of his life graced the seat of the Shankarāchārya of Jyotirmath,[105] a seat that had been vacant for a hundred and fifty years because no occupant worthy of it could be found.[106] The first President of India, Dr. Rajendra Prasad, sat at Guru Dev's feet, and my old teacher, Dr. Sarvepalli Radhakrishnan, who became the second President, addressed him as 'Vedānta Incarnate'. Maharishi's devotion continues. Not a day passes without some tribute to Guru Dev. Whatever he does, whatever he achieves, even what he thinks, he attributes to his master.

With such greatness of soul as Guru Dev's before one, it is perhaps easier to keep one's 'perspective' when the sense of one's own universality dawns. Certainly this was essential in the path that Maharishi chose. Had he been content to sit in a Himālayan cave he could perhaps have afforded to let go and just give himself over to the sense that 'I am Brahman and all else is "māyā"[107] anyway', so common in India. But

---

He told us of Maharishi's closeness to his master and the intensity of his devotion, which was extraordinary, even by Indian standards.

105 Shankara, also known as 'Ādi Shankarāchārya' ('ādi' — original, first; 'āchārya' — teacher), established four principal seats of learning in different parts of India to carry on his teaching. Jyotirmath in northern India is one of them. Those who occupy these seats are known as Shankarāchāryas.

106 Maharishi tells that for twenty years the paṇḍits had tried to persuade Guru Dev, as Maharishi affectionately calls his master, to accept the seat of Jyotirmath. Guru Dev, who from a young age had lived as a strict recluse, always managed to evade them, but finally, at the age of seventy-two, no longer put up any resistance and allowed himself to be installed as Shankarāchārya.

107 Usually translated as 'illusion'; Maharishi translates it as 'that which is not'.

seeing the possibility of helping mankind out of its state of struggle and suffering, he decided to come out into the world and give the ancient knowledge of the Himālayas hands and feet, so that it could travel and be useful to people in active life. For almost twenty years[108] he has been working to this end at the rate of twenty hours a day, much of that time spent with other people. In this work he often seems to want to bridge, even to hide, the gulf that separates him from those around him. Just how successful he has been is shown by the fact that, in working with him, the flow of argument can be quite free and uninhibited. Although Maharishi does his best not to remind one who he is, his true status sometimes cannot help breaking through, even to a comparatively insensitive nature like my own.

I recall particularly one occasion when we were discussing some verses of the Gītā on the lawn of Henry Nyburg's house in Wiltshire, where much of the Gītā commentary was written. I was as usual happily gamboling on the surface, full of quips, when all of a sudden a look came into Maharishi's eyes, or rather the look went from his eyes. They ceased to focus and became liquid, unfathomable. My poor fluttering mind, suddenly out of its depth, almost frightened, recoiled. I thought to myself: 'My God, to whom am I talking?' Fortunately, perhaps, such moments have been rare, or the pages that follow would be bare indeed. But my own lack

---

108 *Editor's note*: Twenty years came to be over 50 years.

of sensitivity and Maharishi's capacity to 'eat rice' have seen to it that they are quite crowded.

It may be said that Maharishi deserved a worthier 'adversary'. This is true, of course, and it is good to see great minds, particularly from the realm of science, now flocking to Maharishi. A unique interchange is going on that will set new frontiers to knowledge. Somehow one always knew that the light of this exceptional being would not remain hidden from the world.

And yet in the context of the work on the commentaries, of which these conversations formed a part, the ordinary intelligence had a role to play.[109] In the early stages of preparation of this book, the following exchange took place.

Maharishi: People will enjoy this book. They will enjoy your insight.

VK: I haven't any insight. It's your wisdom they will enjoy, and they will enjoy it all the more when set against my ignorance.

Maharishi (quick as lightning): See what insight you have!

Mine is a critical rather than a constructive turn of mind. I look instinctively for hidden assumptions or gaps in the argument. This was sometimes useful in our work together because it forced Maharishi to come down to my level of thinking and to elaborate step by step, for the ordinary in-

---

109 For Maharishi's own view of this role, see conversation, 'On the Purpose of Discussion'.

telligence, what from his level is quite obvious and therefore not in need of elaboration. And when I was superficial Maharishi was always there to take my remarks to a different level. Even from the present conversations it is clear that I am by no means alone in filling this role. The freedom that Maharishi allows his questioners and critics must be unique. But I hope it is clear that this freedom is not abused. However sharp our quips, there is only love and respect for Maharishi.

For me these conversations have been a source of pure delight, both when I participated in them and now, in their reproduction. Unfortunately the printed page can give no idea of Maharishi's voice, the variety of its inflexions, the subtle emphases, and the laughter that is a language in itself. But I hope that something comes over of the liveliness, the grace, the joy, the patience and, above all, the generosity with which Maharishi shares his wisdom with others.

THE CONVERSATIONS

I

ON THE NATURE AND
PURPOSE OF DISCUSSION
— AN OVERALL PERSPECTIVE

As a prelude to the Tahoe and Kashmir sections of this book, both originating from the late 1960s, I should like to reproduce two conversations dating from the 1970s. These will help to put all the other conversations into perspective since they set forth Maharishi's views on the nature and purpose of discussion.

The first conversation took place in late 1973 in Vittel, a spa in eastern France, where Maharishi was holding a Teacher Training Course. It was my first chance to tell Maharishi about my progress with the book since he had given his consent to the project earlier that year. In his remarks Maharishi goes deeply into the significance of our conversations. It was a great relief to me that he could see my negativity in such a positive way, though I suspect that in India the vāda (discussion) of which he speaks took place between people of more or less the same level of consciousness.

It may be of interest that immediately after this exchange, undeterred, or perhaps encouraged, by his remarks, I argued with Maharishi about the Veda for at least an hour, bringing out all the 'questions, doubts, challenges, furies' in my armory.

The second conversation, which took place in May 1974 in Arosa, Switzerland, is less complete, but I should like to include it because Maharishi's angle is slightly different from that which he took in Vittel. The short exchange occurred after I had read Maharishi one of the Tahoe conversations which found me in a particularly argumentative mood. The talk is of argument and argumentation rather than discussion, though I think these three terms were synonymous for us.

Vittel, France, 19 December 1973
On the Purpose of Discussion

VK: You see, these are all disparate conversations on the internal mechanics of the Absolute, on shravana, manana, nididhyāsana,[110] on the Purusha of the Sāṁkhya, and all kinds of different things. And it has no overall theme, except your thought.

Maharishi: I think it'll be good enough if from every direction the thought focuses on the desired goal.

VK: Yes. I say in my introduction that, although there is no overall theme, the raising of human consciousness is the theme of all you think and do and are. That is the common theme.

Maharishi: If some of it comes out from everything, then

---

110 Hearing, contemplation, and meditation.

78

every expression is successful.

VK: But what I am unsure about is this: you see, I contradict you very firmly on nearly the whole thing, and especially on the method of translation and this sort of thing. Although I explain your methods I don't know how far you want these contradictions left [in the manuscript].

Maharishi: I think these contradictions are the voice of the age. The message of the Transcendent must be in contradiction with the surface values of life, and unless you voice them the purpose of the speech will be lost. It's in this age that the understanding about everything is so much on the surface. Now, the message of the depth is in complete contradiction with the message of the surface. So, when you voice some value, it's not in contradiction with what I say, but it's the surface expression of that. (Laughter)

You see, neither the green nor the red of the plant, nor the roundness of the stem, nor the flatness of the leaf can be in contradiction with the sap. They are only the other expression of it. So nothing can go wrong as long as we are expounding the truth of the Absolute; nothing can go wrong because everything will fall into place. So it's not contradiction. It's the liveliness which helps to bring up the holistic value of the message. It's not a contradiction — nothing can contradict — the sap stands in no contradiction with the value of the green leaf or the pinky petals.

So you don't contradict. What you bring out is the other

aspect of it, the other side of it. And when the other side comes, then only the understanding becomes more complete. Unless we explore the other side of what we are considering, the consideration will never be complete. For these reasons, it's necessary to go in detail into all the relative values, and when we consider relative values the range of the relative will reach the farthest negativity. (Laughter)

VK: That's a relief.

Maharishi: It's a great relief. And unless the whole range of negativity is covered, the consideration will always be incomplete. This is what has established a sort of tradition, tradition of vāda — discussion. It's an element in enlightening the student. They say, 'vāde, vāde, jāyate tattvabodhaḥ.' It's through questions, repeated questions, 'vāde, vāde', questions, doubts, challenges, furies — 'jāyate tattvabodhaḥ' — that is born enlightenment of the truth. Through discussions, because in discussion one goes so far — as far as the intellect could go. And if the truth will satisfy that farthest negative point, then it's really omnipresent truth. And if it can be bogged down by some negativity, then it's not omnipresent, then it's not truth, then it's not the total expression of truth. And therefore this is a feature of Nyāya, logic. Logic tears everything apart and challenges everything, can challenge everything. And if something is able to satisfy the farthest fury of discussion, then that principle is taken to be victorious.

In India the wise men sit and one challenges the other.

The other tries to defend himself, and the one who is able to defend his point to the last, the farthest end of negativity, he is rewarded.

So there is this tradition of uncovering the depth of knowledge. If bliss and if unboundedness and if eternity — if the Absolute — is omnipresent, it must be possible to locate it in the farthest negative point.

VK: Then one has nothing left to stand on because one is encompassed.

Maharishi: From all directions.

VK: Whatever one says is the truth, even if it's the obverse side. (Laughter)

Maharishi: No. If it is able to resolve the opposite viewpoint, whatever it may be, then the truth is omnipresent, then the truth is an all-time reality. If it is not able to resolve the farthest point, then there is something lacking in the status, in the character, of the truth.

See, consciousness is omnipresent. It's present in whatever a man thinks, it doesn't matter what he thinks — if he thinks rightly, if he thinks wrongly, if negatively, positively — the basis is consciousness. And through whatever thinking the consciousness could be indicated, or realized, that will be the right instrument to dig into the value of consciousness, that will be the path of enlightenment.

See, consciousness is the essence of every thought. If it is the essence of every thought, then, be it a negative thought or a positive thought, a wise man will be able to locate consciousness through whatever the surface value of the thought may be. That is why the message of the Absolute finds nothing contradicting it. It can't. The thorn may be of a different character, a negative character as compared with the tenderness of the petal, but as far as the sap is concerned, the sap is the life of the thorn as it is the life of the petal. Now because the petal is so beautiful and so delicate, if sap is considered to be the basis and the life of the petal that does not mean that that sap which is the life of the tender and beautiful petal can't be the life of the thorn. It doesn't mean that. So whatever the expression in the relative, consciousness is at the basis of it and a wise man should be able to indicate that here is consciousness.

The expression of it, be it a tender wave on the ocean or a tidal wave, the tidal wave and the tender wave both are the expression of the same water. The wise man will be able to show water in the fury of the tidal wave, he'll be able to show water in the calmness of the tender ripple. He'll be able to show the reality. And because consciousness, or the Absolute, is a value of one's own Being, one's own Self, it must be very easy to indicate it, whatever the surface expression of it may be.

That is why vāda, or discussion, is an aspect of the path of enlightenment. It's an essential part. Unless one probes into so many angles of enquiry, it may not be possible to give complete satisfaction, and if a principle is not capable of satisfying completely, then it's not the principle that will be of eternal value, absolute value. That is why discussions are a part of the practice whereby one intellectually locates the farthest end of it and transcends. So discussions are all right.

VK: But discussion can contradict. It's true that nothing can contradict the Absolute because that's on a different level, but discussions are not on the [level of the] Absolute. Even though one person may speak from the standpoint of the Absolute and the other may not, it's still in the realm of discussion, you see, so there can be contradictions.

Maharishi: But the most rewarding aspect of a discussion is that the intellect rejoices in locating something so delightful. When, in the discussion, one raises a point and the other man gets so greatly satisfied — the thrill of satisfaction — 'Ah, brilliant, I never thought of that point.' And then he thinks in his mind on what other point he can attack. He takes some one word of the answer which had satisfied him and attacks on that word. And the other man says, 'Oh, fine, this word means this.' And then he rejoices, 'Ah, what a beautiful point, I never thought of it.' And in this way, every wave of discussion brings a wave of satisfaction to the intelligent man. He understands, but he takes a stand of arguing so as to see how brilliant the other side is. And as they keep on going back and forth and back and forth — it's a great intellectual satisfaction.

And the joy increases when the opponent brings out a point of greater negativity, and all those who are listening think, 'Ah. This must be an unimpeachable point. Let's see how he answers.' And he answers in a simple way and every one says, 'Ah!'.

So discussion is an intellectual process of arriving at the final principle. And the knower of reality should be able to lead a person to that realization. There are so many furies popping up in the Upanishads — take the conversation between Gārgī and Yāgyavalkya. She [Gārgī] stands and challenges [Yāgyavalkya].[111] These are examples to show that the path of knowledge has always been through intellectual activity. Discussion is just intellectual activity to satisfy the rising wave of inquiry. So that is all right.

Arosa, Switzerland, 28 May 1974
On the Purpose of Argumentation

Maharishi: Argument has its validity in the evolution of experience and evolution of understanding. Argument takes one point and crosses it off, and then takes another point and crosses it off. This is the story of evolution. One stage is experienced and then that gets dismantled; another higher stage is experienced and that gets dismantled, and so on. So, the evolution of experience is the basis of argumentation.

---

111 See footnote 113.

One point leads to another point and then to another. This is the natural process of evolution. That is why argumentation is a natural thing where evolution is necessary. Once the climax of evolution has been reached there is no more argumentation. In the Nyāya system[112] the procedure of gaining knowledge ends with 'nigrahasthāna' (the point of arrest), from which no further march of argument is possible.

Argumentation being on the intellectual level, the intellect keeps on proceeding parallel to experience. Just as the experiences keep on being replaced by higher experiences, so the understanding keeps on being replaced by higher understanding.

VK: And so the argumentation changes …

Maharishi: It's a natural thing, just as evolution is natural.

VK: This is the trouble; there's no connection between one state of consciousness and another. If one man argues from one state of consciousness and another man argues from another, it's very surprising that there can be any converse between them at all.

Maharishi: This is what Yāgyavalkya said to Gārgī: 'No more, otherwise your head will get smashed.'[113] (Laughter)

VK: I thought about this when writing the introduction to this book. How is any argument [between Maharishi and

---

112 See MBG, pp. 473ff.

113 See BU 3.6.1, where the sage tells the importunate Gārgī that if she asks any more questions her head will fall off.

myself] possible? And then I thought: Well it's only possible because the higher state of consciousness has enough sympathy to comprehend the lower. Therefore argument is possible.

Maharishi: It's allowed. Argument is allowed because evolution has to be allowed. (Laughter) Intellectual evolution through argument.

VK: Intellectual evolution. Unfortunately that's all it is. (Laughter)

Maharishi: See, how experience and understanding proceed together.

VK: The only thing is, if experience doesn't grow, understanding doesn't grow.

Maharishi: All these scriptures come out to give an expression to experience, to the mechanics of experience, to the process of the evolution of experience. That's why the Vedas are eternal; because the evolution is eternal, the expression of the evolutionary process has to be eternal. They just go parallel. It's experience.

II
LAKE TAHOE, CALIFORNIA: SUMMER 1968

Since he first visited it in 1963, Maharishi has loved Lake Tahoe, and whenever possible he has returned there for his writing. Maharishi finds the lake very enlivening and productive of new and fruitful ideas.[114] He says that in addition to its great natural beauty, the Tahoe area has the advantage of a high altitude (over six thousand feet) without the disadvantages, since one does not feel the height 'because of the ocean-like lake'.

Thus it was at Lake Tahoe that Maharishi decided, in the summer of 1968, to begin his translation and commentary on the Brahma Sūtra. He called me there to join him in this work and he also invited Marjorie Gill and Jemima Pitman, who had been among his first supporters in England.

In order to reach Lake Tahoe by air one has to alight at Reno, Nevada. At the airport I was happy to see Debby Jarvis, whom I had first met in India in 1966 with her husband Jerry, who was the director of the Students International Meditation Society (SIMS) of America. Debby and Jerry had taken a house for Maharishi right on the lake at Crystal Bay. When we arrived, Debby took me straight to

---

114 It is interesting to note that Lake Tahoe was sacred to the American Indians.

the wooden terrace in front of the house and there, after the gaudy lights and the noise of Reno, was the huge lake, very still, bathed in moonlight, so that you could see deep into the clear blue–green water. It was one of those first encounters that are not easily forgotten.

Maharishi was not there when we arrived. He was at the nearby Squaw Valley ski resort conducting a leadership training course for over seven hundred people. It was the largest residential course to date and provided the real reason for his presence at Lake Tahoe — the Brahma Sūtra was a distinctly fringe activity. The course, the first to be video-taped, kept Maharishi busy for most of the day and, besides conducting it, he was giving interviews and private instruction, making films, planning academies, and doing a hundred other things. Yet he still found time at odd moments for the Brahma Sūtra. Some moments were odd indeed. I remember using the car bonnet (hood) as a table, with Maharishi dictating, when he was about to be driven to Squaw Valley by Jerry.

The periods usually set aside for the Sūtra were mealtimes, the early morning, and late evening or night — when Maharishi was not with the course participants. It was good that Maharishi — thanks to the Jarvises' foresight — had a house away from the course. He could not have accomplished so much work on the Brahma Sūtra had he lived, as he usually did, where the course was taking place.

The beautiful wood and stone A-frame house, with its

large living room and huge diamond-shape window occupying most of the side overlooking the lake, was of a type quite common in the area. The houses by the lake were generally subdued in colour and set amongst large trees, so that they blended beautifully with their surroundings. Except for a small stretch on the Nevada side of the lake, the sometimes quite garish hinterland did not obtrude and looking round the lake one might have been in northern Norway, so unspoilt was the view. The lake is very beautiful. Surrounded on all sides by the Sierra Nevada, its central depths were until very recently unplumbed. It could be calm one moment and extremely tempestuous the next. But whatever its moods, the colours of lake and sky were always glorious.

Because Maharishi was so occupied with his other activities, there were at Lake Tahoe none of the longer 'asides' that form the bulk of the later part of this book. For the Tahoe section I have therefore had to rely mainly on the commentaries themselves, but even these tended to be short, and in any case much of the discussion concerned the Sanskrit. Consequently this section may seem rather insubstantial and also rather technical when compared with Kashmir and Mallorca.[115] Maharishi wanted to establish the theme of his commentary and went through the sūtras at a fairly rapid pace, leaving me gasping behind, somewhat aghast at

---

115 The volume devoted to conversations in Mallorca is in preparation.

his radical departure from the usual interpretations, but also full of admiration for the beautiful sequence of his thought and for the insight that enabled him to fit the sūtras to his theme. It is not easy, in these extracts, to convey the thrill of the first encounter with the completely new interpretation that Maharishi unfolded. Starting with the simple premise that the Brahma Sūtra must be about Brahman, the ultimate reality that can be lived by everyone, Maharishi cut right through the irrelevancies of the past and made the Sūtras meaningful for people living today.

Every new interpretation of the Brahma Sūtra has to be judged against Shankara's great commentary, and the difference of approach between Maharishi and Shankara is a constant topic of the conversations. The Brahma Sūtra is the fundamental text of the Vedānta philosophy, which Maharishi has called the 'collected value of knowledge from the Upanishads'.[116] Shankara's first concern is to show that the Brahma Sūtra is a faithful expression of its source — the Upanishads — a concern he shares with other classical commentators, however much they may disagree with him about the meaning of the Upanishads. Maharishi takes the correctness of Shankara's exegesis for granted. He only wants to show how each sūtra crowns with knowledge the aspirant's growing experience of Unity. Shankara tends to take experience for granted. He speaks from the point of view of the goal, whereas Maha-

---

116 See Introduction, p. 64.

rishi always has in view the role of the Brahma Sūtra in enabling those on the path to reach the goal.

In the course of upholding his interpretation of the Upanishads, Shankara refutes other systems of Indian thought, both orthodox and heterodox. The five classical systems of Indian philosophy, as well as the theistic Shaiva and Bhāgavata philosophies, and the heterodox Buddhist and Jaina schools, which do not recognize the authority of the Veda, all come under scrutiny and attack as not adequately representing the highest goals of life.

Maharishi, while holding that the other schools are perfectly adapted to their aims, agrees with Shankara that they are not competent to portray the nature of Brahman. But the refutation of these schools is not his main concern. His emphasis is solely on the nature of Brahman. 'We can very well accept that view and say that here, because multiplicity is being filtered out, what is being filtered out is Sāṁkhya... The description of Brahman is such that it does not accept any division brought about by Sāṁkhya. But it is a description of *Brahman*. The purpose of the Sūtra is not to pull down the Sāṁkhya, but to establish Vedānta.'[117] Again, when the Buddhist doctrine of momentariness seems to be under discussion Maharishi's concern is to show what the Sūtra says about the nature of Brahman, not what it says about Buddhism. The important point here is that Brahman is not

---

117 See conversation, 'Two Ways of Approach to the Brahma Sūtra'.

overshadowed by the mutability of the universe.[118]

Maharishi's commentary, like Shankara's, reflects the need of his time. 'Shankara ... was talking in the language of his time. He had to tell the people that here is the goal of life and Jainism is not going to take you there, or Buddhism is not going to take you there.'[119] But 'the minds of today are not as in Shankara's time. They want something simple and straight ... a simple commentary on the steps of experience leading to the knowledge of Brahman.'[120]

Unlike Maharishi himself, I did not really believe that the author of the Brahma Sūtra had in mind an interpretation like Maharishi's, and I voiced my objections with regularity. I thought that Shankara's more polemical approach was much closer to Vyāsa's intentions. But according to one of the tapes, I also gave it as my opinion that it did not matter what Vyāsa had meant, so long as the Sūtras served as a vehicle to bring out Maharishi's own teachings. All the great commentators, I added, had used the Brahma Sūtra and similar classical texts as pegs on which to hang their own philosophies.

It does appear that Indian commentators, especially the great innovators, are less concerned with taking a historical view of a text than with its usefulness, in the light of their own experience and philosophy, to the lives of their

---

118 See conversation, 'How to Read the Brahma Sūtra'.
119 ibid.
120 See conversation, 'Two Ways of Approach to the Brahma Sūtra'.

contemporaries. But I now think that to speak of 'pegs' is too superficial. It is very evident to anyone who has worked with Maharishi that nothing inspires him quite so much as the ancient corpus of writings of the Vedic tradition, to which the Brahma Sūtra belongs. It seems to me that if the commentator is at home on the level of consciousness that inspired the original text, then that text can speak to him afresh, and he can successfully apply its message to the lives of the people of his day.

Lake Tahoe: Participants in the Conversations

Maharishi
BD: Brahmachari Devendra
MG: Marjorie Gill
JJ: Jerry Jarvis
VK: Vernon Katz
JP: Jemima Pitman

Two Ways of Approach to the Brahma Sūtra:
How to Save Shankara from Contradiction

This discussion raises a number of themes that keep recurring in the conversations: the difference between Maharishi's approach and that of Shankara, the extent to which the Brahma Sūtra is a polemical work directed against other systems, and Maharishi's viewpoint that Brahman is not something only to be thought about but that it has to be approached through steps of experience and be *lived* in daily life.

As already explained, the Tahoe section of this book tends to be rather technical, and this particular conversation fairly bristles with the names of Indian systems of philosophy. A simple explanation of the systems referred to can be found in the appendix to Maharishi's commentary on the Bhagavad-Gītā.[121] However, it is not necessary to know the ins and outs of these philosophies in order to appreciate Maharishi's main point: the Brahma Sūtra is not to be regarded as a Vedānta tract directed against other systems; rather, the nature of Brahman is such that any description of it automatically transcends the categories governing those systems.

In the Vedānta philosophy of Shankara, realization is likened to the recognition that something which in dim light appeared to be a snake is in fact a rope, or string. Once the rope is recognized as a rope, the snake of ignorance simply disappears. Both in this conversation and in the one that follows it Maharishi interprets this analogy so as to illustrate his own approach to the Brahma Sūtra.

In this conversation Maharishi throws more light on the difference between his approach to the Brahma Sūtra and that of Shankara. This theme is also prominent in the first

---

121 MBG, pp. 472–94; see also the Introduction to this volume, section, 'Brahma Sūtra'.

part of the Kashmir section. Maharishi keeps returning to it because it is obviously important to him to show that his commentary is in conformity with that of the great master of his tradition. In my role as devil's advocate, I fasten on the superficial points of difference between the commentaries, while Maharishi brings out the deeper harmony between them and shows that the difference is one of approach dictated by the very different circumstances of Shankara's time and our own.

We were sitting in front of our house on the wooden terrace, which jutted out into the water and gave us an unimpeded view of the incomparable lake. Some young people were water-skiing not far away, and the conversation on tape is punctuated by our inexpert comments on their exploits and Maharishi's sympathetic 'oh, oh, oh's', as one or other of them was about to hit the water.

Maharishi: Even if there is reference to the world in the Sūtra, it has to be translated into terms of Brahman. The teaching is about Brahman; the teaching is not about the world. The teaching is just not about the world.

VK: The world is part of Brahman; the world is an aspect of Brahman.

Maharishi: Nothing other than that. Shankara took the other view. But even from that point of view the purpose is the same. Brahman is full. Whatever the relative [may be], Brahman is full. And therefore we could say that if Brahman is eternal the relative also has to be eternal. Or we could say [with Shankara] that Brahman is eternal and therefore it is not broken down by any relativity.

BD: How does this commentary differ from Shankara's commentary?

VK: I think you had better ask how it will resemble Shankara's commentary. (Laughter)

Maharishi: How can we save Shankara from contradiction? You see, from both angles the purpose is the same: unity — whether we go to prove that all this diversity is unity, or whether we go to prove that unity is omnipresent and eternal and don't talk of diversity at all. We either say that this [world], even though it seems to be negative, negative, changing, changing — but look at that, it is *continuously* changing. Therefore it is eternal. So eternity is the basis of futility [mutability]. Futility does not matter; what matters is continuity, eternity — that alone. So from this side we prove that this [world] is Brahman. Or we say [and this is Shankara's view], that Brahman is eternal and omnipresent; therefore it is all-pervading. This [world] is not important; what is important is Brahman.[122] From both angles we are proving exactly the same

---

122 When this was read to him on 3 February 1974, Maharishi added: 'When Shankara says that the world is not important he is only saying that more important is that wholeness of life which the different aspects of life, put together, are able to project. He only expounds the glory of the whole, which is greater than the collection of parts.'

thing. The difference in the method of approach has no power to dismantle the reality. In this way we understand Shankara. All his arguments are justified. Now, here you are. The Brahma Sūtra has a vision of Brahman. It establishes Brahman.

VK: So, seen from either angle, every statement it makes is a statement about Brahman.

Maharishi: Yes, direct Brahman, Brahman, Brahman. Only they [other commentators] have taken *this* approach; we have taken *this* approach. They are not wrong, and we hope that … (laughter)

VK: What they have done is to try and refute other schools.

Maharishi: They have gone the hard way. But they have been successful in their hard way.

VK: The whole of Shankara's commentary is …

Maharishi: Is very beautiful. This no one could have done except Shankara himself.

VK: He is either refuting the Mīmāṁsakas [the Karma Mīmāṁsā school] or the Bauddhas [Buddhist schools], or some other school of philosophy. That is his point of view, whereas your point of view is simply to make statements about Brahman.

Maharishi: This is a much simpler job. The hard job our predecessors have done. (Laughter) So we don't have to go the hard way.

VK: But just from the very construction of the Brahma Sūtra, it seems their approach is the one that the author had in view, because a lot of the Sūtra is not affirmation at all — a lot of it is argumentative.

Maharishi: Because they [the commentators] took that approach, and they came out to be consistent in that approach.

VK: But when you read the sūtras themselves, many of them are seen to be argumentative.

Maharishi: When we read, it's an angle that brings out the meaning. So they have taken an angle which they alone could have taken. Shankara knew that easier commentaries could be written straight away, but he has proved his point by the toughest possible angle, which needed all scholarship. He has taken the most scholarly approach that there could be and has proved that the consistency of that approach does justice to the Brahma Sūtra and fulfils the purpose of Vyāsa.[123]

Someone of a lesser intellect (laughter) could take an approach from his status and find that it is much easier. The other approach is easier for the scholarly people, but our approach is

---

123 Maharishi added when this was read to him: 'To say that the [red] rose is red is obvious. To say that the rose is a faint red is not so obvious because it is the deeper red on the surface that one is faced with; but the faint red is a reality at the depth of the rose. Now, to say that the rose is colourless is to satisfy the farthest limit of enquiry, for the colourless sap is the ultimate reality of the rose. So, if an argument is able to establish the rose in terms of the colourless sap, then this train of reasoning will be able to satisfy any enquiry between the deep red of the rose and its colourless sap. That is why Shankara went through all this process of argumentation.'

easier for laymen. And in this way we can hold Shankara high, yet establish this [our] viewpoint. And then we can say, 'Yes, from that angle which he has taken no one can refute Shankara; no harder [more rigorous], no better commentary than Shankara's can be brought out because it is the most scholarly, and he has succeeded in maintaining the consistency of his approach.' And this is the greatness of Vyāsa; he can satisfy the layman from this angle and the scholarly man from this angle. And here is Shankara, so many hundreds of years ago, and now ... It is a beautiful vision of the whole. And then with this approach we don't have to shiver on any point.

VK: And just go on regardless.

Maharishi: Yes. (Laughter) Before this, no one brought out the meaning in such a layman's manner because the time was not ripe for it. This is the scientific age. Scientific age means childlike intellect, which would not believe anything that has not been seen or measured. So in this age ... the simplest style of approach and direct realization belong to only this age. Therefore this is the commentary of this age; that was the commentary of that age.

VK: When people had minds.

Maharishi: Yes, when people had minds they could recognize a thing even without seeing it, by inference.

(Maharishi breaks off as we all follow the misfortunes of a water skier.)

I think this morning has been very good. At least we found a way of holding Shankara high. Once we have held Shankara high we are safe. We feel good. Otherwise it won't be right. This was done during lunch on Tahoe Lake.

VK: The most beautiful surroundings possible.

Maharishi: So beautiful ... I think this vision is so clear — about Shankara and this relationship [between his commentary and ours]. Because of Brahman being Brahman we can accommodate between two extreme points. (Laughter) If Brahman can accommodate two different extremes [relative and Absolute], it must also be able to accommodate between the wise and the layman, the ignorant; between the wise and what? Illiterates. This is how we hold on to Shankara and save ourselves from drowning in ignorance. This is how to save Shankara from contradiction.

VK: The point is that earlier on in the section Shankara refuted the Sāṁkhya system by quoting from scripture. And here he is refuting the Sāṁkhya in purely philosophical terms, without reference to scripture. Before, he used texts from the Upanishads.

Maharishi: Having finished that, he now goes on to common sense.

VK: Yes. He goes on to refute the Sāṁkhya in philosophical terms.

Maharishi: Now, our purpose in commenting on this sūtra will be to establish oneness of Brahman. Not refuting any Sāṃkhya or anything; just establishing oneness of Brahman and looking at the world as Brahman, nothing other than Brahman. The point made by Vedānta is that there is only the string and not the snake. Now [in the angle we are taking] we'll see the snake *as* a string. Instead of putting all emphasis on refuting that the string is the snake, we will see throughout the Sūtras that the snake is the string — the world is nothing other than Brahman. That will be a very positive perception of Brahman — through the world. These are two different angles. Rather than saying that the string is not the snake, we will say that the snake is the string; the snake, in reality, is the string.

VK: In reality, yes.

Maharishi: So, no refuting, but positive statements.

VK: This is what we're seeking all the time, isn't it? Positive statements about the nature of Brahman — not negative statements about the nature of Sāṃkhya; positive statements about the nature of Brahman. (Laughter)

Maharishi: It's such a beautiful [angle].

VK: The problem is that when you read the Brahma Sūtra you see that it's argumentative right the way through.

Maharishi: Right, that is the stand that Shankara took.

VK: Well, I mean, that is the only stand one can really take. (Laughter)

Maharishi: If we want a new commentary ...

VK: Then we have to take a different stand. (Laughter)

Maharishi: Not beating about the bush.

VK: But it's a very argumentative work. It's all 'anumāna' (inference) and 'na' (not) this and 'na' that; it's not a positive statement. (Laughter)

Maharishi: But then there is no *Brahma* Sūtra there. The purpose — Brahman — is there, but in such a roundabout way. The scholarly way is such a roundabout way. To see that there is no darkness left anywhere, drive it out from all the corners — this is the scholarly way. Only good minds use that way; they don't want to leave any dark corner anywhere. So, from that angle Shankara has done a lot.

VK: That is not something necessary for the present state of Kali Yuga.[124]

Maharishi: Because it's the state of stress! (Laughter) The minds of today are not as in Shankara's time. They want something simple and straight. So, such ignorant people [as ourselves] can give a simple commentary on the steps of experience leading to the knowledge of Brahman. Simple.

VK: So we'll see if you can bend the Brahma Sūtras to your bow. (Laughter)

---

124 The traditional Indian name for the age in which we are supposed to be living. See conversation, 'Shruti and Smṛiti'.

Maharishi: Now, I think the portion we are working on will be the toughest. Having succeeded in it, the whole thing will be easy. Because this portion is about creation, and if we are able to hold our thesis through this … (Laughter) Now let's start …

VK: In this sūtra [2.2.11] the topic is supposed to change from Sāṁkhya to Vaisheshika.

Maharishi: (Laughter)

VK: Maharishi, I still think …

Maharishi: Now, we can very well accept that view and say that here, because multiplicity is being filtered out, what is being filtered out is Sāṁkhya.[125] We can very well say it. Now, if the qualities [of Vaisheshika][126] begin to be filtered out, we will say, 'Come on, Vaisheshika is being filtered out. And Vedānta remains.' (Laughter) We could say this, but we can't pin down the whole Brahma Sūtra to Sāṁkhya or Vaisheshika or to the other topics which they mention. The description of Brahman is such that it does not accept any division brought about by Sāṁkhya. But it is a description of *Brahman*. The purpose of the Sūtra is not to pull down the Sāṁkhya, but to establish Vedānta.

---

125 The Sāṁkhya system counts the number of components that make up life. See MBG, pp. 480–3.

126 The Vaisheshika system 'analyses the special qualities (vishesha) which distinguish an object from other objects.' See MBG, pp. 477–8.

VK: But to establish Vedānta by contradicting theories that contradict Vedānta. (Laughter)

Maharishi: That is on the intellectual level. It's fine for all those who have enough time to juggle about. But the man of action needs something positive: What is Brahman? Here is Brahman. Finish off. Forget about differences. If [in reality] there is no difference, why talk of differences?

VK: But the terms found in these Sūtras are terms used in logical arguments between systems.

Maharishi: Yes, they are necessary for a very right [meticulous] mind; of course they are necessary. But a bare statement of fact is just enough to give a taste of Brahman.

VK: But one would think that when they speak of all these pramāṇas (means of validating knowledge)[127] it's more complex than just a bare statement of fact.

Maharishi: These pramāṇas are there to establish the truth. So when we establish the truth of the wholeness of Brahman, the indivisibility of Brahman, the evenness of Brahman, then pratyaksha (direct perception) and anumāna (inference) and other pramāṇas [are necessary].

VK: But Maharishi, I still think that the Brahma Sūtra is the document of the Vedānta, just as Jaimini's Sūtra is the docu-

---

127 In Indian philosophy the most commonly accepted means of validating knowledge are direct perception (pratyaksha), inference (anumāna), comparison (upamāna), verbal testimony (shabda).

104

ment of Karma Mīmāṁsā, and so on with the Yoga Sūtra and the Vaisheshika Sūtra and the Nyāya Sūtra ...

Maharishi: Right, right. Now, what they [the commentators] have done is to establish the supremacy of Vedānta intellectually against the five other philosophical systems. What we are going to do is establish the Brahma Sūtra on the level of experience. So, we are only fulfilling Shankara's purpose. That was established on the level of theory; we are on the level of experience.

VK: Yes, but I am speaking of how the Brahma Sūtra was written.

Maharishi: How it came about.

VK: I think it was written just as a tract, just like these other tracts, to refute the other systems.

Maharishi: Right, right, right. Shankara had to establish a philosophy, or a principle.

VK: Now I'm talking of Bādarāyaṇa,[128] not of Shankara.

Maharishi: Oh, Bādarāyaṇa did justice to Brahman! His purpose was plain narration of the characteristics of Brahman.

VK: You don't think it was the same thing — that he too was refuting the other schools?

---

128 The author of the Brahma Sūtra, traditionally identified with the sage Vyāsa.

Maharishi: In the time of Bādarāyaṇa there were no other schools existing.

VK: He mentions Jaimini by name. I'm not sure if he mentions the founders of any of the other systems, but he speaks of their systems by implication.

Maharishi: Jaimini can be mentioned with reference to Brahman, just because the finest karma (action) is that in the celestial.[129] So somewhere, sparingly, he could be mentioned. Jaimini knocks at the door of Brahman.

VK: Well, if you can make your theme fit, why not?

Maharishi: So far the theme is coming on very well.

Superimposition

The conversation that follows is on the definition of 'adhyāsa', or 'superimposition', with which Shankara begins his Brahma Sūtra commentary. Because the conversation is so short and the concept of adhyāsa so important, I decided, when preparing this book, to explain the subject more fully in an introduction. However, not being too sure of my ground, I wanted Maharishi to hear what I had written. I seized my chance when he was a captive audience during a car journey in February 1974. We were driving from

129 The Karma Mīmāṁsā system founded by Jaimini deals with karma, or action, and action in the very subtlest, or celestial, fields of experience leads to the state of Unity, which is discussed in the Brahma Sūtra. See Introduction, section, 'The Brahma Sūtra'.

Hertenstein on Lake Lucerne to Interlaken, where Maharishi was to give a course on Vedic Studies for the master's programme of Maharishi International University. When there was a lull in the conversation I read my piece.

Maharishi made some very enlightening comments about how the rigid boundaries of perception become a means of glorifying the boundless. So the short Tahoe conversation is really a pretext for appending the longer and more interesting one, which took place in Switzerland nearly six years later.

VK: In the introduction to his commentary Shankara gives a very good definition of 'adhyāsa'. He says, 'smṛiti-rūpaḥ paratra pūrva-dṛishtāvabhāsa'.[130]

Maharishi: The whole of avidyā (ignorance) is based on adhyāsa.

VK: Yes, but I was thinking that if it's a memory of something previously observed, from where does that which was previously observed come? The definition begs that question.

Maharishi: It is just that string and snake. From there adhyāsa is defined.

VK: Yes, the previously observed snake is imposed upon the

---

130 The false appearance (avabhāsa) in another object (paratra, lit. 'in another place'), similar in nature to memory (smṛiti-rūpa), of something that has been previously observed (pūrva-dṛishta).

string being observed at present. But in order to have observed something previously, there must already have been some adhyāsa. It's an infinite regress.

Maharishi: There has been a chain of adhyāsa generation after long generation. Always the same thing coming on.

VK: Yes. I think Shankara's presentation is wholly from the point of view of supreme knowledge, really.

Maharishi: It must be. It can't be otherwise.

VK: It's just wholly that. Therefore the question of origination doesn't arise. It's just a state that always is.

Maharishi: Yes, just a description of what is.

Postscript: Switzerland, 13 February 1974

VK: Maharishi, I wrote something on superimposition, on adhyāsa. I would very much like you to comment on it.

Maharishi: Yes, yes.

VK: I wrote: 'The concept of the superimposition of appearance upon reality, of the appearance of a snake upon the reality of the string, is central to Shankara's thought. And it is no mere concept, for, as Maharishi points out, it is possible actually to experience how the snake appears upon the background of the string, how the relative appears upon the background of the Absolute. But in order to experience this, one must first have seen through the snake, have seen it for what it is — an appearance of the string. The tendency to see the string as a snake is woven into our categories of cognition. The ignorance that this implies is basic, but it is remediable. Unfortunately, Shankara's clear intellectual exposition of the mechanics of superimposition has led people to suppose that the remedy was to be found in trying directly to alter our mental categories — the way we look upon the world. One of Maharishi's great contributions has been to reaffirm the physiological basis of mental activity. Without the radical change in the nature of the nervous system brought by the practice of the Transcendental Meditation technique, the truth of Shankara's teaching, however clearly understood on the intellectual level, will simply not be allowed to dawn on the level of actual experience. The rigid boundaries imposed by our mental categories will not permit the unbounded to penetrate through the boundaries.'

Now, this next point I would like you to check: 'It is not the actual nature of these categories, but rather their rigidity that is the obstacle to realization. The physiological changes brought about by the practice of the Transcendental Meditation technique form the essential prerequisite for breaking down these rigid barriers of beginningless ignorance.' Is that right? Is it really the rigidity that is the obstacle?

Maharishi: No. What we can say is that the rigidity might remain there, but there is that influx of unboundedness —

consciousness overtakes — and then it becomes so natural and so profoundly one with one's life that the rigidities, which were thought to have obstructed the influx of the Absolute before, now begin to radiate that unboundedness. Those rigid boundaries become the rigid expressions of the unbounded, so that the unbounded shines so clearly.

VK: Aha, aha.

Maharishi: The rigidity is helpful to make the unbounded spring up in such concrete forms, so that it is the unbounded which is rigidly, or concretely, brought to experience. So, it is not even the rigidity of the boundaries, it is only the lack of the unboundedness [which is the obstacle].

VK: But isn't the obstacle the rigidity of our mental categories, the rigidity of the way in which we impose a pattern on the world? Or do you really mean that this rigidity itself becomes helpful?

Maharishi: We would say [that the obstacle is] lack of the unboundedness, lack of that comprehension of wholeness.

VK: Yes, yes, I see.

Maharishi: Then that lack becomes responsible for the world of differences. And once that lack is removed, the world of differences is the world of wholeness. It's a completely different story.

VK: Aha. So, it's an integrative process in some way.

Maharishi: It's an integrative process, yes. If we say that it is the boundaries that bind, or overshadow, the boundless, it doesn't appeal to logic.

VK: So the boundless has to come first and shine through the boundaries.

Maharishi: And occupy our awareness to such an extent that, whatever we see, we find that that thing represents our own consciousness — unbounded.

VK: Oh, and it is these rigidities which are responsible for the multiple infinities. The fact that there are these rigidities means that one can still see things separately; otherwise, it would all be one.[131] But these rigidities are there, and so, when one sees the boundless in terms of these rigidities, then one experiences these multiple infinities, one upon the other, one object after another seen in terms of the Self, in terms of the boundless.

Maharishi: Right, right, multiple infinities. It's so interesting …

VK: But in that case you're looking upon superimposition in a very positive way. You are saying that adhyāsa is somehow necessary in order to experience the fullness of reality. Yes? Shankara says that we superimpose these categories onto the flat Brahman. Yours is in some way a much more positive conception.

---

131 See conversation on 'The Gap' which discusses the concept of 'leshāvidyā', the faint remainder of ignorance, which makes activity possible in the state of Unity.

Maharishi: That's why it works; that's why it shows results in life.

The Situation that Exists Between Relative and Absolute: The Snake and the String

This is really a commentary on Brahma Sūtra 2.2.15: 'rūpādi-mattvāch-cha viparyayo darshanāt', which was translated at that time as: 'And from cognition it is clear that the opposite arises from the qualities of form and so on.'

Monier-Williams[132] defines 'viparyaya' as 'mistaking anything to be the reverse or opposite of what it is.' Maharishi says that the snake, in the Vedānta analogy, is the viparyaya, the wrong knowledge, of the string. He makes the beautiful point that only when one has actually cognized the situation where the snake, or relative creation, starts to be experienced out of the string, or Absolute, can one understand the Vedānta view that the world is just a superimposition upon the reality of Brahman and that, in truth, all this is Brahman.

Maharishi: Now, come on. Oh, beautiful — Vyāsa — how beautiful!

VK: Let's see what is coming out now.

---

132 Sir Monier Monier-Williams, *A Sanskrit-English Dictionary* (Oxford University Press, 1899), p. 974. See also YS 1.8.

Maharishi: It's so beautiful. Vyāsa has to explain the situation in the world — the field of action. Viparyaya is the snake. The snake is the viparyaya of the string. Why do we say that the creation is the viparyaya of Brahman? Because we have cognized it — darshanat. We have cognized the situation where the viparyaya takes place, where the snake starts to be experienced out of the string. We have seen that, we have cognized that, we have realized that, and that is the realization of supreme knowledge. It has been realized how the water becomes milk.[133]

VK: Things taking form, you mean.

Maharishi: Yes. How relativity starts from the Absolute — that has become a living reality to us. And then only, on this basis of 'darshana', direct cognition, on the strength of this experience, we say that all this visible form found in creation — 'rūpādi-mattvāt' — is the viparyaya of Brahman. Because we have seen it.

VK: You mean, we've seen how the one becomes the other.

Maharishi: How the one becomes the other. And we have seen that the one does not become the other, yet begins to appear.

VK: 'Viparyaya' means something that is opposed, inverted, opposite. You use it as a technical term for this …

---

133 A reference to Brahma Sūtra 2.2.3: The pure water of the Absolute becomes the cloudy milk of the relative.

Maharishi: The Vedantic technical term for this is 'viparyaya'. The jagat (world) is the viparyaya of Brahman. This is the usual understanding. Just as the snake is the viparyaya of the string.

VK: Well, how does this connect with the previous sūtra, which showed that Unity was not on the level of ...

Maharishi: Of action.

VK: Yes, and now ...

Maharishi: Now then, from where does action come? That action is *there* is a reality. And the previous sūtra has said: 'Don't bring Unity to be lived in the field of action. Live it in the field of consciousness. The unity of Brahman is lived on the level of consciousness and not on the level of action.' But now, the level of action has to be completely negated. And how does it exist? It exists as the viparyaya. All this action is just the apparent phase of this [Absolute], because we have cognized that [truth]. We have cognized that viparyaya is not an intellectual conception, but is the expression of the reality of the situation that exists between the Absolute and the relative. That has become a perceived reality; that has been cognized.

See, that is why Vedānta cannot be understood by those who try to understand on the intellectual level. How could the snake come out from the string? When one has not seen how the transformation from the Absolute to the relative [takes place] — that it [the relative] is not there, that it's a superficial imposition, that the whole thing is Brahman, [then one cannot understand Vedānta]. And that makes it clear how Brahman is never to be lived on the level of action, because action is just so futile [mutable]; action is empty Brahman. The snake is empty. And if we start to live the string on the snake … it's not possible.

VK: No. It's just a different realm altogether.

Maharishi: A completely different realm. And that is the realm of ignorance. And when Brahman has become a living reality, that realm vanishes. It's beautiful.

VK: It's very good. 'In Rome do as the Romans do.' In ignorance, do as the ignorant. (Laughter) I mean, you must use the behaviour which goes with that realm. You cannot have immutability in the changing field of action.

Maharishi: It's so beautiful. This is how it connects with the previous sūtra.

VK: It's very nice, the way you explain it.

Maharishi: This is the simplicity of Vyāsa. Only he wrote in Sanskrit. If he had written in English he would have written in simple English. Shankara made it …

VK: Complicated?

Maharishi: Scholarly, scholarly. Because he was born to do that.

VK: But Maharishi, these terms in the Brahma Sūtra are all technical, philosophical terms.

Maharishi: Yes, yes. This is the perfection of Vyāsa. He could explain Vedānta to a child and to a venerable intellect, a mature mind.

Proving Brahman from Fault

This is a commentary on the next sūtra (2.2.16), 'ubhayathā cha doshāt', translated at a later date as: 'And because of defect in either case.' The basic argument is that from the recognition of the fault, or mistake, in thinking that there are two — the relative and the Absolute — in the state of Brahman, there emerges the recognition of the wholeness of Brahman.

Whether or not it constitutes Maharishi's final say on the sūtra, the commentary illustrates both his brilliance and the one-pointedness of his vision, which sees Brahman everywhere, even in defect.

Maharishi: Oh. Beautiful. Vyāsa's intellect — such a beautiful thing. Now listen. 'Doshāt' — Brahman; from defect, or fault — Brahman. He is establishing the nature of Brahman. He is negating that both things are present in Brahman.

VK: Karma and ...

Maharishi: Karma (action)[134] and bhāva (existence).[135] Both are not in Brahman.

---

134 See BS 2.2.12.
135 See BS 2.2.14.

VK: Bhava is not in Brahman? Existence is not in Brahman?

Maharishi: No, *both* are not in Brahman, both.

VK: Both together; one …

Maharishi: Yes. Only one is there, not both. (Laughter)

VK: You *are* clever.

Maharishi: See, in the previous sūtra he said 'viparyayo dar-shanāt';[136] and here he says 'doshāt'.

VK: It's all part of the same argument.

Maharishi: Same argument, yes. Now the beauty of Vyāsa is that he is creating Brahman from dosha (defect). (Laughter) Where is the dosha in Brahman? If the two are put together, then that will be the dosha in brāhmī-sthiti (the state of Brahman). That will defeat the purpose of brāhmī-sthiti.

VK: Only one is there.

Maharishi: So from dosha he is proving the unity of Brahman. You see? He is finding Brahman in fault. And what is the fault? The fault is to see the two, both relative and Absolute, as being there, in Brahman. That is the fault.

VK: You're really being too clever, Maharishi. How do you think out these things? It's unbelievable. (Laughter)

Maharishi: (Laughing) We are stuck, we are stuck with the

---

136 See preceding conversation.

wisdom of Vyāsa. Now, in the previous sūtra he established Brahman on the level of cognition. But cognition itself is a phenomenon which establishes the trinity of experiencer [along with experience and the object of experience]. So he finds some fault in the previous sūtra. And this is just the fault of language. That reality is transcendental, and here is language which is [necessarily relative]. So now, this point is dominating in his mind. So when he writes the next sūtra, he brings out Brahman from fault. (Laughter) You see how the sūtras are [composed], how they come out of the mind?

MG: It's fascinating, I am trying to follow.

Maharishi: Having established Brahman on the level of cognition in the previous sūtra, he now feels, 'Oh, some mistake has been made — doesn't matter; that fault is there.' And then he says 'Fault? Fault of [there being] the two, and by virtue of [the recognition of] this fault, Brahman is found to be without the two. The fault is there in the two. And therefore, in the fault of there being two,[137] brāhmī-sthiti is present. When, by mistake, two begin to be felt, then brāhmī-sthiti is disturbed.' We'll put it beautifully, nicely, but this will be the sense of this sūtra. When someone finds that the-relative-and-the-Absolute-together is a mistake, that mistake will prove the unity of Brahman. Here you are. Marvellous. Come on, next sūtra.

---

137 That is to say, in the fact that duality is faulty.

Brahman Is Found Between Two Teachings

This conversation took place during a car ride along the lake to Emerald Bay, a beauty spot in a uniquely beautiful part of the world. It was one of those rare days when Maharishi did not go to the Squaw Valley course in the morning. He had been enjoying his commentary on Brahma Sūtra 1.1.24, which he translated as: 'Light is That, because of taking recourse to Its feet.' Maharishi explained this as follows: 'Vyāsa says, "Light is the feet of Brahman. So, if you want to ascend to Brahman, hold on to his feet." That means, come to that celestial light and you will have him.'[138]

The day was exceptionally fine and I suggested that it might be the right moment for the outing that had been promised for some time. It was decided to go by car to look at some land for an academy, at a place called Tahoma, before going on to Emerald Bay.

I remember the visit to Tahoma chiefly for our encounter with a very nice lady, outside whose house we had stopped to ask the way. She asked Maharishi how he liked California and told us about the deep snow at Tahoma in winter. What I found so interesting was the perfectly natural way in which she, and for that matter other Californians, treated

---

138 The meaning is that when one has been living the celestial light of God Consciousness for some time, one becomes aware that this is not different from the light of one's own pure consciousness. The message of the sūtra is: live the state of God Consciousness first if you want to know Brahman. In conversation, Brahman is often referred to as 'he', although the word is neuter.

Maharishi, who is not the sort of person one would normally expect to see at one's front door. On another occasion, we had taken a boat ride, and, because of a sudden squall, had to make an emergency landing on the Nevada shore. We were sitting somewhat disconsolately on the grass when some boys came up to Maharishi and spoke to him as man to man in an open and friendly way, asking all kinds of questions. Their self-possession was in sharp contrast to the stares which one often met even in sophisticated parts of Europe as the white-clad figure emerged from the car.

Much of the time the road to Emerald Bay ran fairly high above the lake, which reflected such a variety of shades of blue as I have never seen in water before or since. There were turquoise, azure, peacock, cornflower, royal; there were tints of lilac, indigo, and near purple. At Emerald Bay, which is joined to the lake by only a narrow opening, the colour of the water changed to deep emerald. From a windy promontory we looked down on the white-topped waves of the stormy bay — in the distance, the calmer waters of the illimitable lake receding in its shades of blue towards the horizon. Below us, set in the middle of the bay, was a rocky island crowned by what seemed to be a ruined castle — but it could not have been, for this was California.

I had remembered the conversation in the car as having been highly enjoyable. Listening to it recently I found that much of it was about the scenery, when it was not about Sanskrit words. Several sūtras were discussed. I have reproduced here the only extensive commentary, which turns out to be quite short after the discussions about the Sanskrit have been omitted. The outing must have been near the beginning of our stay, for Maharishi was still on the first section of the first chapter, and he was particularly happy about the way in which each sūtra seemed to confirm his view that Vyāsa was making 'simple statements about the nature of Brahman'.

I will try to summarize the 'simple statements' Maharishi makes in his sketch for a commentary which follows. From my level of consciousness they were far from simple, but then the first point that Maharishi makes here is that at each level of consciousness a different teaching has to be given. For example, there cannot be the same teaching for someone who is experiencing increasing separation of Self and activity as he is approaching Cosmic Consciousness and for someone else who is experiencing increasing unity when approaching Unity Consciousness.[139] But whereas the difference in teaching may give rise to the state of Brahman, that state itself is to be found beyond these teachings, in the sense that the whole is more than the collection of its parts. However, it is necessary to go through the different steps of teaching in order to pass beyond the teaching, and Brahman can only be located when one realizes that there is no opposition between finding it within the steps of the teaching and beyond them.

Maharishi: On this beautiful excursion, I got into the spirit

139 See Introduction, section, 'Higher States of Consciousness'.

of Vyāsa's teaching, and this I got from going into the meaning of the twenty-seventh sūtra. And it's such a beautiful meaning.

MG: This is called Inspiration Point. (Laughter)

Maharishi: And this is?

JJ: Emerald Bay.

Maharishi: Emerald Bay — Inspiration Point of Tahoe lake. And here I got into the spirit of Vyāsa's teaching. And this came out of Brahma Sūtra twenty-seven of the first pāda (section) of the first chapter.[140]

VK: You're up to a beautiful commentary, Maharishi.

Maharishi: The sūtra says that for every state of consciousness there is a teaching, and by this difference of teaching Brahman is gained. Brahman is born out of the difference of the teaching.

VK: You mean, step by step.

Maharishi: Step by step, step by step. At every level of consciousness there is a teaching. There is one teaching at one level of consciousness, another teaching at another level; so by virtue of this difference in the teaching, eventually Brahman is born.

---

140 This was provisionally translated as follows: 'That is on account of the difference in teaching. Should this statement be denied, the denial would be incorrect, there being no conflict between the two even in this case.'

VK: It's very good.

Maharishi: But he says, 'The difference of the teaching is not the end. You'll not get Brahman in the difference of teaching; you'll have to go beyond that' — this is what he means. 'Don't think that in the difference of the teaching you will find Brahman.'

VK: So, what you said before is really being denied, that from the teaching of difference Brahman is born.

Maharishi: No, it is born out of the teaching of the difference, but it won't be located right there. You go beyond and you'll find it.

VK: It's very subtle, that.

Maharishi: It's very subtle, but it's the expression of the state. And then he says, 'You will find the state of Brahman in the non-contradiction of these two statements.'

VK: There's no contradiction between the two, you mean — between finding it in the difference and beyond the difference?

Maharishi: Yes, in the two states there is no difference, and in that non-difference you will find Brahman. In the non-difference of the two teachings you will find Brahman. This is the insight into Vyāsa. See how he writes? How he writes!

VK: Well, yes. Marvellous.

Maharishi: It's excellent! It's just superb! It's such a perfect vision. Look at it. First he says, 'In this', and then he says,

'Wait on, wait on; not in this, but in this.' And then he says, 'If you don't see it clearly, now I am telling you that these two statements don't oppose each other and in the non-opposition of these two you find Brahman.'

VK: Ah, yes, in the non-opposition.

MG: This has never been written before.

Maharishi: Oh, no, no. Had Shankara been driven on the Emerald Lake, (laughter) he would have found Vyāsa's spirit [here]. See this difference [among the three statements above]? It's such a beautiful exposition.

VK: Yes, Maharishi, you find it in between. I mean, there is the fact that different levels of teaching lead you to Brahman and that at the same time you have to go beyond these levels of teaching.

Maharishi: Yes.

VK: And then you have to see that there's no difference between …

Maharishi: Between going beyond [the teaching of difference] and [remaining] in that [teaching].

VK: But there is a difference, no?

Maharishi: No.

VK: They both lead to the same, you mean, or what?

Maharishi: There is no difference because in between them is the state of Brahman.

VK: No, beyond is the state of Brahman, isn't it? Beyond the teaching.

Maharishi: The difference in the teaching just describes the situation — this situation and this situation; in between them you have no situation, and that is the field of Brahman which is beyond the two, beyond the two. Look at that view.

VK: It's beautiful; just so fantastic.

MG: The colouring of the lake!

Brahman Displays Itself

In this short commentary Maharishi makes the important point that Brahman is not realized: it displays itself, for it is of the nature of one's own Self. The sūtra in question (2.1.34)[141] is usually said to deal with the inequality and cruelty found in the world, whereas Maharishi sees it as referring to Brahman alone. Maharishi never wavers from this standpoint, even if he changes the details of his interpretation, as he was to do with this sūtra in later years.

VK: 'Darshayati' is causative. It means 'causes to see', 'shows'.

Maharishi: Yes, this is how Brahman is displayed. This is

---

141 This was later translated as: 'On account of dependence there is no unevenness or lack of compassion, and thus indeed he shows.'

how Brahman is seen — that's all. Without unevenness and without any relativity is Brahman perceived. It's beautiful. Vyāsa says that this is the state of consciousness through which Brahman is lived, or seen. So, 'cause to see' means this consciousness. It's such beautiful perfection of expression. Because Brahman is not seen. Brahman is not realized.

VK: It is displayed.

Maharishi: Yes. This is the state of consciousness in which Brahman displays itself as Brahman. This is the state of consciousness which knows no roughness. It is even and there is no relativity in it; it is pure consciousness.

VK: This is how Brahman causes itself to be seen.

Maharishi: That's it. Such perfection of expression. Darshayati — causes to see. It's not that Brahman is experienced by someone, or anything like that. It causes itself to be seen. And this refers to the clarification of how the Self is Brahman. Vyāsa has established that the nature of the Self is the eternity of Brahman itself. Now he says that Brahman itself causes itself to be seen in this state of consciousness which knows no relativity, which is not uneven, and which is devoid of any roughness — even, serene, absolute Unity ...

VK: And it doesn't refer, then, to the previous sūtra?

Maharishi: No, it doesn't. It's a statement.

VK: It is completely the opposite of what all these fellows [other interpreters] are saying about cruelty in the world and

126

inequality among different creatures. I just hope that this whole thing holds water. It's so …

JJ: Full!

VK: It's so unbelievable!

Maharishi: See, we are commenting on the *Brahma Sūtra*. And they are men of the world trying to give a meaning to something that is not on the level of the world or the intellect, but is the expression of Brahman. I think the Brahma Sūtra should relate to Brahman and not to clarify behaviour in the world — cruelty and all that. It's so, so … This is what brings the tragedy of knowledge. (Laughter) Vyāsa wrote from one level; he was seeing [the truth, but his words were misinterpreted by those on a different level of consciousness]. This is how truth is lost. I think Vyāsa will rejoice in our doing the commentary. (Laughter)

VK: Maharishi, we've only two or three more sūtras and then we've finished that pada (section).

Maharishi: Let's read the next sūtra.

How to Read the Brahma Sūtra

Here Maharishi speaks about three consecutive sūtras from the second section of Chapter Two (2.2.31-3). Various topics are discussed, including once again Shankara's conception of the Brahma Sūtra. But perhaps the main theme is one which will be developed more fully in Kashmir, namely, that knowledge is different in different states of consciousness. I make the point that Maharishi may be misunderstood when he says that all is Brahman and there is nothing else. Maharishi replies that all is Brahman only for the one who is in Unity Consciousness. If people who read the Brahma Sūtra have not at least gained God Consciousness and started to approach Unity, there is a danger that they may make a mood of the whole thing.

When I read him the conversation, Maharishi added the following comment: 'The Brahma Sūtra will have significant meaning only for those who are in Unity or are approaching Unity. For others it will have a meaning in the sense of showing them that there is more to life [than they are at present experiencing]. It is like a game. One who is not a champion also enjoys the game, but the real joy comes only when one is at the top. Like that, the description of any state of consciousness will be truly enjoyed only by those who are in that state of consciousness. Others too will enjoy it in a way, but the top level will not be there.' So those of us who are not yet champions should read the Brahma Sūtra to learn of the possibilities that are open to us, but not as having immediate relevance to our present state.

During our conversations at Lake Tahoe, Maharishi emphasized the importance of God Consciousness for understanding the Brahma Sūtra. This is because God Consciousness is the immediate precursor of Unity, and at that time the state of Brahman was broadly equated with Unity Consciousness. Later, when Maharishi was able to go into the details of the state of Unity, it became clear that 'Brahman is structured out of the segments of Unity.' That is to say, the experiences in the state of Unity itself were recognized as the immediate precursors of the state of Brahman.

Maharishi: This sūtra [2.2.31][142] means that we cannot say Brahman is missing just because of the momentariness of the universe.

VK: This word 'kshaṇikatva' (momentariness) is so much a Buddhist term.

Maharishi: No, it's [an expression of the truth]. The omnipresence of Brahman was described in the previous sūtra. Now Vyāsa is saying that the omnipresence of Brahman is not overshadowed by the futility [mutability] of creation. That means, he is establishing the same conclusion as the previous sūtra by another argument. Even the momentary nature of the universe establishes that Brahman is eternal and omnipresent because existence cannot be denied, 'isness' cannot be denied — 'sarvaṁ khalvidaṁ brahma'.[143] Because existence is not missing, even the momentary nature of the world establishes Brahman as infinite.

VK: I was just thinking this commentary will not do much good.

---

142 'And on account of momentariness.'
143 'Truly all this is Brahman', CU 3.14.1.

Maharishi: Why not?

VK: Because it brings us right back to the doctrine of māyā (illusion), even though you put it in its highest form. But they'll all say, 'Oh, it's the same thing again: All is Brahman and there is nothing else.'

Maharishi: No. We are talking of the ultimate reality of it. This ultimate reality can only be recognized by our taking our consciousness to the highest in the relative, the most glorified state of life in the relative. So raise the level of relative life to such great heights ...

VK: People with very profound experiences may accept this, but ...

Maharishi: No. In the introduction we are going to hammer hard the point that this Brahma Sūtra is the study for those who have gained God Consciousness.

VK: But if somebody picks it up and opens it at random it will give the wrong impression — to the beginner, anyway.

Maharishi: No, we will leave a margin at the top and repeat in italics on every page: 'The Brahma Sūtra is for study after one has gained God Consciousness.'

VK: But Unity is not a goal to which most people look forward. Maybe if one has meditated for some time and experienced the various stages and levels of consciousness. But you have always put this emphasis on the two hundred per cent of life [one hundred per cent Absolute and one hundred per cent relative]. But now you come out with something which is the same thing as they have all been preaching, except that it's totally different.

Maharishi: Ah.

VK: Because it's produced in another way. The others put unity right at the beginning: make a mood of unity, and that's it. But superficially it's the same thing — the idea that only Brahman exists and there is nothing else. So two hundred per cent of life is meaningless at that level.

Maharishi: No. Two hundred per cent we say for Cosmic Consciousness. And then we'll say three hundred per cent for God Consciousness and Brahman is four hundred per cent. (Laughter)

JJ: But people may say, if this is the goal ...

VK: I don't want it.

JJ: Yes, I don't want it. Just as happened at this course when two people started saying, 'I don't want Unity. I like the relative field.'

Maharishi: Yes, I like the best in the relative. I don't mind if the worst is annihilated to bring out the best of the relative — and then on to Unity.

VK: It's not something that people are ready for.

Maharishi: They should not read it.

JJ: That's all you'll have to put in the front: 'Do not read this unless you are in God Consciousness' — and then the book will sell millions of copies, Maharishi. (Laughter)

VK: It's good to do the commentary, but I am not sure if it's wise to print it at this stage.

Maharishi: Wherever such things come we give a big footnote: 'If by chance a reader who has not gained Cosmic Consciousness or God Consciousness picks this up, see that you don't fall into this mood-making.'

VK: You'll have to do it on every page.

Maharishi: Keep on doing it like that all along.

VK: It's something the ordinary person is completely unready for. He will *imagine* it, and will imagine it as some unity.

Maharishi: So what we will do is to bring out this point: 'The danger is that if a man who has not gained Cosmic Consciousness or God Consciousness reads this, he may conclude this and this … Beware of these points because this is a state which is never on the level of mood-making. When you come to God Consciousness and enjoy the world in the celestial light, then this text will become a living reality for you, and not otherwise. Because as long as a man has not gained the highest status in the relative field, he can't possibly live the Absolute in his day-to-day life.' Keep on doing this at various points in the book and then we are safe. And

then we will have brought out that real living Brahman, that
state of real Brahman. The mistake in the usual commentaries on the Brahma Sūtra is that they all talk in terms of the
study of Vedānta, *study* of Brahman. Brahman is *life*. It has
to be understood on the level of living.

So kshaṇikatva (momentariness) is all right. The temporary nature of the relative itself establishes the permanent
nature of Brahman. Now in the next sūtra [2.2.32],[144] the
non-existence of creation, which becomes a living reality in
the state of Brahman, also establishes the eternity of life. Before we had the momentariness of creation, now we have
its complete non-existence. So after talking in terms of the
temporary nature of creation, he now says that this temporary nature does not exist.

VK: This idea that temporary nature does not exist — if
people read this they will misinterpret it.

Maharishi: This temporary nature does not exist *in that state
of Unity of life*. What doesn't exist is the temporary nature;
what exists is the permanent nature. So if the vision is gained
on the permanent level — fine.

VK: In this sūtra [2.2.33],[145] according to Shankara, we come
to Jainism.

Maharishi: Shankara had to do this because he was talking

---

144 'And entirely on account of not coming to be.'
145 'It is not any one thing by reason of impossibility.'

of these principles in the language of his time. He had to tell the people that here is the goal of life and Jainism is not going to take you there, or Buddhism is not going to take you there. It's a brilliant piece of …

VK: So you really think that Shankara is the brilliant one, not you? You are taking the obvious meaning, and Shankara read into the text the brilliant contradictions of other systems. (Turning to the others present) Maharishi is taking the obvious meaning, which every child could see. (Laughter)

Maharishi: Yes, obvious. Shankara is for the learned. We are for the simple, the innocent …

VK: You are taking the immediate view of the thing.

Maharishi: Yes, because Shankara has contradicted all these, there cannot come out any philosophy to say that Brahman is not there, or not there — he has refuted all possible arguments that might arise at any time. That is the value of Shankara. It is very, very beautiful. But in the absence of *our* viewpoint it is not applicable to all times. But this and that together will form a … Only, the translation will have to be redone for Shankara, because the translators have misinterpreted his ideas. They must have, because they went by the word meaning, and the word meaning could go a little bit this way, and this way — and it will distort the whole meaning.

VK: They give an accurate account of Shankara.

Maharishi: No, if we translate Shankara we will see that just by a little word here and a little word there the real vision is not available in the translations, because the translators went by the grammar, by the word meaning. If they had had that *state* [of Brahman] in mind then the translation would be different.

VK: But Shankara did not have that state in mind.

Maharishi: Of course he did. Shankara was absolutely true, true to the vision of Vyāsa; only, he took a scholarly view. If I had studied a lot of Sanskrit I would have taken the same view, fallen into the same rut. (Laughter) So we go by the vision and not by the grammar. We don't lose the grammar. So long as we have the vision, we will be able to translate Shankara very profoundly. These commentators did not have this division in mind [between other states of consciousness and Unity, the stage where Vedānta comes to be true]. Just that one verse of the Gītā: 'Na hi gyānena sadrisham pavitram-iha vidyate; tatsvayam yoga-samsiddhaḥ kālenātmani vindati.'[146] Just that one verse, that one verse. Any commentator who has done that verse properly, who had defined 'yoga-samsiddha' as we have defined it, is capable of doing these Brahma Sūtras and the Upanishads. Because that is the key to the vision — if he has it, he has it; if not, then not.

---

146 'Truly there is in this world nothing so purifying as knowledge; he who is perfected in Yoga, of himself in time finds this within himself.' MBG 4.38, p. 311.

VK: Yoga-saṁsiddha?

Maharishi: Yoga-saṁsiddha. 'Yoga' is Transcendental Consciousness; 'yoga-siddha' (accomplished in yoga), Cosmic Consciousness; and 'yoga-saṁsiddha' (perfected in yoga), glorified yoga-siddha — God Consciousness. And he who is yoga-saṁsiddha gets this knowledge of Unity within himself in the course of time. Just that one thing, that one vision.

Doing Justice to the Brahma Sūtra

The short selections that follow are extracted from a two-hour quick running commentary by Maharishi on most of the first section of Chapter Two. I marked the tape 'wholly delightful', but on listening to it again later, I realized that its delights are not easy to convey. A good deal of it concerns the interpretation of Sanskrit words, and Maharishi's actual commentaries are quite short. However, in these extracts I have tried to give an idea of that happy session, while leaving out most of the discussions about the Sanskrit.

The conversation is pervaded by laughter, much of it, I am afraid, at the expense of previous translators and commentators. Maharishi is showing how the words of the Brahma Sūtra confirm his theme that each sūtra makes a statement about the nature of Brahman. If he is hard on his predecessors, it is only out of his zeal to explain the true nature of Brahman and the Sūtras that bear its name.

It Keeps On Fitting

VK: You have to go very carefully, but anyway, this sūtra follows.

Maharishi: It follows our theme, absolutely. This is Brahma Sūtra, which brings fulfilment: the state of Brahman.

VK: I think Vyāsa must have come to visit you too, Maharishi.[147] (Laughter)

Maharishi: He'll be happy; he'll not be required to do 'shāstrārtha' with me, because he'll find that this is a simple explanation of what he meant. (Laughter)

VK: 'Do shāstrārtha?' What do you mean?

Maharishi: The 'artha' of the 'shāstra' — the truth of meaning [artha] brought about by scripture [shāstra]. Shāstrārtha means close analysis of the situation by argument proceeding on a sequential basis from one stage to the other. This is it. See, it [the argument from one sūtra to another] is just so well connected.

VK: I can't follow it completely, but shall we see if it …

---

147 Maharishi tells the story that when Shankara was returning from Jyotirmath after having completed his commentary on the Brahma Sūtra, Vyāsa appeared as an old paṇḍit and challenged him about his interpretation. Shankara was able to satisfy him, and it appears that the old man was pleased. But perhaps this was not so much because he found that his own meaning was brought out, as because Shankara, throughout, was able to sustain the stand that he, Shankara, had taken; for Brahman, being omnipresent, can be approached from many angles.

Maharishi: If it fits the next one, yes. This sūtra [2.1.7] says that there is negation without an object which can be negated because, in the realization of Brahman, objectivity is found to be just nothing but the extension of the Absolute, or one's own Self. When this is the experience — that it [the object] is the Absolute — then it is not right to say that the object is negatable. It cannot be negated. Once it has been experienced that the object is the extension of the Absolute and therefore can't be declared 'asat' (non-existent), then it's not asat; it is Brahman. That means the sūtra is emphasizing that even this obvious [surface] reality is Brahman. Even though it seems to be perishable, it has been experienced to be the extension of the Absolute. It's beautiful. It supplements the previous sūtra.

VK: A completely new interpretation of the Brahma Sūtra.

Maharishi: But it fits, it keeps on fitting. (Laughter)

VK: (Spoken with surprise) Yes, it seems to fit.

Maharishi: It keeps on fitting itself.

VK: Fantastic. (Turning to the others present) I tried to find a difficult passage for Maharishi, to test the interpretation, just at random, to see if it would fit. (Much laughter)

Maharishi: See, the whole translation [at which we were looking] is absurd. From that translation, you can only take out that commentary. So the translation is absolutely ...

VK: But the other translators all agree …

Maharishi: It is lacking vision. The translation is lacking vision.

VK: But these sūtras all seem to be directed against different schools of philosophy.

Maharishi: No one will be able to stand against this complete top level of Unity. All that which they are saying doesn't come into the picture at all. They [other interpreters] just stand on the ground and look — like that — and they don't find the peak.

The Status of Brahman Is Not Jeopardized by the Dissolution of Creation

Maharishi: Two or three sūtras before [2.1.5], Vyāsa said that that which is all-pervading, that which is transcendental, is Brahman. And then he added that that which is obvious is also Brahman. So the question may arise: 'What will happen when this obvious [aspect] disappears at the time of the dissolution?' So he says [2.1.8–9]: 'The situation does not change when the manifested world dissolves. Brahman remains Brahman, whether the obvious is there or is melted into oblivion.' So, there are these two aspects of Brahman, the omnipresent and the obvious. When one aspect gets dissolved, even then the status of Brahman is not jeopardized, even though the dissolution of the manifest reality is the dissolution of one's own status. Read the sūtra.

VK: (Reads the Sanskrit and one of the translations.)

Maharishi: (Laughing) There is no connection between the two minds [Vyāsa's and the translators].

VK: There is no connection between the two reasonings [Maharishi's and the translators].

Maharishi: No, there is absolutely no connection. It's just the plain status of Brahman that is explained. But look at Vyāsa's intellect. He makes it so clear. One aspect is gone and then, if that is gone and that was the aspect of Brahman, what has happened to Brahman? Vyāsa says that his status is not jeopardized.

JJ: The commentator's status has been jeopardized. (Laughter)

Maharishi: They'll all go into the caves and meditate. Hide themselves. (Laughter)

VK: From you? Maybe, you'll have to hide yourself from them. (Much laughter) They'll come at you with hammers.

JJ: That's why Maharishi has television in mind.

VK: So they can't get at him. (Much laughter)

Maharishi: I think we'll flood the market with wisdom.

Understanding and Liberation

Maharishi: Now he [Vyāsa] says [2.1.11]: 'If your logic does not accede to this demonstration of the eternity of Brahman, and if you cannot conceive it intellectually, then you will not get liberation.' If your logic is not able to comprehend that, and if your imagination, even intellectually, is not able to reach that which we have established before — that Brahman is there whether the world is there or not — then you cannot get liberation. That means, if your logic is not profound and is not able to comprehend, then you will not get release.

VK: But you don't get release through logic, do you?

Maharishi: No. It means, you just can't get on to the field of Brahman.

VK: Why? Because of lack of logic?

Maharishi: Lack of logic means lack of understanding. All understanding should be such that it leads to Brahman. We can interpret the whole of the fourth chapter in this way. All your logic, or all your imagination — that means, all your powers of apprehension — if they don't discover this reality, then you don't get liberation.

VK: But you say — you remember we discussed it before — you say that Cosmic Consciousness is liberation. But that is gained long before the knowledge of Brahman.

Maharishi: Now we could say that from this point on, Vyāsa wants to establish freedom; having established Brahman on the level of existence, he now comes on to liberation. He proclaims that Brahman is eternal liberation. He means thereby that even logically one could arrive at the truth that Brahman is liberation. He brings in ill-logic and ill-imagination, just to show that proper logic and proper imagination — that means, proper understanding — will fathom this truth of Brahman as eternal liberation. Direct experience will certainly reveal it, but even the understanding will usher in this truth; understanding will reach it. We'll have to look into the sūtra from the point of view of grammar, but this is the meaning. Such a beautiful sūtra. Now let's see the next one. What is next?

Brahman as the Supreme Authority

Maharishi: The sūtra means that the proper understanding of this status of Brahman provides the criterion of whether the authority is valid, authentic, or not. The authenticity of a principle is weighed against this nature of Brahman. If the authority comes up to this mark, then it is an authority which is acceptable, and if it does not, then it is not. That means, Brahman is not established by authority. The authority is established by this nature of Brahman. If this nature of Brahman is accepted by the authority, then it is authority;

if not, then the authority is not. That means, this previous sūtra, which speaks about logic and imagination, is valid if it is acceptable to this structure of Brahman. The authenticity of the scriptural authority is by virtue of its ability to establish Brahman in this way. We are commenting on the *Brahma* Sūtra. It shows that Brahman, and not scripture, is the supreme authority. The state of Brahman is that which gives authority, gives a status, to the authenticity of the scriptures. Not that the scriptures prove Brahman; just the other way.

VK: It's very nice. It's not the scriptures that prove Brahman …

Maharishi: But Brahman gives life, or validity, or authenticity, to the scriptures. This is beautiful. This is Brahma Sūtra, which upholds Brahman above everything. It's so enjoyable.

VK: I'll have to get my Sanskrit grammar to be sure.

Maharishi: We'll verify the Sanskrit grammar. And whatever is the grammar, we'll have this suited to the grammar, and it'll suit it. Otherwise, it would not fit, sūtra after sūtra, in a very logical way.

JJ: If they [other interpreters] can fit that commentary to it … (Much laughter)

Maharishi: If they can do that …

VK: It should be child's play. (Laughter)

Maharishi: And then? The next sūtra?

Brahman Is Realized on the Level of the Intellect

Maharishi: Now, this is beautiful. Such a precious thing. It speaks of the dawn of Brahman in the intellect. Shankara said: 'bhāvādvaitaṁ sadā kuryāt, kriyādvaitaṁ na karhi cid.' That means, always have non-duality on the level of consciousness; never bring non-duality into activity. This non-dual Brahman is realized on the level of intelligence, on the level of the knower himself; it has nothing to do with the level of action. The revelation, the realization of Brahman takes place on the level of intellect. It is gained through intellectual revelation. On the level of intellect alone, on the level of thought alone, one realizes Brahman. It's so beautiful.

VK: That's what you were saying, that supreme knowledge is on the level of intellect.

Maharishi: Ah. That's why the Gītā says: That is found within oneself, in time.[148]

VK: Time finds it …

Maharishi: Yes. Time finds it within oneself. A very beautiful sequence is coming on. It's so simple and it has been so much rounded about, so much distorted. Continuum of distortion. Distortion continuum in the eternal continuum of Brahman. (Laughter) How can Brahman be brought to light on the basis of guesswork? This is that which we call

---

148 4.38, see MBG, p. 311.

the tragedy of knowledge. Vyāsa wrote something. Shankara brought it to the suitability of his own time. But where is the suitability of the time [in the commentaries of today] when the whole simplicity of the expression, the exposition of reality, has become muddled?

VK: But Maharishi, you talk about suitability of time. Surely Shankara's time was more suitable for an exhaustive explanation than our time?

Maharishi: But we have created a world on the path to realization. We have created a world on the path to enlightenment.

VK: But in Shankara's time too — look at the devotion, look at ...

Maharishi: Oh, Shankara himself was beautiful, but he had to just give an intellectual gloss for the sake of all the paṇḍits who were following Buddhism. So he brought them back.

VK: Many paṇḍits followed him [Shankara].

Maharishi: Because they couldn't ...

VK: Understand him? (Laughter)

Maharishi: Refute him. He was a very great intellect, a mastermind.

VK: He was. His commentary ...

Maharishi: Is very beautiful.

VK: Yes, I mean just the ingenuity of it, the way he refutes these views; all the possible objections to his point of view that he raises and then refutes; an infinite number of objections.

Maharishi: That establishes him without a doubt.

VK: His mind is marvellous.

Maharishi: And because at that time people did not have much knowledge of the texts dealing with ultimate reality — the Upanishads — he had to raise the points. And when he raises the points, people say, 'It seems to be all right.' And when he cuts them all down, people say, 'Ah yes, this is it', even if they are not conversant with the original text. (Laughter)

JJ: They would never have raised those objections.

Maharishi: No. And to his time he could not have conveyed what he wanted to convey without following this system of raising the doubt himself and then demolishing it, because the people had not ...

JJ: He had a double job. At least Maharishi doesn't have to raise doubts. Others take care of that. (Much laughter)

Maharishi: Simplicity is our mark. Simplicity. No complication.

VK: But even Shankara ...

Maharishi: He was not complicated.

VK: No, he also had one view, only he saw all the possible objections. His view was straightforward and, just as you do, he imposed it on the text. (Laughter) In just the same way. Every commentator must do that; he must have a view of his own, and from his own experience ...

Maharishi: Otherwise, how will the commentaries come out?

VK: I mean, all these people who look at all the different books — as I was doing when writing my thesis — and try to get a synthesis; they are just people who haven't got any ideas of their own. (Laughter)

Maharishi: We have one thing. We found a book of study on the level of Unity — this Brahma Sūtra. This is the text on the level of Unity.

VK: That means that the Upanishads are really all on that level too.

Maharishi: And the Upanishads will be very intelligently, very clearly and profoundly understood when one understands the Brahma Sūtras. Because they are so simple.

VK: The Brahma Sūtras?

Maharishi: Are so simple. In the light of the Brahma Sūtras, the Upanishads will be more clearly understood. That was the purpose of the Sūtras. Vyāsa made Brahman so clear, so simple. This being the time of the predominance of material values, reality must be explained in terms of the surface values of life. Only simplicity can work in these days. Simplicity is our mark.

Eternity Is Established in the Field of Change

Maharishi: ... That means, the realization of Brahman is established on the level of the intellect cognizing eternity in the field of futility [mutability]. In the unity of Brahman eternity is established in the field of change. This is it.

VK: (Reads out another translation)

Maharishi: Oh, they are talking of the unmanifest before creation. And what we bring out is that the unmanifest — that eternity of the unmanifest — is imprinted on the manifest field; and that is the state of Brahman.

VK: You mean that it's imposed?

Maharishi: That the state of Brahman *is* that. The state of Brahman means cognition of the field of eternity, even in the field of change. We have done the Brahma Sūtra. (Laughter)

VK: You've just done a few verses from Chapter Two.

Maharishi: But the whole trend of thought — it suits the next verse, and the next verse, and the next verse. Each verse fits. It goes on and on and on.

MG: When you were discussing it yesterday, I thought you had finished with philosophy; that it wasn't any use writing any more books and philosophizing.

Maharishi: But this is not philosophizing; this is just cognition of the reality. (Laughter) And what we have found in other commentaries is confusion continuum. (Laughter)

VK: As Jerry says, at least they are consistent in their confusion. (Laughter)

Maharishi: Confusion continuum. No wonder people run away from Indian philosophy, due to such commentaries on the Brahma Sūtra. (Laughter)

VK: But all academic philosophy has been like that, not only Indian philosophy …

Maharishi: All un-understandable.

VK: Dry, very dry.

Brahman Is Found Within the Sound

Maharishi: The sūtra [2.1.18] says that through the technique it is found located within the sound; through the technique of Transcendental Meditation, Brahman is found located within the sound.

VK: Not found within the sound; it's found beyond the sound in the technique of Transcendental Meditation.

Maharishi: Here he gives the whole technique of Transcendental Meditation. Go deep within, go deep within, and there you will find transcendental Brahman. There you will find that which is Brahman. It supplements the previous sūtra, where Vyāsa talked about the gross, changing aspect of life. Now he's showing Brahman within the changing features of life. Through the technique you find Brahman within sound, form, smell, touch — with every perception.

VK: You are supposed to find it beyond the sound; not within the sound.

Maharishi: (Laughing) Through the technique, you find Brahman within the sound.

VK: Within the sound also. That will be another technique.

Maharishi: Within the sound, because you have to go within, within, within, and then in the innermost area [you will find it]. What is next?

VK: The next sūtra says: 'And like a piece of cloth.'[149]

Maharishi: See, we connect this with the previous sūtra, which said: 'It is found within the sound.' How is it found? As flat, pure consciousness, unbounded. Within the sound it is found. And how is it found? Just like a flat cloth. So pure awareness is just like a flat field of life; that is the experience of pure awareness.

---

149 BS 2.1.19, 'patavach cha'; also see conversation, 'Brackets Are a Cage'.

Activity Does Not Obstruct
One's Becoming Brahman

Maharishi: In the previous sūtras Brahman has been described as the whole and as the ultimate. Such a description apparently puts Brahman further away from the individual. Now this sūtra brings him down to the intimate relationship with the Self within. That which is the whole, and that which is divided — it's strange, it's wondrous that it is present there within the Self.

VK: Now [2.1.28] Shankara quotes the Brihadāraṇyaka Upanishad, which speaks of chariots, horses, and roads, which the dreamer creates in the dream state. Similarly, gods and magicians create elephants and so on without losing, without doing damage to their own nature. So the diverse creation may exist in Brahman also without impairing Brahman's real nature and unity.

Maharishi: Such a beautiful thing. We underline that thing which he says: 'without impairing its real nature and unity'.

VK: It says that dreamers, gods, and magicians create without losing the unity of their own nature.

Maharishi: This is it. That means the whole thing can be created and yet one doesn't lose the unity in Being. Even though engaged in a vigorous kind of completely original activity — creating means original activity — even then … It's beautiful.

VK: But what has that to do with the Ātmā (Self)?

Maharishi: That is the nature of Brahman.

VK: Brahman, yes, to create individual souls you mean, or …

Maharishi: No, no, no. See, the previous sūtras have not got Brahman into any intimate relationship with the individual. And now this sūtra connects Brahman so intimately with the individual that it's the individual himself, it's the innermost aspect of the individual himself. That is Brahman.

VK: But what has that to do with Shankara's commentary about creating things without losing the unity of one's being? It's a nice thought, but is it relevant to this verse?

Maharishi: It is, in the sense that the whole multiple creation, all the activity of the outside, doesn't obstruct one's becoming Brahman. Oh yes, it does connect. Even though Brahman is wholeness and without parts and omnipresent, as the previous sūtras describe, even though the individual as an individual is completely engaged in time and space, even then the individual lives that Brahman. And that is realization of Brahman.

VK: And that in itself is wondrous.

By Thought Things Get Done

At the start of this conversation Maharishi speaks of the awareness being dominated by the unity of life. Here the context is the transition from God Consciousness to Unity.[150] Maharishi emphasizes the naturalness of this transition, and when he describes how, once it has been made, the whole of life settles down, his voice changes and one can almost feel this process of settling down. At such times it becomes clearer than ever that such descriptions are, for Maharishi, no mere exercises in conjecture.

The volume of sound swells during the last part of the conversation when the laughter of Maharishi and Jerry Jarvis erupts in concert and fills the air. The topic is the activity, or absence of it, of the man who has reached supreme knowledge, and the explosion of laughter comes as Maharishi makes the point that activity is simply due to the inability to get things done by thought alone. Maharishi is here foreshadowing his later teaching of the Transcendental Meditation-Sidhi programme.

Maharishi: Here Vyāsa is describing that transition from the celestial to [Unity].

VK: But you say that even in the state of Unity we continue to live differences on the sensory level, while recognizing

---

150 This topic is discussed at greater length in the conversation 'The Transition from God Consciousness to Unity'.

Unity on the level of awareness.

Maharishi: Awareness is dominated by the unity of life.

VK: So in the awareness the unity is dominant, but as far as action is concerned, you act as if there were diversity. It seems like splitting the mind, in some way.

JJ: Oh, you don't act *as if* there were diversity; your actions are by nature diverse.

VK: They're diverse, yes, because they're in the realm of relativity. But if you can act, it means that you must continue to *recognize* diversity in some way. And you also continue to recognize God, just as you did in God Consciousness. If you continue to recognize a tree, you must continue to recognize God.

Maharishi: Now, the thing is, pure consciousness is much more alluring, much more fascinating in itself than even the celestial. Therefore, the slipping of life [from God Consciousness] into that [state of Unity] is just a very natural thing. The very nature of life is towards evolution. Just that one factor explains it: the whole relative life is proceeding in the direction of evolution. Now, transcendental pure consciousness, being infinite and absolute, has much more value; it is a much higher state of evolution than the celestial. And the brightest celestial and this [transcendental pure consciousness] are almost one. Because the celestial also has various phases — gross and subtle, subtler, subtlest. And by the time one arrives here [at the subtlest celestial], this is seen to be almost one [with transcendental pure consciousness] and here, at this junction, it is recognized that these two are the same.

So, even the state of God Consciousness, from here to here to here [from its grosser to its subtlest levels] takes time [to traverse]. By the time one gets more and more used to it, more and more and more subtle aspects and more brilliancy are revealed — more celestial and more celestial. And then the *most* celestial and this [transcendental pure consciousness] — they are [recognized to be] the same. This is what takes time. And this is what the Gītā says: In time one finds that within oneself.[151] *In time.* Shifting from here to there, living the gross celestial, and subtle celestial, and subtlest celestial; by the time life comes here [to the junction point], it is almost one with it [transcendental pure consciousness]. And then it settles down — the whole life settles down.

VK: And this is not possible in Cosmic Consciousness because the ...

Maharishi: Great activity is possible in Cosmic Consciousness.

VK: But in the state of supreme knowledge, can you still have great activity?

Maharishi: Then one would not be required to be active.

---

151 4.38, see MBG, p. 311.

Then thought flows and the whole thing is done, gets done just [by itself].

VK: Because otherwise the contrast would be too great.

Maharishi: Yes. The contrast will be very great. See, the metabolic rate in this state is almost nil. It's so powerful — any impulse [that arises] immediately gets done [transformed into action]. Activity is due to inability of performance by will. (Loud laughter) It just comes to that.

VK: So, the recluse state would be the natural state for such a man.

Maharishi: Not recluse. The monarch of all the universe.

VK: Just the one who gives instructions.

Maharishi: He does not have to speak, even.

VK: He has just to think.

Maharishi: And thinking also is on that level — subtlest level — because the metabolic rate is not high.

VK: He can't think on a gross level, can he?

Maharishi: No, he can't, because the breath doesn't go up [sufficiently to permit this kind of thinking]. Look at the height of possibility! Gross activity is just due to inability of performance by will. (Laughter)

VK: It's just something one has to make do with.

Maharishi: Yes. See, as one grows higher and higher and

higher, activity does become less and less, and then the expansion is more and more and more. This is so in every business. He thinks more. He thinks more. By thought things get done. By thought things get done.

Time Will Catch This Wisdom

This short exchange is interesting in that it foreshadows the establishment of Maharishi International University[152] three years later. Maharishi begins by repeating the words of a sūtra (2.2.22), as he often does prior to commenting on it.

Maharishi: 'Pratisaṁkhya apratisaṁkhya. Pratisaṁkhya apratisaṁkhya nirodha.' This is how the children who study Sanskrit grammar repeat the words again and again. (Laughter) 'Pratisaṁkhya apratisaṁkhya nirodha.'

VK: One wishes one had learned it that way as a child, so it would be part of one.

Maharishi: It becomes a part of you, and then later you see what it means.

VK: There's very much to be said for learning by repetition when one is a child.

Maharishi: In the early days, oh yes. That sustains wisdom throughout life.

---

152 Later renamed Maharishi University of Management.

VK: I still remember all the nonsense, the silly nonsense rhymes I learned when I was a little boy; so, if one had learned something sensible, it would still be remembered.

JP: Shall we start a kindergarten, in which we …?

Maharishi: You start a university. Higher education for higher consciousness. We'll see that this generation gets this wisdom, somehow or other. Because it's such a nice thing; only we have to be speaking aloud and there's no doubt that the time will catch it. It *has* to catch it, it has to. It's just … we have solely to keep on speaking. That's all.

VK: You think the time is ready for it?

Maharishi: Absolutely ready.

III

SRINAGAR, KASHMIR: SUMMER 1969

Almost a year has passed. The Brahma Sūtra has lain dormant. For my own part, I had listened to most of the Tahoe tapes and had written summaries of the main points; but no new work had been done. Maharishi had been occupied with the training of teachers, the foundation of all his work of regeneration, for, as he once said, he could only reach the whole population of the world by multiplying himself. The training of teachers coming from all over the world was a full-time job, especially when the courses were held in India. It involved looking after their physical as well as their intellectual and spiritual welfare and left no time for even a passing glance at the Brahma Sūtra. The main centre of teacher training was the academy at Rishikesh, but because Rishikesh became unbearable during the hot months, participants and paraphernalia would be moved en masse at the end of March to Kashmir, where the course would be continued on the houseboats and hotels of Dal Lake.

There was a hiatus between courses when Maharishi called me to Kashmir to continue work on the Sūtra. I reached Srinagar at the beginning of July 1969. To arrive there as I did, by air, is surely an opportunity wasted. I have often imagined how it must feel to descend from one of the passes into the huge Vale of Kashmir after making one's way gradually through the hills and mountains from the parched and dusty plain — perhaps rather like suddenly chancing upon Holland in the middle of the Alps. The Vale, itself nearly six thousand feet high and formed by the basin of the upper Jhelum river, is a blissful oasis — green, lush, and fertile, crisscrossed with innumerable waterways. Tall poplars planted by the British accompany the roads and streams, and the splendid, dark green chinar trees, cousins of the London plane, give strength and comfort in the heat of the day. Families of ducks pass in grave procession along the waterways and there are geese everywhere — fat creatures waddling around in the rivulets that run under dark trees at the backs of houses. In the distance, surrounding the valley on all sides, are the snowy peaks of the Himālayas. During our stay they were all too often obscured by the summer haze, but when one did catch a glimpse of them, immensely high above lotus-covered waters and rice fields of a fluorescent green, the sight took one's breath away.

Srinagar, a city of palaces and tightly packed clusters of wooden houses, with the meandering Jhelum as its central highway, is flanked by two imposing hills — the Shankarāchārya Hill, with its ancient temple, and Hari Parbat, with its fortress. The outskirts of the city wind round the beautiful Dal Lake, whose indolent waters reflect with great clarity the two strangely shaped hills and anything else that comes their way. Dotted around the lake are the famous Mughul gardens — Nasim, Shalimar, Chashma Shahi, and perhaps loveliest of all, Nishat Bagh, the Garden of Breezes, which rises in ten luxuriant terraces of trees, flowers, and fountains against the gaunt hills. I remember a view of the lake at sunset from Nishat, with the great pale pink orb slowly disappearing to leave delicate silhouettes of distant trees and strips of land mirrored in the sheet-like water.

To be deposited in the middle of it all straight from New Delhi was to miss the whole context of this wonder. Yet arriving by plane had its compensations. After being very nearly arrested in mid-air for daring to film the innocent Himālayan peaks, which towered beside us, I stepped from the aircraft to be met by a guard of honour formed by a large number of wild-looking gentlemen sporting an assortment of wool caps and shouting 'Kashmir Zindabad, Kashmir Zindabad'[153] at the tops of their considerable voices. As we passed with some trepidation through the ranks, the Englishman walking beside me wondered if this unlikely reception committee were meant for us. But the object of its fervour turned out to be the portly personage who had occupied the seat in front of me on the plane. He happened to be a former chief minister of Kashmir.

There was indeed no one to meet me, not surprisingly, because the plane had decided that morning to leave New Delhi more than an hour before its scheduled time — the only aeroplane in my experience ever to leave early. I took a taxi at the airport. Fortunately, the driver knew where

---

153 'Hail Kashmir.'

Maharishi was staying, for I didn't. I asked him where one could get some flowers for Maharishi. He said there were no flower shops, but the head gardener of the Oberoi Hotel was his good friend, and for a consideration I could pick my fill of flowers there. There I stood in the grounds of the palatial hotel — it was a converted palace — sheepishly and furtively directing the gardener as to which flowers I wanted picked. Once again, as at Reno, Nevada, I was approaching the Brahma Sūtra through a rather strange gateway.

Maharishi was staying on the outskirts of Srinagar, not far from the hotel whose garden I had despoiled. This time he was at home when I arrived. Home was a pleasant, rambling, white-painted house which had been taken for him by Richard Aaron, a lovable and rather imaginative young American who will long be remembered by the merchants of Kashmir for his purchases.[154] The house was set in green

---

154 It was Richard who went round the motor showrooms of London inspecting Bentleys and Rolls Royces, giving out that he was Maharishi's secretary. Though he was only intending to buy such a car on his own account, it led to reports that Maharishi was ordering one — or it may have been a fleet. This fiction went around the world, a toy for journalists to play with, joining many similar stories based more on imagination than fact. One newspaper went so far as to write that Maharishi, who was in Kashmir at the time, had been seen, dressed in white robes, touring one of the leading London showrooms. I brought one rather witty article about the proposed car purchase with me from London. Filled with righteous indignation I read it to Maharishi but he only laughed, saying that the man wrote very well and ought to start Transcendental Meditation and use his talent constructively. I have never heard him complain of the treatment accorded him by some of the media — he does not react to hostility — but it is strange how often they will fix their attention on inessentials: anything rather than come face to face with Maharishi's simple message that each one of us can with ease realize our

fields with steep hills rising behind it, and in front of it lay Dal Lake, about one hundred and fifty yards away. From the lake and the lakeside road, the ground fell somewhat towards the house and this gave it a very secluded feeling.

For some reason Maharishi insisted on calling this unexceptionable dwelling 'the cowshed'. I never quite discovered whether this epithet referred to its origins, its present condition, or its location — there being real cowsheds in the vicinity; probably the first, because it was rumoured that the place had indeed started life as a cowshed. I thought it a pleasant enough house and, by local standards, very comfortable. There were one or two snags, mostly connected with the profusion of fauna so characteristic of the sub-continent. Thus, when I awoke one morning to discover what looked like a small pile of sawdust in front of my rubber-type sandals, I found on closer inspection that I had only one and three-quarters sandals left. Yet it was at 'the cowshed' that I spent what were probably the happiest two months of my life. The main reason for this was nearness to Maharishi — living in the same house, spending a large part of the day in his company and, above all, working with him on the Brahma Sūtra, for many hours. Not since the early sixties, when we were working on the Gītā in private houses in England, had I been so close to him, and then never for so long a period at a stretch.

Furthermore, I was again surrounded by old friends. Mar-

---

potentialities and live a life of fulfilment.

jorie Gill and Jemima Pitman arrived a fortnight after I did. They too were present at most of the sessions on the Brahma Sūtra, and somehow the joy was multiplied because they were there to share in it. Ulla and Nikolaus Blücher, good friends since we first met on the Black Forest course in the winter of 1960 and among the first to support — and translate — Maharishi in Germany, arrived later with their son Lukas and stayed nearby. Brahmachari Devendra was there, as were Florence Kaivani from Geneva and David Fiske from South Africa.

On 'Guru Pūrṇimā' — the July full moon, which is dedicated to the guru — we all went out on Dal Lake in a large boat. Many course participants had stayed on in Kashmir and, with local meditators also joining in, we were quite a large group. There was singing and music-making by local musicians, and the occasion was graced by the presence of Lakshman Joo, a great authority on Kashmir Shaivism. Both Maharishi and Lakshman Joo spoke, and it was a great joy to see them together. On that day Maharishi also gave a short but matchless talk on the growth of consciousness to a small group of meditators at his house. Even more than what he said, the way he said it was impressive. He seemed to have retreated deep within himself and then come out just enough to speak these very quiet words.

Maharishi also joined us on two excursions which were to enable us to see something of Kashmir beyond the immediate environs of Srinagar. One was to Yusmarg, a small open valley in the Himālayan foothills; the other to two of the lovely lakes of Kashmir — Manasbal and Wular. These expeditions were much enjoyed. I remember in particular a picnic by the rest house overlooking Lake Manasbal. We sat there on chairs brought out by the attendant — Maharishi, Mrs. Gill, Jemima, and I quite near the precipice, talking of ultimate things, with the lotus-covered lake far below us. It is one of those incidents which time has dimmed only a little, a moment of closeness to Maharishi in a natural setting of great beauty. In later years, with the world making ever-increasing demands on his time, such moments became more rare.

Maharishi would usually work alone before lunch, though sometimes he would have a young Indian student of Sanskrit read him passages from the classical commentaries or other Sanskrit writings. After lunch he would show us the results of the morning's work with much enthusiasm and joy. In such quiet hours of thought, Maharishi brought out the hidden depths of the wisdom of the past, showing their relevance to our own needs and aspirations.

Although it was an all too rare period of comparative peace and freedom from responsibility for Maharishi, his work of regeneration was never far from his thoughts. While in Kashmir I received a letter from a friend who was much involved with Biafran relief. She asked me if Maharishi would make a statement on the situation in Nigeria. After I had read him the letter, he was silent for a long time. Then he said: 'Day and night, day and night, I think only of how to relieve the suffering of the world more quickly, and I always come up with the same answer: train more teachers, train more teachers.' Nothing could better illustrate his conviction that problems cannot be solved on the level of problems, that one has to go to their underlying cause — the stress and lack of fulfilment of the individual.

I do not know how much of what Maharishi spoke and wrote in Kashmir will be incorporated into the final version of the Brahma Sūtra commentary. The essence will be there but, as explained in the Introduction, Maharishi's teaching was a living process; new breadths and new depths were continually being revealed. And Maharishi was not really interested in what he said or thought in the past. He lived in the present and for the future. However, I hope that by means of this book at least some of his thoughts during the summer of 1969 will be preserved. It may be that his teaching reached greater splendour during large courses where he was inspired by the questing minds and deep experiences of so many meditators. But I cannot remember any teaching quite so intimate and charming and happy as that given during those two months in Kashmir. Maharishi was a living testimony to the truth that life is bliss, in all circumstances, but it was a precious opportunity to be with Maharishi when that bliss could flow in knowledge without having to address urgent business. I hope some of this happiness, which spread to Maharishi's surroundings, comes over to the reader.

These conversations were, of course, never meant for publication. They are so diverse and many of them range over such a wide variety of topics that it is hard to put them into any logical order. I have grouped all the conversations concerned mainly with the character and purpose of the Brahma Sūtra at the beginning. These are followed by the conversations dealing with the nature and growth of higher states of consciousness and with the ultimate goal of life. Finally, there are a few conversations in which a tender level of feeling predominates. I hope this proves to be a satisfactory order.

Kashmir: Participants in the Conversations

Maharishi

NB: Nikolaus Blücher

D: A Kashmiri Doctor

MG: Marjorie Gill

VK: Vernon Katz

JP: Jemima Pitman

An Introduction to the Brahma Sūtra: Experience and Understanding I

Eleven months after Lake Tahoe and we are back on familiar territory: what is to be the distinguishing theme of the present commentary and how does our approach differ from that of the great Shankara? The present conversation and others that follow it deal mainly with such general questions. As they took place at different times over a period of some two months, a certain amount of repetition is inevitable, but each conversation yields insights of its own.

In these talks Maharishi elaborates on the distinction, which he made at Lake Tahoe, between experience and understanding, and he again affirms that while there is a difference in emphasis, there is no essential difference in import between Shankara's commentary and his own. The summer air of Kashmir finds me at my most polemical and I dispute Maharishi's thesis whenever I get a chance. In retrospect it seems that once or twice I put my views rather too harshly or even with a touch of sarcasm, but Maharishi seemed not to notice and sweetly answered my points, often giving them quite a new dimension as he does so. At such times one is very much the northern barbarian at the court of an oriental monarch.[155] But I should add in self-defence that in the context of the light-heartedness of our talks, my remarks did not really seem out of place. Cold print just cannot fully convey the atmosphere of lightness and laughter in which the profound work of interpreting the Brahma Sūtra for our age was carried on.

---

155 But on one occasion, the barbarian, always on the hunt for truisms or tautologies, became the object of gentle reproof. Apropos of something Maharishi had said in the course of a commentary, I let fall: 'We don't need the Brahma Sūtra to tell us that what is without parts is whole.' Maharishi laughed heartily and through his laughter repeated what I had said, and then he added: 'This is your ripe and full understanding about Brahman — you don't need words.'

During the conversation that follows, Maharishi sketches out a theme for the introduction to the Brahma Sūtra. The points he makes, whether or not they will appear in the published commentary, are valuable and ought to be recorded.

Maharishi: This will be our stand, in the introduction to this commentary: 'There are two aspects of knowledge, one is understanding, the other experience. So far, commentaries have stretched more along the lines of understanding. This is a commentary to bring out that phase of the Sūtra which is more concerned with experience.' It will be a very good distinction. For everything to do with the understanding aspect, which needs quite a lot of referring to the [scriptural] texts, the commentaries written so far [will be useful]. It will be a very fair distinction, and it will make our angle stand out.

VK: And there is this aspect of understanding in the Brahma Sūtras, otherwise almost every other sūtra wouldn't have 'As is clear from the statement.'

Maharishi: Yes. It has its significance in the Sūtras. And then we say: 'Come on, now have the practice; this is the age of the practice' — finished. Now, if we are going to take this stand, we will comment on the Sūtras with this in view right from beginning to end. It will be brilliant — [we emphasize] experience.

(Maharishi starts writing as he speaks.) It appears that former commentators exposed the meaning of the Sūtras mainly in terms of understanding. Therefore, it was vital for the justification of the great knowledge contained in these Sūtras that the phase of experience be brought to light. For this, this commentary. Today, because Cosmic Consciousness and God Consciousness — what to say of Unity? — are regarded as speculation, not as concrete reality on the level of experience, it is very necessary to bring out the experience aspect of the Sūtras on that height where the experiences culminate.

VK: It's a very good point.

Maharishi: Even in order to restore [recognition of] the necessity for intellectual understanding of the ultimate reality of life, the time demands that ultimate reality be brought to light and exposed on the level of experience, so that it is possible for everyone to experience it.

So, we don't deprecate anyone. 'You [the former commentators] said that because that was your angle. But time demands that this aspect of experience should be brought out also.' And we justify their angle, elevate them and uphold them. It's very beautiful. And then the readers of our commentary will simply run to Shankara's commentary to see to what intellectual heights he has gone in expressing the reality of experience and understanding. And there they will find that [those heights]. Beautiful. And then, whatever difference there is from all the traditional thinking, we'll justify it.

VK: Save ourselves.

Maharishi: Save ourselves. In upholding others, we save our life.

VK: I don't know if we've saved our Sanskrit as well. We may have saved our intentions, but …

Maharishi: No, the Sanskrit is all right.

VK: I am not so sure, Maharishi; it's a bit bruised.

Maharishi: But the structure is bruised, it's not broken. (Laughter)

VK: No, just bent.

Maharishi: Just bent; not fallen apart. It's there. Its bones stand, (laughter) the bones are not taken apart … It's a very beautiful point. This point we will make right in the first paragraph of the introduction and immediately it'll catch the reader, right at the first paragraph.

VK: Show them straight away what angle we are taking.

Maharishi: And *why* it is that angle. This will interest any intelligent man. (Maharishi is writing as he speaks.) The Brahma Sūtras have been the reading of the seekers of knowledge and seekers of truth in all times, and not only of the most highly evolved but even of the beginners, for even a beginner wants at least to have a vision of his goal. This has been the range of the Brahma Sūtras. And they have been the reading, not only of the seekers of knowledge but also of those who wanted to abstain from trying to reach any unknown goals of life and were satisfied with increasing joy in the present. Even such people wanted to see what those seekers were seeking. So, even for them this has been the book of reference, if not the textbook. In this way, the Brahma Sūtras have been bringing to light the hidden reality, the ultimate goal of life. They are designed to give a complete knowledge of that ultimate reality. And complete knowledge comprises experience and understanding.

VK: But what the commentators have done is not only to give an understanding of Brahman; they also give an understanding of all the different parts of creation, all the 'tattvas' [categories of creation], everything that is there. So, it's not just a question of their emphasizing understanding and our emphasizing experience. Their subject matter is different.

Maharishi: The thing is, when we have to tell people about the hundredth story of the building, as a context to what we want to say we have to tell them what lies in the first, second, third, ninety-ninth storeys. So, wherever there is a reference in the Sūtras to different levels of creation, it only is to take the awareness of the people, the intelligence of the people, step by step, to ultimately fathom the unknowable Absolute, take the expanded ...

VK: How does it help people to know which species are water-born and which are moist-born and where they go after death?[156]

---

156 These are subjects discussed in the commentaries.

Maharishi: No, the details of that are not the concern. Say we want to give the understanding about infinity to a man. So we tell him, 'Here is an inch, and twelve inches make a foot, and so many feet make a yard, and so many yards a mile, and so many miles ...' and we keep on increasing his awareness till he finds that it's not within the capacity of the mind to comprehend any more. And then he reaches the Infinite. And we tell him that this is the Infinite. But we start from something that is comprehensible.

VK: But Shankara starts from Brahman and then goes on to the creation.

Maharishi: That is the brilliance of teaching. If you want to teach about the sun, fine; say something about it and then start from the earth. And then go on through all the different strata till you reach the sun.

VK: All right, you win, Maharishi.

Maharishi: Mention the Absolute and then start from the relative. Then say something about what is nearest and then get on to the ... The theme of the Brahma Sūtra is a theme which wants to restrict itself within the field of ultimate Unity. That is the range of the Brahma Sūtra. But because its language is such that it will be intelligible to any level of consciousness, it will have some bearing on knowledge at every level. And that is why people of all levels of consciousness derive some inspiration from this text of supreme knowledge.

In our commentary on the Brahma Sūtra, all the knowledge of life will be given out — the whole thing — all the six systems of philosophy. Even though the Brahma Sūtra is the text for Vedānta only, in proving the state of Unity we lay open the significance and the validity of all the other five systems as well.

VK: As long as we don't have to prove every sūtra by the sixteen criteria of the Nyāya, I shall be happy. Otherwise, we will still be doing it at the end of the century. (Laughter)

Maharishi: Maybe we can do the first sūtra, or second sūtra, and lay out all the details according to these [criteria].

VK: Just as an example again [as in the appendix to the Gītā commentary].

Maharishi: Just as an example again, and we say that this is truth.

VK: Better choose a long sūtra, Maharishi.

Maharishi: Even the first sūtra. We can lay out the whole thing. The original sūtras have that profundity of the experience of reality. So the criteria established by the Nyāya Sūtras, and for that matter by the Sūtras of Vaisheshika, Sāṁkhya, Yoga, and Karma Mīmāṁsā, will be shown to be capable of meeting the dignity of the Brahma Sūtras.

Experience and Understanding II

Maharishi again elaborates on the distinction between experience and understanding. His conception of the Brahma Sūtra and method of translating and commenting on it are discussed in a lighthearted way and I look back longingly to the easier verses of the Bhagavad-Gītā.

Maharishi: The thing is, we don't have anything from previous commentators which we can consult.

VK: We have broken away from everything.

Maharishi: Not actually from everything.

VK: But at least from grammar. (Laughter)

Maharishi: We have to stand on our own and create our own air. See, there are two phases to knowledge — experience and understanding. The commentators so far have emphasized the understanding aspect of the knowledge of Unity; we are emphasizing the experience aspect of it. And therefore, whereas the commentators so far, following Shankara, have gone more for scanning the different scriptural texts because their aim was to clarify the understanding about Unity, our aim is to bring out those standard experiences which Vyāsa has laid out in his Sūtras for the practical guidance of those who are in God Consciousness and are passing on towards Unity. Vyāsa has laid out standard experiences, true for all times and for all seekers. This aspect has not been brought out so far and that is our contribution. And we see the meaning is so obvious from the experience point of view and so complicated when we twist it to fit on the level of understanding. So we are doing justice to the Sūtras straightaway [in an immediate way]; others have laboured hard to bring out a meaning in them.

JP: It's not that the sutras fall into two categories, one based on understanding, the other on experience?

Maharishi: The beauty is that each sūtra presents both levels. So our commentary will not exclude the understanding level, but will give the understanding of the experiences in a clear way, and this will be more of a practical guide. In all those commentaries on the Sūtras, Unity Consciousness is not established because its basis, which is that gap, is not brought out.[157] It's missing. It's not brought out in the clear way in which we show it.

VK: I've been reading the Gītā. What a pleasure it will be to translate the Gītā again after these Sūtras. It seems so much simpler.

Maharishi: It's so much simpler because the Gītā has good long verses and the Brahma Sūtra is so concise. Our technique of translating is to read the sūtra a few times and sense

---

157 The gap referred to is that between Self and non-Self, which is appreciated in Cosmic Consciousness. See conversation, 'The Gap'.

the meaning of it, and then to tally the words with the meaning through grammar. So grammar is not our first attack, not our first consideration.

VK: That we've gathered.

JP: 'Secondary.'[158]

Maharishi: It [grammar] is secondary. It has to be satisfied, but we work from a different angle.

VK: We let our fancy flow.

Maharishi: As long as the flow of fancy is in the direction of more refinement it will be justified. Grammar will take care of itself. It can't run away from its goal. The breath of grammar is also evolutionary, so it can't shy away from the right direction.

* * *

VK: This is the beauty of these sūtras, that they give you the inspiration. One shouldn't be concerned too much — as I've often said before — about whether we interpret Vyāsa correctly or not.[159] (Here I address the others) The Sūtras seem to be the starting point for Maharishi's inspiration. (Maharishi laughs) This old wisdom inspires him in a way nothing else does.

Maharishi: Maybe by the time we have done these com-

---

158 A reference to BS 1.1.6, which we had just been discussing, and which was translated as: 'If it be considered secondary, not so, on account of the word "Self".'

159 This was my view, but it was certainly not Maharishi's.

mentaries, we'll be able to show them in a flash, so that in a single vision one will be able to see all the Brahma Sūtras. All the Sūtras in one vision — in three or four pages.

VK: It will have to be a very good, longish introduction. You will need this to explain your methods — even methods of translation. And then all your terms, like 'transcendental', 'cosmic', 'relative', 'Absolute' — all this sort of thing. This will give people a vision of the whole thing.

JP: The visions of the teaching you put at the beginning of each chapter of the Gītā were marvellous.

VK: They were very good. And this time the visions will be done while the commentary is being written, whereas in the case of the Gītā they were done after the commentary had been completed. And they will be even more necessary for the Brahma Sūtras, because, compared to the Sūtras, the Gītā is child's play.

Maharishi: We'll have our divisions [into chapters] and then, just in one flash, the whole scheme — in one flash. In every chapter we'll flash that principle of direct experience.

VK: In what seems to be the most unlikely of all works. I think you take delight in interpreting what seems such a dry and cold work and making it relevant to life.

Maharishi: One has just to *read* the Sūtras. I think we'll give the vision of the teaching.

VK: I think that will be much more important here than in the Gītā, because the Sūtras, read by themselves, are unintelligible — they just are. Even if they're put into good English they're still not intelligible.

Maharishi: Intelligently they become unintelligible. But this is such a beautiful thing; our Brahma Sūtra commentary has a purpose — it is all about Brahman.

VK: Other commentaries also speak about Brahman, but more in a textual context, in relation to the shrutis.[160] Their concern is whether or not the 'golden Purusha in the eye',[161] or some other principle mentioned in the shrutis, is Brahman or not. But today people couldn't care less whether this text or that text speaks of Brahman or not. But if someone can show them the way to realize, to make a better life for themselves, that will interest them.

Maharishi: At least that much …

VK: It's marvellous to think how you got the idea that the Brahma Sūtra could be interpreted in this way. I mean, you've taken the most unlikely text possible [for showing the actual experiences leading to the knowledge of Brahman]. If you had taken the Upanishads …

Maharishi: It would have been nearer the imagination.

---

160 The shrutis are the Vedic texts. See conversation, 'Shruti and Smṛiti'.

161 See introduction to 'Shankara's Commentary and Maharishi's Own'.

VK: It [the Brahma Sūtra] is the most unlikely text possible, and you are positively drawing Brahman out of it.

Maharishi: Or showing it to be within the fold of Brahman.

The Significance of Maharishi's Commentary for the Modern Age

Although Shankara's commentary, based on his philosophy of non-dualism (advaita), is the most important and the oldest extant, each school of Vedānta has produced its own commentaries on the Brahma Sūtra. I mention Ramānuja, whose commentary, the 'Shrī-bhāshya', is based on qualified non-dualism (vishishtādvaita). This philosophy holds that the world and individual souls are to Brahman as body is to soul; they are united with, and yet different from, Brahman. There are also commentaries from the point of view of dualism (dvaita), dualism-and-non-dualism (dvaitādvaita), and pure non-dualism (shuddhādvaita). But though these commentaries differ in their interpretation of scriptural texts, all are agreed in referring the Brahma Sūtra to these texts. Maharishi here contrasts this approach with his own, which, emphasizing as it does the aspect of experience, brings out the Sūtra in a form suited to the present day.

The favourite number 'sixteen' comes up again, though not this time with reference to the Nyāya philosophy.[162] Maha-

---

162 Nyaya, one of the six classical systems of Indian Philosophy, recognizes sixteen ways in which to test the procedure of gaining knowl-

rishi, interpreting the Sūtra for a practical age, sees the first section of the first chapter (1.1.1–1.1.31) as answering sixteen practical questions about Brahman. It is a good example of how Maharishi draws Brahman out of the Brahma Sūtra, or, as he would say, shows 'it to be within the fold of Brahman'.

During the conversation Maharishi lists the sixteen implied questions, but only in two or three cases does he also give the answers proposed by the Sūtra. However, on going through my notes I found the full list of questions and answers, and I am appending this to the conversation. At the end of the conversation Maharishi outlines a possible plan for printing the Sūtras in such a way that the reader will get an immediate overall view.

Maharishi: It will be a joy for the paṇḍits to see that the Brahma Sūtras could be interpreted in a way other than Shankara's, because the tradition has been to follow Shankara. For all these two thousand years these wise people have been so much entangled in Shankara's thought, that they never thought originally.

VK: Yes, that's very true.

Maharishi: And this is because the tradition said that nothing more could be brought out about the Brahma Sūtras

---

edge. See appendix to MBG, pp. 473–7. Maharishi often referred to these sixteen ways.

than Shankara brought out. They say this about any of these [texts] — Gītā and so on — but people have tried to comment on the Gītā from their own level. But the Brahma Sūtras nobody has tried. Only Shankara has been followed.

VK: Ramānuja has done something.

Maharishi: Ramānuja tried, but he didn't have the essence of the whole thing. He wanted to refute Shankara. But has he refuted Shankara? I don't think he could, in a nice way. And he has done great damage by not holding Transcendental Consciousness as the basis[163] — and that is a great loss.

VK: In any case, he also goes in for the same thing — interpreting the Sūtras in terms of different verses, different bits of shruti (scripture).[164]

Maharishi: So he is following Shankara in his ...

VK: Only, he interprets in his own way, in his 'vishishtādvaita' way.

Maharishi: He followed the same pattern.

VK: Yes, same pattern.

Maharishi: Rational thinking belongs only to this generation, to this age. (Laughter)

VK: And what was the characteristic of the other age?

163 MBG Preface, p. 13.
164 See footnote 190, in the conversation 'Shruti and Smṛiti'.

Maharishi: To follow.

VK: 'Anugamāt.'[165]

Maharishi: 'Anugamāt.' (Laughter)

VK: Well, it must have been. If our age had been the same, people would have continued to take the moon for just a beautiful orb in the sky. But they wanted to find out, to go there.

Maharishi: Find out — think differently — straightforward — go.

VK: In some way, of course, you must be a product of your generation.

Maharishi: Of the time, of the time. It's the time. It's not the individual; it's the time.

VK: But is this way of thinking better than the other? We can't say which is better and which not better.

Maharishi: No, it's not better. It's only the truth coming out once again — in modern language. Truth coming out once again. Now, what we have to find out is the development of thought on the chapter-to-chapter level. It's a very beautiful thing. That's why they have been grouped together.

VK: The chapters?

---

165 'On account of following', a reference to Brahma Sūtra 1.1.28.

Maharishi: Yes. Now, in the first section of the first chapter there are these sixteen points in their progressive subjects. This section deals with all these questions: What is the basis of knowledge of Brahman? It is present here and now. What is Brahman? How is it realized? Benefit of realization? Simplicity of realization? Proof of realization? — direct experience and 'shruti'. What is its nature? How does it differ from other things — what is it? Where is it? Means of realizing it?[166] — ākāsha (space), prāṇa (breath), jyotih (light). Practical method of realizing it? How does the experience become permanent? The principle of realization? Does it become a living reality? Example of one who has lived Brahman in daily life? And the last question: Can everyone realize Brahman?[167]

These sixteen questions have been explained in the first section. This is analysis of the Sūtras in understandable language. And whatever reference is made to the shrutis, and all that, is valid in terms of these questions. Then it is understandable.

At the time of Bhagavan[168] Shankarāchārya there was so much less stress that he didn't have to go through all these details, childlike details, (laughter) but we have to come down to that level.[169] Shankara is for the great people of all

---

166 That is, the different experiences, or stages, which lead to Brahman.

167 See appendix to this conversation.

168 'Bhagavan' is an honorific, meaning 'worshipful', 'adorable'.

169 Maharishi has said: 'Our role is to bring the awareness of the people from the gross, surface level of multiplicity to the Transcendent and then gradually to show that this [state] is Cosmic Consciousness,

generations, and this [our commentary] is for the man in the street of every generation. And this will save us, (laughter) save us from being thrown out.

VK: From the company of the wise.

Maharishi: It's very beautiful, very beautiful. This is our speciality: we are bringing out things in the perspective suited to modern thinking, and [at the same time] holding fast to the tradition. That is our strength. It's very beautiful, very creditable. This thing will become very clear in this commentary on the Brahma Sūtras, much more than in the Gītā.

VK: You reveal a little bit more each time.

Maharishi: The whisper of the silence. So this is a beautiful thing. We have yet to write down everything. (Laughter)

VK: There's a long distance between the ideas and putting them down.

Maharishi: We should print the Brahma Sūtras like this: one here, one here, one here — print so that people can read properly [that is, get an overall view]. They read all the four

this is God Consciousness, this is Unity Consciousness, this is Brahman Consciousness. Shankara must have done the same thing for his disciples to whom he taught meditation, but he didn't have to do this when he wrote his commentaries on the Upanishads and the Brahma Sūtras — though he must have prepared quite a lot of this groundwork in his commentary on the Bhagavad-Gītā. But he went deep into whichever lake he dived — whether Upanishads or Brahma Sūtra or Gītā.' (Quote drawn from additional material in the conversations transcribed for this book.)

sections, here, here, here, and then turn the page here, here, here. It'll be such a beautiful presentation. And if the commentaries are short, they could even be printed [with the sūtras in this format].

Appendix to the Significance of Maharishi's Commentary for the Modern Age
Questions and Answers: A Vision of Chapter 1, Section 1
(1.1.1 - 1.1.31)

Below are listed the implied questions, and the answers given to them by particular sūtras. The numbers of the sūtras are in parentheses.

1. What is the basis of the knowledge of Brahman?

It is present here and now. (1)

2. What is Brahman?

It is the ultimate reality, the source of scripture, the synthesis of all. (2–4)

3. How is Brahman realized?

By direct cognition supported by scripture. (5)

In terms of the Self — not as an object, not secondary. (6)

4. What is the benefit of realization?

Brahman becomes a living reality of daily life in eternal

liberation. (7)

It is exclusive of nothing, inclusive of all. (8)

5. Why is it simple to realize Brahman?

Because it is realized as the Self. (9, see also 6)

Because realization comes in a very natural way. (10)

6. What is the proof of realization?

Direct experience and shruti (scripture). (9–11)

7. What is the nature of Brahman?

It is blissful because of practice. (12)

It is abundant. (13)

It is the ultimate cause. (14)

It is indescribable — what the scriptures describe is just the mantra and not Brahman. (15)

It is without a second. (16)

8. How does it differ from everything else — what is it?

Oneness is found by way of different layers of creation, one within the other. The teaching of difference is that of different layers of creation. Ultimately there is the one, indivisible, non-relative, absolute Brahman. (17)

One knows through one's desire. All desires lead to the final goal in which no desire is left. The field of no desire, of fulfilment, is Brahman. (18)

Desire is the natural tendency of life, and this is enough to realize Brahman. (19)

9. Where is it?

It is within. (20)

And even without. (21)

10. What are the means [stages] of realizing it?

Ākāsha (space). (22)

Prāṇa (breath). (23)

Jyotiḥ (light). (24)

11. What is the practical method of realizing it?

Surrender of the mind through the recitation of the mantra and thereby direct cognition. (25)

Experience of beings as the ray of Brahman; that is, when one comes out [of Transcendental Consciousness] everything is in terms of Brahman. This experience is supported by shruti. (26)

12. How does the experience become permanent?

The inward stroke (25) and the outward stroke (26) together make the state of Brahman permanent. (27)

13. What is the principle of realization?

Prāṇa (breath) following the field of Brahman: the impulse of individual life merging into the universality of Brahman. This is a natural principle of evolution. (28)

14. Does Brahman become a living reality?

Yes, the speaker is Brahman. This is how it becomes a living reality. It penetrates all layers of life. (29)

15. Is there an example of someone having attained the state of Brahman?

Yes, Vāmadeva. This is an authentic example from the shruti. (30)

16. Can anyone realize Brahman?

Yes, because prāṇa[170] is the sign of Brahman, and prāṇa can be cultured in any state, whether under the influence of sattva, rajas, or tamas.[171] (31)

Shankara's Commentary and Maharishi's Own

This is one of those discussions where I use all the weapons in my armoury to try to disprove Maharishi's view of Shankara. Seen in cold print, some of my remarks in this and the next conversation seem to exceed the bounds of common politeness, and when I read him the text, I asked Maharishi if I should expunge such remarks. He replied: No, let them be. These are conversations.

The idea mooted here of a detailed reconciliation of Maharishi's commentary with Shankara's still fills me with

---

170 *Editor's note*: For further understanding of prāṇa, see the section, 'Prāṇa and Being', in Maharishi's *Science of Being*.

171 The three basic impulses [guṇa] of nature.

apprehension because of the work that would be involved. But I now think that Maharishi is right in denying that there is any inherent contradiction between the two commentaries. (It is not really surprising that Maharishi should be right, but in our civilization we are brought up to bow to evidence rather than authority, and one has to be convinced on that level.)

In my attempt to disprove Maharishi's view I refer to Shankara's practice of connecting the Sūtras with such Upanishadic notions as the 'she-goat' and the 'Purusha[172] in the eye'. The three-coloured she-goat is said to represent nature in its primal state. But on studying Shankara's commentary a little more closely one finds that the whole point of his teaching is to show that nature is not to be regarded in the Sāṃkhya manner as an independent and ultimate principle, but rather as the power of the ultimate — Brahman.[173] Similarly, he says that the golden Purusha in the eye does not refer to an individual self, human or divine, but to Brahman.[174] Shankara, in his own way, is doing what Maharishi is doing — letting the Brahma Sūtra explain the nature of Brahman.

Maharishi: This morning the idea came that whenever we find that we seem to be deviating from Shankara in our analysis, we will show in the footnote how his meaning is also

---

172 The principle of subjectivity, often translated as 'person'.
173 See SBS 1.4.8-10.
174 See SBS 1.1.20-21; 1.2.13-17.

implied in our commentary.

VK: Maharishi, if you do that you'll have nothing but footnotes. (Laughter) Show me one verse in which we say the same thing as Shankara.

Maharishi: But the sense will penetrate into Shankara's wisdom.

VK: If you do that you'll be doing just what the others are doing and Shankara will be your — exactly your 'pūrva-pakshin'[175] (laughter) — but you'll also be making your commentary into an exegesis rather than letting it be a direct statement of something applicable to present-day life.

Maharishi: All right, in our introduction we'll pay tribute to Shankara and just don't …

VK: If you have these footnotes, you will never get out of the morass. I think you have to do as you did in the preface to the Gītā — make a general statement about Shankara. You made quite a lot of statements about him while commenting on the Sūtras at Lake Tahoe. I've written these down.

Maharishi: That is enough for the introduction.

VK: Let's not get drawn into commenting on Shankara, because it will take you away from your theme.

Maharishi: No, it may supplement the theme. (Laughter)

---

175 The *prima facie* objector whose views are answered in the commentary.

Then the translators of Shankara will be embarrassed.

VK: Why?

Maharishi: Because then Shankara will have a different meaning than that brought out by the translators. We connect our theme with the details of Shankara's interpretation. It's so simple; one word we take and set it to work. (Laughter)

VK: But you'll have to re-explain every sūtra. In what Shankara says there is practically nothing that in an obvious way corresponds with what you say.

Maharishi: I think if we scan Shankara's depth we will find that he is saying just what we are saying. Only we are speaking without going into details and he has gone deep into the details. Because, if our commentary is a deviation from Shankara, then it won't be truth. Shankara is truth and ours is not a deviation from it. It will appear to be a digression from Shankara if people don't have our vision, and certainly from these translations they don't get Shankara's vision. These translators are just … Whatever they have done they …

VK: No, it is not the translators.

Maharishi: But just one small thing will … Just one angle, just one fine angle and it [the true meaning] is gone.

VK: Then you have to read through this voluminous …

Maharishi: We have to read Shankara.

VK: Every voluminous page.

Maharishi: I think that will not be necessary.

VK: That in itself will be a work. It will be one work bringing out your teaching and it will be a far greater work reconciling it with Shankara. How do you reconcile what you say with what Shankara says about the she-goat and the Purusha in the eye and all that? (Laughter)

Maharishi: The Purusha in the eye, we will say, is the seat of cognition; only it is brought on a very intimate personal level. We just give a vision from that angle.

VK: First you have to go to Shankara and then from Shankara you have to go back to the passages in the Upanishads to which Shankara refers.

Maharishi: Then we'll have to say what Shankara means from the point of view of the Upanishads.

VK: That is the point I wanted to make: we have to explain our method.

Maharishi: We'll say to the scholars who find in our commentary some contradiction with Shankara that they should please wait until we have reconciled our thought with Shankara — for this is just the truth.

VK: Shankara was writing for monks, and maybe this is something that is just not valid today.

Maharishi: But as Shankara expounded it, it is the truth of all time. The tradition of Brahman knowledge is the truth of all time.

VK: But all the conclusions he drew from it were about people qualifying for knowledge of Brahman.

Maharishi: That is misinterpretation of Shankara's thought.

VK: I did that for my thesis. I followed it right through. He actually says that one has to renounce the householder's fire[176] before one can start on knowledge of Brahman. Householders can practise karma yoga (the yoga of action) but Shankara connects gyāna yoga (the yoga of knowledge) with physical renunciation. Maybe he thinks that at the time of renunciation one is also qualified [for gyāna yoga].

Maharishi: I think we'll interpret this renunciation as an intellectual recognition of the separation that one experiences in the state of Cosmic Consciousness. (Laughter)

VK: I had no doubt that you would get round that one, Maharishi. (Laughter)

Maharishi: Because from the angle of truth, truth only can survive.

VK: You have a fixed idea of what truth is and Shankara, because he is Shankara, has to conform with that. (Laughter)

---

176 A fire is always kept burning by the householder.

Maharishi: Shankara doesn't have to conform with that. He innocently expounds just that.

VK: Because he is Shankara he must be truthful, and therefore he must be saying this. (Laughter) You don't argue from the facts; you argue from principles always.

Maharishi: From principles. And the facts don't deviate from the principles. (Laughter)

VK: You argue from 'as it ought to be', and you make the transition from 'as it ought to be' to 'it is'. (Laughter) The Gītā commentary is beautiful as it is, but you have forced some of the meanings.

Maharishi: No, no.

VK: Yes, but for a good purpose.

Maharishi: Then we have brought it back to the main path, which has been forced by other people, who have deviated from the route. (Laughter)

VK: I can't win. (Laughter)

Maharishi: See, this is the time of revival. And these are the basic themes of revival which we are bringing out now. Having established the validity of our revival, we are now establishing the ... The spirit of revival is established; the principle is established. Now what is needed is to show that it is deeply rooted in eternity. And this work we'll do. Once this commentary goes out there'll be a great demand for a commentary on the Upanishads, because the whole teaching is so clearly set out. We can comment on even a few Upanishads, but do them thoroughly.

Interpretations of Shankara, and the Ancient Indian Stages of Life

The earlier part of this conversation is in much the same vein as the preceding one. Loath to waste my research of bygone days, I again refer to my findings about Shankara's advocacy of the recluse way of life. But this time my remarks lead to a very interesting explanation of the ancient social order of India as expressed in the stages of life (āshramas). There are four such stages: the student's life of celibacy (brahmachārya), the householder's life (gārhastya), the life in the forest, where husband and wife retire to meditate (vānaprasthya), and finally, the life of the homeless wanderer who has renounced everything (sannyāsa). Maharishi relates these stages to different states of consciousness, but unfortunately the conversation is interrupted before he has fully developed his theme.

VK: Not for hundreds and hundreds of years has anybody written an original commentary on the Brahma Sūtras.

Maharishi: No, no, the very attempt was not there. Our commentary is opening a new gate for future generations. And now there will be research on this [commentary] and people will try and do something original, because there is that, here is this. Out of the two somebody may think up something.

VK: Out of what? Yours and …

Maharishi: Out of the two. There are two pictures available, [ours and the generally accepted one] and both are grammatically right. This will inspire some geniuses to put out something of their own. But it will be difficult to deviate from ours.

VK: The only trouble with ours might be that it could be repetitive in some way, because other commentators have various themes relating to different parts of the scriptures, whereas our theme is just one Brahman, and the two aspects of Brahman as inclusive of this world and as beyond.

Maharishi: The Brahma Sūtras have to be within this narrow gauge, otherwise they become *jagat* sūtras.

VK: (Explaining to the others) The 'world' sūtras, the sūtras of the world and not the sūtras of Brahman. (Laughter)

Maharishi: And all these themes are so hopeless because they don't do justice to Brahman. But Shankara wanted to make the teaching more clear to the people of the world and he took them from here [the world] on to the reality. But these commentators, being hinged only to the surface value of the translation, the insight into the meaning of Shankara, which supposedly we are able to have, [got lost]. (Laughter) They got entangled in the word meaning.

VK: I think you are doing an injustice to the translators. I think they have translated *Shankara*.

Maharishi: No. Shankara can be translated, but one word of Shankara missed for its proper sense and the whole thing [goes wrong]. Then they will have to adjust the meaning, having lost the spirit of that one word, and in their attempt, yet to have the sequence of thought, they will fail. To translate or comment on Shankara, the commentator must have Shankara's consciousness.

VK: But if you look at Shankara's commentary, he speaks about the Purusha in the eye[177] and other such notions that occur in the Upanishads. That is not a question of translation. He sees the Brahma Sūtras as connected with these various scriptural passages. That is not the translation, that is Shankara.

Maharishi: But there would be one word here and there which would go beyond these material expressions [of the translators].

VK: What you mean to say is that you could do with Shankara what you have done with Vyāsa [that is, interpret him in your own terms]. (Laughter)

Maharishi: And then Shankara will be happy, because he has been miserable for these last two thousand years because

---

177 See preceding conversation.

of what his followers have done to him. His teaching is mutilated. And that is why some philosophers of today even find Shankara a little short of top merit. There is a lot of criticism of Shankara and that criticism holds good, not of Shankara, but of the translators and interpreters of Shankara. Because his thought is sublime and simple and pure and glorious. It is just the truth that he speaks. He was not responsible for what his words would be understood to mean — very misunderstood. And this is what I said in the preface to the Gītā. It is the perfection of Shankara's expressions which is responsible for the downfall of his teaching. His followers could not hold on to that height of perfection and just interpreted his expressions this way and that way.

VK: This is the real Shankara you are talking about, Maharishi, not the Shankara in the mind? (Laughter)

Maharishi: No, the real Shankara.

VK: Not as he ought to be but as he is? (Laughter)

Maharishi: As he is. And it is the Shankarāchāryas[178] of these many centuries past — they, being recluse people, did not bother much about the world and the angle [of teaching] with which the people in the world have to be raised.

VK: Shankara was the same. He was a recluse and he was writing for recluses.

---

178 As explained in footnote 105, Shankara, or Shankarāchārya, established four seats of teaching in different parts of India; each such seat is headed by a Shankarāchārya, therefore the plural.

Maharishi: No, he was not writing for recluses; he was writing the truth of life. He was writing the truth and that is a universal thing.

VK: But he was advocating the recluse life.

Maharishi: No.

VK: Oh yes. I spent a lot of time during my thesis collecting all those passages where he said that karma (action) was only for the unenlightened — karma in the literal sense of acting in the world. And he meant actually leaving the world and becoming a sannyāsī (homeless wanderer) — literally, not metaphorically.

Maharishi: No, the thing is, the social order of India is the expression of the truth on all levels, relative and Absolute. The very social structure gives a picture of the truth of life as it is lived in different levels of consciousness. So, the recluse life represents the state of Cosmic Consciousness. [In Cosmic Consciousness] there is that gap, there is that void. From where does it come? It is that way of life which is represented in a recluse way of living. It's very perfect.

VK: You mean it's expressed …

Maharishi: It's expressed in its concrete form in the ancient social order. The whole structure of life, the structure of living, is just the picture of life at different levels of consciousness.

VK: But it needn't be lived like that, need it?

Maharishi: If lived like that it will be perfect.

VK: *Sannyāsa* as an expression of Cosmic Consciousness?

Maharishi: As an expression of unity of life — top level, not Cosmic Consciousness.

VK: But this separation?

Maharishi: Cosmic Consciousness is represented by vāna-prasthya, where one both lives a worldly life and yet does not live it — where that gap is established.[179] *Sannyāsa*, on the other hand, is all Unity. See, rightly a man should be enlightened up to the state of Brahman by the time he is twenty-five. And it's very reasonable. About twelve years of life are enough to raise a man to that level — starting from eight or ten, up to twenty-five. It's very ideal and very beneficial. Look at the freedom from stress and strain [that there would be].[180] There was much less stress and strain a hundred years, two hundred years ago. But as life is demanding more of man it is necessary to go back to that state of life.

VK: But it's not necessary to be a sannyāsī in order to live the unity of life.

Maharishi: If the elderly people become sanyāsīs they leave

---

179 Husband and wife retire to the forest together to pursue spiritual enlightenment.

180 Maharishi has returned to this theme a number of times — his vision of the full sunshine of the Age of Enlightenment when children with very pure nervous systems will be born.

younger generations to handle society and do whatever they want to do — progress and all that.

VK: But those who have supreme knowledge are just the people who ought to be *in* society.

Maharishi: Ah, and that is the reason why sannyāsa is not for all; only for one class of people, Brahmins, that's all; no others.

VK: But that is worse, because the Brahmins are just the wise men who ought to be in the society and not out of it.

Maharishi: They are in the society so long as they are young. Because all the people in the society don't have to go one way, otherwise there will again be disorder in society [because people are by nature diverse]. And then, people in the society should have some wise people coming to them unasked.

VK: What do you mean?

Maharishi: Sannyāsīs come into a home unasked. A wise man with full experience of spirituality who has also lived in the world, he comes to a home and he comes feeling obliged that he has come to this home and will get bread from there. And if there is some advice [needed], here he is, available for any questions. The whole order is very sublime and realistic.

Shruti and Smṛiti[181]

W hat follows is a good example of how light conversation can give rise to profound teaching when Maharishi is present. On this occasion Maharishi and the three of us — Marjorie Gill, Jemima Pitman and I — had resorted to the small back room on the ground floor, where the work on the Sūtras was usually continued after lunch. In the afternoon heat this was the coolest room in the house, though even here it was still uncomfortably warm. Yet despite the heat, how much beautiful teaching emerged during those days in Kashmir, when Maharishi enjoyed a certain amount of freedom from organizational matters and could go deeply into each subject even with only a few people present.

The conversation begins on a somewhat personal note, but as usual Maharishi does his best to bring the topic back from the person to the teaching because for him it is the teaching that is important, not the person. In much the same way as in the previous conversation he took the chance to expound the stages of life, he now seizes on my bantering remark about smṛiti to launch into his beautiful exposition of what distinguishes the categories of scripture known as 'shruti' and 'smṛiti'.

---

181 *Editor's note:* Maharishi's later discussion of smṛiti (memory) can be found in his book *Celebrating Perfection in Education*, pp. 14–17. In this context, Maharishi defines smṛiti as total memory on the level of unmanifest self-referral intelligence, which maintains the complete sequential order in the unfoldment of natural law itself, on the basis of the perfect sequential flow of shruti — Veda — in the form of sound.

The Indian cyclical notion of time, where each period of manifestation is followed by one of dissolution, also comes up in connection with shruti. (I wish I could give an adequate impression of the sound of Maharishi's voice as he speaks about the freshness and purity that characterize the beginning of each creation — one can almost sense them as he speaks.) The cycle of four 'yugas' is a sub-cycle within the larger period of manifestation,[182] and the present revival is seen against the background of Kali Yuga, the last and least fresh period of the cycle and the one in which we are now said to be living. Maharishi holds out the possibility of a better world through the practice of Transcendental Meditation by generation after generation — 'but it'll be a rare achievement. It will be the sunshine coming through the clouds of Kali Yuga.'[183] Only five years or so after this conversation took place, Maharishi, through what he likes to call 'the window of science', caught a glimpse of the dawn. There are indications that he once again read the signs correctly, but as he himself said: 'The dawn has to be inaugurated during the night. The proof of the dawn is only when the day comes.'[184]

Maharishi: It [the work on the sūtras] is becoming easier all the time.

---

182 See BG 8.17; also MBG 4.1, pp. 253-4.
183 *Editor's note:* In 2005 Maharishi inaugurated the Dawn of Sat-Yuga — see appendix.
184 Conversation, Courchevel, France, 18 August 1975.

VK: When one is awake[185] it's very exhilarating.

Maharishi: Very. You feel like doing more and more.

VK: It's very exhilarating to be in the company of a completely original mind. It's very rare. Everybody follows everybody else's thought, looking at what others have done, but when somebody thinks completely differently, thinks for himself ...

Maharishi: It [the work] is so exhilarating. And the best part of it is that the teaching is linked in such a natural way by onward steps. This alone is the right meaning. (Laughter)

JP: *Which* alone is the right meaning?

Maharishi: What we say.

JP: (Turning to the others) Maharishi comes to one conclusion and the next day he comes to quite a different conclusion — and it's the translation of the very same verse.[186]

VK: Because it [Maharishi's teaching] is smṛiti and not shruti. (Laughter)

Maharishi: The truth is one, even though it is said in many ways. It becomes valid when it can be proved from any angle. The smṛitis[187] are the teachings of the saints from time

---

185 ... as one often was not, because of the heat.
186 For Maharishi's method of commenting, see Introduction, section, 'Maharishi's Approach to the Brahma Sūtra'.
187 The plural is also used, as in the case of the Vedas and the Brahma Sūtras and, later in this conversation, the shrutis.

to time; shruti[188] is the teaching of the eternal truth of life, which never changes. Smṛiti is about the same truth [as shruti but] applied to the lives of the people under various circumstances. The same one truth. See, like this (pointing to a flower): The sap is the basis of this green and white — this is one truth of the existence of this flower. Another truth of its existence is that the sap, when it manifests into the stem, is green; when it manifests into the petal, it is white. These are the two realities about the sap. But the one reality about the sap is that it is neither green nor white, it is neither the petal nor the stem — it is unmanifest. This truth is eternal truth; it is true for all time. And the truth that it is green here, white here, that it is soft here, hard here — these are relative truths, which keep on changing. If you put the flower in the sun this will no longer remain green and this will no longer remain white — it will change.

So there are realities which change and there is one reality which never changes. Shruti deals with that reality which never changes; smṛiti deals with the same reality but [with respect to] its changing phases. And these relative truths of smṛiti have been dealt with by different seers. They have spoken; there are written words, and this is called scripture. Shruti speaks of the one reality, non-changing, ultimate, and eternal. That is also scripture, but is said not to be the prod-

---

188 The word 'shruti' derives from the root 'shru', to hear. The word refers to the sounds actually heard, on a subtle level of consciousness, by the Vedic seers (rishis), and found in their written form in the Vedas.

uct of any one mind. It is the revelation in the perfect minds
at the beginning of creation when the whole atmosphere is
so fresh and pure — no stress, no strain in the atmosphere.

JP: Which scriptures are shruti then?

Maharishi: The Vedic texts are shruti — the Ṛig[189] Veda,
Sāma Veda, Yajur Veda, and Atharva Veda. The smṛitis [on
the other hand] are the teachings of the saints from time
to time. They speak of the relative truths in life, but of the
absolute reality of these relative aspects — the applied value
of the absolute truths expressed in the shrutis — so that this
reality is an all-time reality in every generation. Generations
may go, thousands and thousands of years may pass, but the
teachings of smṛiti are standard teachings; they won't deviate
with time and with place in different parts of the world.[190]

---

189 Maharishi later spoke of 'Ṛk Veda'.

190 When I asked Maharishi — this was at Vitznau, Switzerland, 25
February 1975 — where the Brahma Sūtra stood in relation to shruti
and smṛiti, he replied: 'The shrutis of the Vedas describe total reality —
the relative and the Absolute. They are compact expressions meaningful
for all states of consciousness, and their purpose is the establishment of
brāhmī-sthiti, the state of Brahman. The Brahma Sūtra gives direct expression to this ultimate focal point of all the shrutis, brāhmī-sthiti. The
smṛitis are the fundamentals of living which will always form the basis
of all aspects of life in motion and guide its flow to the supreme value of
evolution — that reality of wholeness, Brahman, which is expressed in
the Upanishads and made clear by the Brahma Sūtra. The smṛitis bring
out the practical theme of the shrutis, so that day-to-day life may reflect
Brahman Consciousness. The smṛitis have their breath in the shruti —
they are not separate. Their source and their course are the laws of nature
expressed by the shrutis. The Brahma Sūtra, the direct expression of the
knowledge of Brahman, may be said to express the goal towards which
the smṛitis flow and the knowledge which is the purpose of the shrutis.
It explains the ocean which is the goal of all the shrutis and the smṛitis.

So the shrutis and smritis both are authentic records. But the shrutis speak of the top-level value of life; the smritis speak of the relative values of the same ultimate reality.

JP: The Bhagavad-Gītā comes into the smritis, then?

Maharishi: The Bhagavad-Gītā is a very peculiar thing. Because it is spoken by Lord Krishna, and Krishna is [the] Absolute, the status of the Gītā [is such that] I wouldn't put it in the field of smritis; and there will be a hesitation to put it in the field of shrutis because it's the spoken word. Because it's the spoken word of the Absolute Himself, it could be put in the field of shrutis, yet it's difficult to do so because the shrutis are revelations and not the spoken word.

VK: The Gītā is generally said to be smriti.

Maharishi: We would hesitate to put it in the family of smriti. It is said to be smriti just because it can't be accepted as shruti since it is the spoken word.

VK: It sounds absurd to say that it is spoken by the Absolute.

Maharishi: Yes, it is something inconceivable. That's why it has a very special status.

JP: The shrutis are also written words. Is there a distinction between the written word and the spoken word?

Maharishi: No, no. It [shruti] is not spoken or written. It's a revelation. The shrutis are heard. It is shruti — it is heard,

---

This is how we connect them.'

and yet not spoken. (Laughter) It's difficult to come down to a very specific determination, but it is heard and that is why it's called a revelation. See, if it's a spoken word, then it has its time and place; it has a status in the relative. And if it has a status in the relative, then what will happen to its structure when the dissolution comes and the reality of existence has to continue for another creation? So, even in the state of dissolution something has to continue in order to give rise to the next creation. And this something is indeed indestructible; it is absolute. How the creation is to come up, and how it is to manifest, and how it is to evolve progressively for the next creation — all that also has a legal status.

JP: A legal status?

Maharishi: A legal status means that the whole thing has to be in a very perfect order of creation and evolution. The natural laws are not made anew in every creation — the same old thing comes up, manifests again and again. So there has to be some intelligence to continue it after the dissolution, until the next creation, and that is shrutatva ('shruti-ness'). Shruti is just that aspect of intelligence which manifests creation according to set laws.

VK: And this is apprehended ...

Maharishi: At the beginning of each creation.

VK: But the fact is that in this particular case shruti is written in Sanskrit. It's about a particular type of people.

Maharishi: Particular type of people. And the peculiarity of these people is: fresh, clean, neat, unstressed nervous systems in the beginning of creation — that purity of the atmosphere, purity of creation.

VK: But they must, at some particular time, put it into their own words, governed by their own conditions and sphere of influence. The impulse may be there but the same words won't come down for every creation.

Maharishi: Same words. That is the 'apaurusheyatva' of the Vedas.[191] It's that impulse, that sound.

VK: But that impulse is always translated into human terms. People may be very pure and at the beginning of creation, but they apprehend that impulse at a particular time and place, according to their social structure and so on. And you could very well imagine that the same impulse at another creation could ...

Maharishi: Could be different?

VK: Well, the impulse would not be different, but its translation into human terms would be different.

Maharishi: No, it can't be, otherwise eternity would be disturbed. The eternity, the infinity of the shruti would be dismantled if it were in any sense different. If it is to be eternal, then it must maintain its structure and its spirit, and every-

---

191 Their character as not being humanly created, their 'non-humanness'.

thing that there may be between the structure and the spirit. It must maintain itself in its entirety, otherwise it won't be truth, it won't be eternal truth. The laws of nature would be different each morning. (Laughter)

VK: That would make life very difficult, wouldn't it! It's difficult enough when the laws of nature are the same. (Laughter)

Maharishi: Seasons change; different laws of nature are exposed at different times. Those which are not exposed on cloudy days remain dormant and start to function when the clouds are not there, when the day is bright. So they remain there. In the shrutis everything must be there, because it is the thrill of pure consciousness which says this and this and this in the shrutis. So, nothing is different. It's the same thing in each creation. That is why the Vedas have their own grammar — if at all, for the sake of understanding, grammar can be said to apply to this [field of shruti].[192]

JP: The Vedas only therefore comprise shruti, or do they comprise smṛti as well?

Maharishi: No, all the Vedas are shruti.

---

192 When this was read to him, Maharishi added: 'The cognition of shruti is the source of grammar, and then grammar becomes the means of understanding the various aspects of the cognition. So grammar is of no use to those who actually saw or heard it [shruti], but it is of great use to those who don't have that level of awareness and now want to comprehend as much as can be comprehended of shruti. The source of grammar is shruti and the goal of grammar is the total exposure of shruti to those who want to understand it.'

JP: But I thought it was said that Vyāsa wrote ...

Maharishi: He wrote it [the Veda] down, he wrote it down.

JP: Was he therefore the one who received the direct perception of all this, or ...

Maharishi: No, that came much before. He just wrote it down.

JP: So it was passed on ...

Maharishi: From the beginning of creation to ...

JP: By word of mouth.

Maharishi: By word of mouth — by the ability of the human consciousness to catch those eternal impulses at the basis of all existence.

VK: So we may not have the original shrutis even now. They may not be the same as when they were written down, just as your words in future generations may not be the same as those you really spoke.

Maharishi: Revival of a great deal of the meaning is possible, as we are doing now, but cognition of the original impulses of the Vedas is not possible. The cognition of the Vedas, which happened at the beginning of creation, is not possible now because of the stress in the atmosphere, the pollution of the whole creation. The nervous system is not so pure; it cannot be so pure now as it was in the beginning of creation. It's not possible. What is possible is that much of the *meaning* can be revived, but the structure, the very form of it [shruti] in the completeness of its original shape — it's not possible. [193]

VK: What do you mean? It's not possible to understand ... ?

Maharishi: To cognize it. The impulses — they are not found. The system is not so pure.

JP: We're not on the same wavelength, so to speak.

Maharishi: The system has to be purified. It will take a few generations — the people keep on meditating, and their children and their children and their children — and the whole atmosphere will become purer and purer and purer.

JP: But that does not belong to Kali Yuga.

Maharishi: It's not a characteristic of Kali Yuga.

JP: And therefore it's not going to happen through these generations meditating.

Maharishi: The possibility we can accept, but it'll be a rare achievement. It will be the sunshine coming through the clouds of Kali Yuga.

---

193 *Editor's note:* In his later teaching, Maharishi expanded on the role of experience in relation to Veda. For example, in his book *Maharishi Vedic University: Introduction* (Holland, MVU Press, 1994), Maharishi defines Veda as 'the structure and function of the organizing power of Natural Law' (p. 4) and describes how the 'lively Home of all the Laws of Nature is available in [the] holistic field of consciousness' (p. 8). He explains that individuals can spontaneously enjoy the practical benefit of this organizing power of natural law on the level of experience, through practice of the Transcendental Meditation and Transcendental Medition-Sidhi programme.

JP: But how can we accept the possibility when according to …

Maharishi: Because we have something good in Kali Yuga — the means of communication of the present day. This is the one thing that is good in Kali Yuga [because our message can spread quickly].

VK: Cognition of the impulses of the Vedas would mean being aware on the very, very subtlest levels.

Maharishi: On that level where the revelation took place.

VK: And that really needs a nervous system of such purity …

Maharishi: That great degree of fineness …

JP: Not only that. The nervous system also has to have a certain environment to be able to receive those impulses. This is the difficulty, I am sure.

Maharishi: Environmental purity is very, very necessary, but that will grow naturally with individuals growing in pure consciousness.[194]

---

194 Here is a foretaste of Maharishi's teaching about collective consciousness.

The Roles of the Teacher and of Shruti Compared

The discussion is about a phrase that recurs a number of times in different sūtras: 'tathā hi darshayati' — 'thus indeed (third person singular) shows.' Because Sanskrit normally uses the verb form without personal pronouns, this can be translated as 'he', 'she', or 'it' shows, according to taste. The importance of this short discussion lies in Maharishi's description of the differing roles of the teacher and of scripture. The teacher is needed to enable one to apply the wisdom of scripture to one's present need. Maharishi returns to the role of the teacher in other conversations.[195]

Maharishi: We'll either be making Vyāsa very happy or we'll be annoying him. But I think he'll be happier when we say 'the teacher says', because that makes the meaning lively, it brings life to it. [On the other hand] when we say 'scripture says', there is some inertia.

VK: The trouble is that there is so much about scripture here that it does point to Shankara's type of interpretation.

Maharishi: And that type of interpretation will be valid once we say that the word of the teacher is the speech of shruti.

VK: Because what Shankara does everywhere is to take some text of shruti and refer the sūtra to that. And from the num-

---

195 See conversations, 'The Gap' and 'The Mahāvākyas'.

215

ber of statements about 'statements' and 'declarations' and 'shruti' and 'smṛiti' and all that, it would seem that Vyāsa has this scriptural reference in mind.

Maharishi: Now, in the world of today everything is sought in terms of *direct experience*, direct teaching, liveliness. And once the teacher is defined as someone who speaks the thought of shruti and smṛiti, then when we use 'the teacher says' the whole thing becomes lively. Otherwise it remains on a very abstract level of possibility but does not come onto the level of living.

VK: I agree with what you say from the practical point of view. I was only thinking of what Vyāsa, or whoever wrote these Sūtras, actually had in mind when he was writing them. He had scripture in mind.

Maharishi: No, it's not a matter of scripture. He had in mind the validity of scripture as spoken by a practical teacher. And the beauty of the words used in the Sūtras is that they have both the meanings: Shruti says it and the teacher says it. There is a sūtra that says all teaching is from the knowledge of the scripture. So the basis of the teaching is scripture. Now, the teacher makes the scripture lively and speaks it on the level of the need of the aspirant. Just this is the difference between shruti and the teacher, that the teacher says something when it has to be said. Shruti is there; it could be read by a man to whom that knowledge is not applicable right away, or by a man who has gone beyond that knowledge. So by oneself [without a teacher] it is difficult to apply the practical utility of shruti to one's level of need [at this moment in one's development]. Particularly when we are taking the stand of practical experience, we take it to be said by the teacher. It's very beautiful.

VK: Only, I don't think Vyāsa had this practical experience in mind, somehow.

Maharishi: Of course he had, because the Sūtras are on the practical level. They are not just for scholars; they should go to all the people.

Translating and Commenting on the Brahma Sūtra

There follow a number of short and often rather light-hearted exchanges, which in the course of dealing with the structure and mode of expression of the Sūtras and the problems involved in their translation, help to throw light on the subject of the Sūtras — Brahman.

The start of the first conversation finds Maharishi wondering why Vyāsa has gone round and round a particular point. He answers his own question by showing that Vyāsa had to write sūtras — phrases or sentences that could be easily memorized. He then goes on to distinguish sūtras from shruti. Although sūtras may be perfect in their meaning they cannot equal the perfection of shruti, in which sound and meaning correspond.

The latter part of the conversation, which arises from my *cri de coeur* about the seemingly less than perfect explicitness of the Brahma Sūtras, is pervaded by Maharishi's gentlest and most heartfelt laughter.

The Nature of a Sūtra

Maharishi: This is his [Vyāsa's] positive approach. But why has he gone round and round like that? In order to make it a sūtra. If he writes a sentence, then it becomes a form of the sūtra that the wisdom could go on generation after generation. People can remember sūtras.

VK: The Upanishads are big. They are not easy to memorize.

Maharishi: The Upanishads are as they are. And their value is that they are the expressions of the Absolute; they are non-created.[196] But in the case of the Brahma Sūtras, Vyāsa is a man; he is writing. So, the wisdom here is not as perfect as the shrutis are. The wisdom here is perfect in the sense of the meaning. But in the sense of expression, in the value of expression, the Sūtras can't be equated, or put on a parallel with the shrutis. They could be very near to the shrutis but just not on that level, because they are spoken, human. They are human expressions. Maybe they are spoken by the top

---

196 The Upanishads are also considered shruti. Each Upanishad belongs to one of the four Vedas.

human mind, fine. But yet, they are spoken and they can't match the grandeur of the shrutis.

VK: Well, these Sūtras could have been a little more explicit, just the same, even if they're short.

Maharishi: No, they are very explicit.

VK: If they can mean so many different things to so many different people — different things to Ramānuja, different things to Shankara, and different things to you — they can't be so explicit. (Laughter) Vyāsa could have been a little bit more clear.

Maharishi: No, we are talking the same thing as Shankara, only we talk in layman's language. (Laughter)

VK: For the world of today.

Maharishi: For the world of today. Layman's language.

VK: Yes, in India there's never any denial; there are only different points of view. It's always a question of different levels of understanding.

Maharishi: That's it. That is the glory of the vision.

VK: Yes, this is Indian philosophy. Not a clear 'yes' or 'no' as in the West. In India it's always 'yes and'. Isn't that so?

Maharishi: That's it. Fullness of ... The ocean is flowing and it is still. That's the situation — what to do? As is the structure of life, so is the structure of the *knowledge* of life. It is still and it is flowing. Still and flowing. So let's have that [translation]. Do justice to the English language. (Laughter)

VK: There seems to be a contradiction between doing justice to the English language and . .

Maharishi: And yet not mutilating the sūtras. (Laughter)

VK: [Between doing justice to the English language] and doing justice to Vyāsa.

Maharishi: Not mutilating the Sūtras in our attempt to expose the dignity of Brahman.

Without Deviation There Won't Be Regeneration

Maharishi: But then, [if our interpretation is wrong] the Brahma Sūtra is not for this generation, not for this world. Maybe our crude intellect of [the age of] Kali Yuga does not fathom the fineness and the depth of Vyāsa. But if that is the case, then it's not for this age.

VK: If that [Maharishi's] intellect is crude, what can one say of other intellects? There wouldn't be any name for them.

JP: They wouldn't even be recognizable as intellect.

Maharishi: We are interpreting the Sūtra on the level of experience, and who can challenge us? Otherwise [if not related to experience] it's useless talk.

VK: At least we are consistent in our deviation [from other interpreters].

Maharishi: We must deviate from them. Without deviation there won't be regeneration.

How the Inexpressible Is Expressed

(Maharishi has been explaining the Sūtras as the translations were read to him. This whole conversation is also pervaded by laughter.)

VK: These Brahma Sūtras must also be a way of realization because all reality is ...

JP: Turned upside down.

VK: It's vanishing under one's feet.

Maharishi: It has to be turned upside down because from ignorance to enlightenment [there have to be constantly changing instructions according to one's level of consciousness].

VK: There is nothing one can hold on to. As soon as one thing is said it's denied again.

Maharishi: And that's how the inexpressible is expressed.

The Sequence of the Sūtras and Their Translation

Maharishi: Every expression guards against so many points. The Sūtras are very careful in their expression, and even then the full meaning is not brought out in any one sūtra. Something is left out and in order to compensate for that, the next sūtra comes. It is a very subtle thing. After all, the sūtras are trying to describe the indescribable, and trying to reach those whose consciousness is far, far away from this reality. To picture the situation of Brahman, to picture the complete reality is so difficult, is so difficult, because words have a specific range of meaning and beyond that they don't see. That is why it is better to sacrifice brevity to clarity, than clarity to brevity.

VK: It is difficult enough to describe the indescribable in Sanskrit, which is at home in those dizzy regions. To do so in English presents quite a task.

Use of the Ablative for Describing the Indescribable

(The Brahma Sūtra consists, for the most part, of a 'string' — sūtra — of ablatives. Maharishi here explains why this is so. The ablative is usually rendered in translation as 'on account of' or 'because of'.)

Maharishi: Vyāsa means to say that Brahman is universal, but if you consider this thing, then on account of this it is like that. On account of your angle pertaining to this, Brahman is like that; otherwise it is universal.

VK: That's a limitation in the …

Maharishi: That is a limitation. He is indicating that if you

222

consider Brahman like this, you are giving it a localized state. But if you give it this localized state, it is because of this angle, because of this consideration.

VK: That's the only way of talking about it.

Maharishi: That's the only way of talking about it, and yet doing justice to it. It is so on account of that angle; otherwise it is not that. If you hold on to this angle, then from this angle you find it like that.

VK: Difficult to ...

Maharishi: To express that thought. Let's put it something like that. (Writing as he speaks) 'The "on account of" form, which occurs in so many sūtras, has been used to indicate that the description of ... '

VK: Of Brahman has to be from a particular point of view.

Maharishi: Yes, even though it is an inexpressible, universal reality.

VK: From one point of view it is on account of this, from another on account of that.

Maharishi: That is why everywhere the Sūtras say, 'on account of this, on account of this'. This is the marvellous and extensive vision of Vyāsa: when he says one thing he sees that some other aspect is lying untouched; so, take that also, include that also. Insofar as speech can encompass the universality of Brahman, Vyāsa has done it.

The Normality of Brahman

(This snatch of conversation reveals one of the most beautiful and fundamental points of Maharishi's teaching: to live the state of Brahman, to live the wholeness of life, is a natural, normal state of affairs. There is nothing to make a fuss about. Brahman is nothing other than what one is.)

Maharishi: This sūtra teaches the normality of Brahman and warns the aspirant not to make any fuss about Brahman. It is a normal, natural state. Live it as it is. Finished. (Laughter)

VK: I wish we had something to make a fuss about. (Laughter)

Maharishi: It's a normal, natural state. Live it as it is. Finished.

JP: Well, it sounds good enough, Maharishi, but ...

Maharishi: We have only to start living it.

VK: Maharishi always sounds good. (Laughter)

Maharishi: So, what is the translation? Let's come down to earth. We have to live it as it is.

There Are No Degrees of Brahman

Maharishi: This sūtra teaches the absolute state of Brahman without any trace of anything else. He says, 'Either you are this, or you are this. There is no room to establish a situation in between.' That means, the state of Brahman, when it is reached, is the state of Brahman. It is not associated with ignorance; it is enlightenment. And if it's not reached, then it's not reached. The rule is either you are this way or you are that way — that's all.

VK: Considering how short and concise the sūtras are ...

Maharishi: How long are the commentaries that are needed!

VK: I mean, that's a very long sūtra to say something so simple. I'm sure there must be more to it than that, Maharishi ...

Maharishi: No, I think it is that. It means that there is no situation of ninety per cent of Brahman or ninety-nine per cent of Brahman. It's only one hundred per cent; either one hundred per cent or no per cent.

VK: So it's not like Cosmic Consciousness ...

Maharishi: Which grows by degrees. It [the state of Brahman] also grows by degrees, but once it is there, it is there. And in that state, it won't allow anything else to be in it. Either it is attained or it is not attained.

The Smashed Seed and the Sprouted Seed

VK: Whereas philosophers can understand these commentaries, only people in Unity can understand Vyāsa himself. (Laughter) The sūtras are so cryptic.

Maharishi: We will show that it is due to the nature of Brahman that Vyāsa had first to say one thing and then had to say completely opposite things. Because, if Brahman is the ultimate reality and the All-pervading and the eternal truth, then — and this is a very beautiful point — it should be possible to bring out the knowledge of Brahman within the expressions which convey the field of possibility, and if there is a field of impossibility lying beyond the field of possibility, then even that field should be incorporated into the nature of Brahman. Vyāsa wrote this sūtra just to prove that Brahman is an all-inclusive wholeness and fullness of Unity which does not exclude any aspect of life, be it within the range of possibility or, transcending the range of possibility, in the field of impossibility. Such a big, huge construction in one sūtra.

JP: Maharishi, I think an intelligible translation of that is: 'In Brahman, anything goes.' That, at least, would be intelligible from our level. (Laughter)

VK: That's marvellous, Jemima.

Maharishi: We will make even our translations [as distinct from the commentary] give some knowledge about Brahman. Our translation will produce a sprouted seed in which the big tree can be visualized. But this will be a sprouted seed, whereas with others it's a smashed sprouting. The sprouting has been smashed before it came up, so there is no possibility of the proper vision of the tree. Now, this will be a sprouted seed. The Sūtras are the seed, and if it has sprouted then we can see the possibility, 'Ah, some day it will be a big, big tree.'

VK: Yes, I see what you mean. In other translations the points so often made in the past are just repeated, whereas this commentary is creative in some way — out of it something can come. Yes?

Maharishi: Something can come out. We see something coming out. And then, that will come out in the commentary — the big tree. But the sprouting will be witnessed here.

JP: In the translation?

Maharishi: In the translation. There'll be some indication of the tree coming out, some meaningfulness.

The Tragedy of Simplicity

Maharishi: This is what we call the tragedy of knowledge. The speaker speaks from his level; listeners then reproduce it from their own level. They [the other commentaries] are so [incomplete]. In so many cases we have seen [in our own commentary] that immediately after the commentary on one sūtra, the next sūtra follows [quite logically]. Once we have the meaning, the sūtra follows, it just follows.

VK: Not always.

Maharishi: 'Not always' means there is some gap. (Laughter) There is some gap still left. And when that gap is levelled out, then it's clear. The Sūtras are simple expressions of the supreme knowledge. Simple, clear, concise expressions of supreme knowledge.

VK: When Maharishi starts talking about simplicity, I don't know what he means by it, but I like to hear the simplicity established. What to him is simple! This is the tragedy of simplicity. (Laughter)

Maharishi: At one end it is found to be hard, and then it becomes simple.

VK: From your level it's all simple. Now I know why Maharishi says 'simple' ...

Tearing Apart and Reassembling

Maharishi: ... from God Consciousness to Unity. So, 'from the way of getting near' pictures the situation.

JP: Maharishi, don't you translate it according to the way it's written and then in your commentary, bring out what you want to convey?

Maharishi: Yes, 'upāsa' in Sanskrit means, 'being near'.

JP: 'Being near'? Not 'worship'?

Maharishi: It is also commonly used as 'worship', but the literal word meaning of it is 'upa-ās' — 'sitting near', 'being near'.

VK: What Maharishi has done in this case is more allowable than what he has done in some other cases where he has taken the word to pieces and reassembled it to suit himself. (Laughter) He has taken it to pieces and reassembled it!

Maharishi: As long as they are the same words, and remain in the same sequence, so long tearing apart and reassembling only amount to diving deep into them. Tearing apart comes in the line of analysis and reassembling takes the shape of synthesis, and this is how the complete meaning comes out. Otherwise they remain empty expressions.

Brackets Are a Cage

(I do not really think that it is possible altogether to avoid the use of brackets in translating the Brahma Sūtras, owing to their terseness. But Maharishi may well be right in saying that brackets can be misleading, in that they limit, or localize, Vyāsa's meaning. I appear as a tempter, offering Maharishi visions of the limitless use of brackets of his own, but he will not be tempted. This conversation, again, is permeated by laughter.)

Maharishi: What did you say about these brackets? That they make it readable?

VK: Yes, they make it readable.

Maharishi: But the fact is that it is these brackets which imprison Vyāsa's spirit. These brackets are a cage for Vyāsa to be lost in, for Vyāsa's teaching to be localized in ignorance. (Laughter)

VK: But as a new commentator you could make your own brackets.

Maharishi: No. Brackets mean localization in ignorance.

MG: I think that's so good. You could put that in your introduction and then avoid all brackets, in a very superior way.

Maharishi: We can just take delight in all the translations made so far but say that these brackets have engulfed Vyāsa's spirit in ignorance. When I saw these brackets in that translation — it becomes so meaningless.

VK: But our translation is also meaningless without the commentary.

Maharishi: But it's meaningless in the spirit of the Sūtras; so the sūtra [form] is not lost and Vyāsa is not lost.

VK: Yes, that's right. It's meaningless only in the sense that one cannot understand the meaning without a key. If you read the Brahma Sūtra and you didn't have the key it would have no meaning. So all we have to do is to put it into English sentences.

Maharishi: Instead of Sanskrit grammar we put it into English grammar. At least we are preserving Vyāsa. [Today]

Vyāsa's meaning is just lost in ignorance and that shows the gap between the two states of consciousness — that of the writer [Vyāsa], and that of the reader of today; the original head and the stressed, strained head of the commentator of this age.

VK: It's not true, Maharishi. It's being unfair to them, (laughter) because all that they put into those brackets comes from their reading of Shankara's commentary. Everything that they put into those brackets comes from Shankara's commentary.

Maharishi: Now, the vision of Shankara is equally lost in the gulf between the two levels of consciousness. Shankara is lost to his commentators …

VK: Because today they can't understand him, you mean?

Maharishi: Yes, they can't understand him. See, there was one word, 'within', and I said, 'Ah, he uses this word because two sūtras later that [something else] follows — and immediately one gets a glimpse. Now, this is Shankara's comprehensive vision.

VK: But I am sure that all that they repeat about gods and palaces [while commenting on the sūtra under discussion] is in Shankara too.

Maharishi: Having done the commentary we can show that the spirit of Shankara is maintained in these expressions of ours and it is lost in those expressions of the other translators. Even when Shankara speaks of 'pradhāna'[197] and other things, his vision on this is the same as ours.

VK: You put Shankara into your mould in the same way as you put Vyāsa. (Laughter)

Maharishi: Yes, we are innocently truthful to Vyāsa. And we'll hold that Shankara also, while going into all these details, gives the same thing [meaning]. See, in the case of 'patavach cha',[198] what we said was the essence of Shankara; only, he brought out two or three points which we didn't.

VK: And we brought out two or three points that he didn't. (Laughter)

Maharishi: He brought out that folding and unfolding[199] — it's very lovely. We got into the structure [of the sūtra] more than he did, but he showed the meaning in the structure. It's very heartening.

VK: It will be a beautiful commentary.

Let Vyāsa Decide

Maharishi: You are doubtful about that [translation]? It's very satisfactory. If Vyāsa, while writing the sūtra, did not

---

197 Nature in its primal, undifferentiated state. See above, introduction to 'Shankara's Commentary and Maharishi's'.
198 'And like a piece of cloth', BS 2.1.19.
199 Briefly, the cloth when unfolded (the effect) is not different from the cloth when it was folded (the cause).

mean what we are saying, I am sure he'll change his mind. (Laughter) Because it's such a marvellous meaning — the individual realizing Brahman, holding [maintaining] individuality yet established in Unity.

* * *

Maharishi: [Apropos of another translation] We can't say 'in spite of' …

VK: Vyāsa doesn't say 'in spite of'.

Maharishi: Let's read the Sanskrit.

VK: We should have Vyāsa here, to decide.[200]

JP: I think so too.

VK: Maharishi, why can't you call him.

JP: I think he may come before the …

VK: Before the month is out.

JP: To defend his position.

Maharishi: I think he must be feeling relieved that his sūtras are coming out of the confusion which has covered them for so many thousands of years.

---

200 See conversation, 'It Keeps on Fitting'.

Ways of Transcending in Indian Thought

Although it is in some ways rather personal, I have included this conversation because it touches upon a subject that tends to be taken for granted in our discussions but which forms the basis of the whole grand edifice of higher states of consciousness: the principle of transcending. Transcending is such a natural phenomenon that it can take place quite spontaneously, even where no systematic practice of any kind is being followed. A surprising number of people, when they first transcend after learning Transcendental Meditation, report that the experience is not unfamiliar. Such spontaneous transcending — Eliot's 'moment in the rose-garden'[201] — is especially common in youth. Often people yearn to repeat it, but the harder they try the less they succeed because they have no systematic procedure of 'not-trying'.[202] They have transcended by accident, as it were.

Transcending can also be accidental in another sense. It can be the result of systematic procedures whose overt aim

---

201 T. S. Eliot, 'Burnt Norton', *Four Quartets* (London, Faber and Faber, 1950), p. 11.

202 In 'The Spiral Path', the second of his two memorable 1966 BBC radio programmes, J. M. Cohen described some youthful moments of stepping from time into timelessness. The clearest such experience happened to take place as, crossing the college court late one evening, he came upon a still, cloudless, moonless sky. 'In my Cambridge days, I did not know what my experience was, or how to find it again. I looked up into the sky again and again, night after night, and nothing came. Hardly even the memory of that surprising state of other consciousness was to be found.' Only when, many years later, Maharishi had taught him to meditate, did he recognize these moments for what they were and understand the principle whereby he could 'lay himself open to their return'.

is not Transcendental Consciousness at all because the principle of transcending is not understood. Thus concentration can lead to transcending if one forgets to concentrate. Maharishi's unique grasp of the principle of transcending has enabled him to give us a way that is systematic, that is to say, repeatable, and at the same time extremely simple because cleansed of everything extraneous, so that each instruction given as one learns Transcendental Meditation conduces only towards transcending.

The short conversation on transcending that follows may be said to start the section of the book that is most directly concerned with higher states of consciousness. The principle of transcending is also examined, a little more fully this time, in the next conversation. Then follow some conversations centered around the theme of the autonomy of different states of consciousness, and after that come the more detailed discussions about Cosmic Consciousness, God Consciousness, and Unity Consciousness.

VK: 'If it be said, not by virtue of taking recourse to the metre, not so, because in whatever way the mind becomes surrendered through recitation, in that way indeed lies cognition.'[203]

Maharishi: It's just Transcendental Meditation explained.

VK: But it says 'in whatever way'. So does that mean by whatever mantra, or does it mean in whatever way one transcends?

---

203 BS 1.1.25, as translated at that time.

Maharishi: Not particularly mantra; whatever way one transcends, we would say.[204]

VK: But you say there is only one way.

Maharishi: There is only one way in the sense that one has to go through the experience of gross and subtle and subtlest.

(Side A of the tape ends here. I must have forgotten to change the tape immediately, but the beginning of Side B is still on the subject of different ways of realization.)

Maharishi: Rāvaṇa was the wisest of his kind. He was a rākshasa, a giant, or what do they call it in English?

VK: A kind of demon, wasn't he?

Maharishi: Demon. He was the head of all of the demons. (Laughter) And he was a great paṇḍit of the Vedas; he knew all the Vedas — everything. And he took a whim that he would fly in a rage against the Lord; through anger he was going to win him. 'Through whatever way the mind gets

---

204 When this was read to him at Arosa, Switzerland, 31 May 1974, Maharishi commented: 'In whatever way one *is*, one is transcending. Transcending happens automatically with every step of progress, or evolution. Evolution means that one thing has gone — it has developed into other things. So life has transcended boundaries. It keeps on transcending boundaries. Every step of progress, or evolution, every stroke of change giving rise to the next evolved state, is dependent on transcending. It is so universal, it is such an all-time reality, that, going through it all the time, one does not even always recognize it, so much is it embedded in one's own nature. So, the process of transcending is one with the evolutionary process. What we call Transcendental Meditation is natural to the human mind.'

surrendered, in that way lies the cognition.'

VK: So anger becomes more subtle and subtle ...

Maharishi: Subtle and subtle, and then one gets out of anger and ...

JP: Did he succeed?

Maharishi: He did.

VK: A former teacher of mine, a lady professor called Betty Heimann — she's dead now — wrote a book on Indian thought[205] where she showed that Indian thought was always taking something to its ultimate conclusion, and going beyond that to its infinity. This was a very good thought ...

Maharishi: Beautiful. Beautiful.

VK: And she traced it right through every point of Indian thought.

Maharishi: Beautiful. That book would be worth reading.

VK: You might not agree with all of it, but that particular thought, that intuition ...

Maharishi: Then she would have learned Indian philosophy from some realized Indian paṇḍit.

VK: I think, yes, she was taught by some such man.

---

205 *Studien zur Eigenart Indischen Denkens* (Tübingen, Mohr Siebeck, 1930). See also the same author's *Facets of Indian Thought* (London, Allen and Unwin, 1964).

Maharishi: Because this one thing just can't dawn in the mind of anyone non-Indian.

VK: She was so kind to me. I came to her in desperation about my thesis. She received me so kindly and I used to go to her every week. It didn't help me much with my thesis, but …

Maharishi: But even then, there was someone to talk to, to consult. While doing the thesis did you feel that you should have taken some other subject?

VK: Very much so.

Maharishi: (Loud laughter)

VK: Very much so.

Maharishi: Because Indian philosophy … Only from our angle it's very rich and sumptuous and delightful and practical. From other angles it's so dry and breath-consuming and impractical.

VK: I never regretted anything more than doing that thesis.

Maharishi: (Loud laughter)

VK: And it put me permanently off the academic life, too, because I found it was such a …

Maharishi: Bore.

VK: Oh-h. Terrible. One reason why I became a businessman. (Laughter)

238

Maharishi: Then the teaching of the Gītā [about the need for action] worked. (Laughter) No, you did it because you had to do Brahma Sūtras. It gave a beautiful background to … the very thinking — the direction of thinking and going deep into the subject — that's the effect of it.

Hearing, Contemplation, and Meditation

This conversation will be of special interest to students of the advaita (non-dual) school of Vedānta, founded by Shankara, which assigns a central role to 'shravana', 'manana', and 'nididhyāsana',[206] here translated as 'hearing', 'contemplation', and 'meditation'. Maharishi is refuting the accepted view that meditation is merely an intensified form of reflective thinking, or contemplation. He makes the very interesting point that hearing is concerned with both sound and meaning, contemplation with meaning only, and meditation with sound only. Maharishi's use of the words 'contemplation' and 'meditation' may differ from certain accepted usages in the West, which associate meditation, and not contemplation, with reflective thinking. But this is unlikely to cause confusion because he defines his terms quite clearly.

Those who practise Transcendental Meditation will know what is meant by 'slipping' from one level of awareness to

---

206 The series derives from BU 2.4.5.

another. However, there is an important distinction, which owing perhaps to the limitations of my own experience I failed to draw in the present conversation. The mind can 'slip' when the system is tired, in which case the experience will lack clarity, or it can slip when the system is alert and well-tuned, in which case 'the mind gets fresher and so becomes sharper and sharper, and then hits hard, clear' — that is, increasingly fine levels of experience are appreciated until there is a clear awareness of the process of transcending the finest level to reach Transcendental Consciousness.

Maharishi: These people [who interpret the Vedānta] have the angle that the state of Brahman comes out of contemplation, out of thinking, out of reading the shrutis, and analyzing, and classifying.

VK: Shravaṇa (hearing), manana (contemplation), nididhyāsana (profound meditation).

Maharishi: Now, nididhyāsana is that about which we are speaking [that is, Transcendental Meditation]; it is the field of experience. See, shravaṇa demands shabda (sound) and meaning both. Manana is on the level of meaning; shabda has not much to do with manana. And nididhyāsana is not on meaning; it is on shabda. For hearing about Brahman, sound and meaning, both are necessary because the meaning rides over the sound, and we hear. For contemplating, sound is eliminated; it is the meaning on which the contemplation grows. So meaning is useful on the level of manana, that is, contemplation. And sound and meaning, both, are necessary in the first instance, to hear. But sound alone is necessary for nididhyāsana, for experience. For through sound — 'svāpyayāt'.[207] One comes to oneself through the sound, minimizing the sound, experiencing its finer states. So this aspect of nididhyāsana is not understood properly. I have talked to very good Vedāntins and they say nididhyāsana is only the intensified state of manana. I said, no, here you are wrong. Nididhyāsana is not the intensified state of manana; it is a completely different process. See, if it were the intensified state of manana it would be like sugar and saccharin: they are two different things but one is more intensified in sweetness than the other. This is not the case with nididhyāsana. The method of nididhyāsana involves, not manana — not the meaning of the sound — but the sound itself.

VK: Couldn't it be that if you think about something, and think about it, and think about it, there comes a point when the intellect won't take, won't give any more, and then you sink?

Maharishi: Now, where do you sink? You sink in the fort of your imagination where nothing else can pierce through. Thinking, and thinking, and thinking, and mood-making, and mood-making — such intensified mood-making [to

---

207 'On account of coming into one's own', BS 1.1.9.

the effect] that that [which is thought about] alone is right. Hypnotism.

VK: It might be that, or it might be that the meaning is transcended altogether in the way of those who do 'japam'. They repeat the name of the Lord, and repeat the name and then, eventually the mind gets tired and it slips. And the same with this kind of nididhyāsana.

Maharishi: No. If nididhyāsana is one of the three means of attaining transcendental pure awareness, then it's a systematic process, not an accidental slip. It must be a systematic procedure. Slipping because of not knowing and after getting tired is no procedure. It may be counted as a procedure of slipping but it's not a procedure; it's an accident. There is a custom in India that if one is walking by the Ganges and accidentally slips and falls into the Ganges, he says: 'Ah, Mother Ganges, now purify me.' He didn't intentionally step into the water to take the bath but he happened to slip here. And he is purified. But this is not the procedure of gangāsnāna (bathing in the Ganges).

VK: But even Transcendental Meditation is an accidental slip.

Maharishi: It's not accidental. (With great emphasis) It's a systematic procedure; it goes step by step. Three things have been counted as procedures — shravana, manana, and nididhyāsana — three different procedures.

VK: Transcendental Meditation is also the mind getting tired — same thing.

Maharishi: No. It is not that the mind gets tired, but that the mind gets fresher and becomes sharper and sharper, and then hits hard, clear.

VK: But it also can be accidental; sometimes it slips, sometimes it doesn't slip.

Maharishi: When it is rainy and slippery it slips. (Laughter) And rainy it becomes because it becomes sarasa (full of charm) — more rasa (charm) and more rasa, and then it slips.

VK: Just what we were saying yesterday. Take anything to its farthest limits and then you transcend. And you could do this even through contemplation. I think this is how they usually interpret nididhyāsana.

Maharishi: No, then it won't be through contemplation. It will be through accidentally slipping out of contemplation.

Ultimate Reality and Different States of Consciousness

A kindly and intelligent Kashmiri doctor had come to visit a member of our household. After completing his ministrations he went to see Maharishi, who explained the work on the Brahma Sūtra to him. Out of this arose a very interesting discussion on the nature of Unity and the autonomy of different states of consciousness.

Maharishi: The level of the sap is the level of unity, existing in the midst of the diversity of the tree. So the Brahma Sūtras deal with the level of the sap — unity of life, Being — and they establish that flower, fruit, branches, tree are nothing but manifestations of the sap. The reality is the sap; flower, fruit, and so on are just its phenomenal aspects. If we analyse the flower we see that every fibre of the petal is nothing but sap. So, in reality, the flower is the sap. And if every fibre of the flower is the sap, then the sap has not become the petal. For if it becomes the petal, then the sap will not be found in the petal. When milk becomes curd, then in the fibres of curd milk is not found.

D: It's a form of energy change.

Maharishi: Not change. That is the main point. It does not change. It does not become transformed.

D: But taking another shape. The basic thing remains the same but it has to take the shape of this and that.

Maharishi: No, it has not. That is the main point, that it has not taken a shape. For if the sap has become the flower it will not be located in the flower. The truth is that when we analyse every fibre of the flower, we find the sap.

D: What we see as flower, is that hallucination?

Maharishi: This is what it comes to (Laughter) No, it is a

244

reality of relative life; the Absolute is the reality of all relative life, just as the sap is the reality of the flower.

D: But when we see the flower, touch the flower, smell the flower, taste the flower, the sap in fact is the flower, in the form of flower.

Maharishi: And this is in our waking state of consciousness. But when our awareness gets submerged in that transcendental pure awareness, then nothing of the relative can be perceived.

D: But you see only the sap.

Maharishi: Only the sap. Now this is in the beginning [early stages] of experience. But when transcendental pure consciousness becomes a living reality in the relative, then the diversity of relative existence no longer remains dominating. It remains, but no longer dominates in our awareness. The unity dominates on the level of awareness. And this is the field of the Brahma Sūtras. They establish the need for that experience and show that it should be a normal experience for everyone. It is not difficult at all. It's a natural thing. And Transcendental Meditation is the way. (Laughter)

D: You explain it so simply, but when we come to the reality, we see the leaves. Sap has become the leaves.

Maharishi: Now wait on. We see the leaf — depending on our level of awareness. We see the leaf when we are clear. We see the leaf when we are dull. We see the leaf when we are so dull that we are going to sleep. The leaf is the leaf, but the quality of perception changes according to our level of awareness. So, when that pure awareness dominates our vision, the reality of the leaf is not hidden from our vision. That signifies Unity; that is Brahman, brāhmī-sthiti (the state of Brahman).[208]

D: In other words, the leaf is the leaf, but in fact it is the sap. The sap has taken temporary form.

Maharishi: On the basis of the reality of the sap the leaf appears to be. This is how we could put it.

VK: Yes, and then That dominates. And this means that in your consciousness, when you look at the leaf, That dominates. But this does not mean that the leaf is not there. It just means that when you are looking at it you are so dominated by the awareness of Unity ...

Maharishi: Right, right.

VK: That you see the leaf as sap. But it doesn't mean that the leaf is not there.

Maharishi: But look at that. The ornament seen by the expert vision of the goldsmith — he sees the design, but he sees the quality of gold at the same time. That means the surface value of the object is not eliminated when the reality of the

---

208 As pointed out in the Introduction, Maharishi nowadays speaks of the state of Brahman as the climax of Unity.

object is cognized. This is what we mean when we say, 'That dominates'.

D: That is very clear; though there are impurities, the man who can see finds out of what carat the gold is. Now the leaf, it is made of sap, but the leaf in reality exists.

Maharishi: The leaf exists but the reality …

D: Is sap, because it's made of sap.

Maharishi: And the reality of the leaf is just a seeming reality — the seeming reality of a mirage without a drop of water.

VK: The design of the goldsmith, this is a real design. He cuts something into that gold and makes it into a design.

D: It's not a mirage, it's a reality.

Maharishi: The thing is, we know this leaf. And someone who doesn't know that there is sap underneath, show him the sap. Take him to the fine roots, and finer roots, and the finest hair of the root, and show him the pearl of the sap. And then he knows: this is all sap. This trunk and leaf and green and red and blue and flower and fruit — they are nothing but this. Now if, in his vision, this sap, this colourless, formless sap starts to dominate, then the domination of the green and the red of the tree and the leaf will become overshadowed by the domination of this colourless quality of the sap. Let the man see the sap and see this thing [leaf, tree, and so on] and again see the sap and again see this thing; let him bring his awareness to the sap and the tree, one after the other, alternating the experience. A time will come when he will start seeing the leaf in terms of the sap. And when it happens that the sap dominates the vision, and the leaf and this colour and all these distinctions, all these differences become overshadowed by the domination of the colourless quality of the sap, then Unity is said to be established in life. Now what is Unity? It is immortality, eternity, unboundedness. Life is then established on that level of immortality, eternity, bliss. That is the practical value of Brahman dominating the vision. Life will be there — the symptoms of life which are in the field of relativity will be there — only it will be dominated by that value of Unity.

D: I agree, sir, the main thing is the sap. This cloth is made of thread …

Maharishi: Eventually cotton and eventually earth.

D: Now, the threads made this handkerchief and I can see with the microscope that this handkerchief is nothing other than threads. So I purify myself and I see the leaves as nothing other than sap — because I can see with the microscope that this rectangular form is nothing other than threads — but this is a leaf also.

Maharishi: Right. This is a leaf when the leafhood is dominating, and this is sap when the sap is dominating the vision.

D: I get your point. With a microscopic eye I see the handkerchief as threads, and in the same way I will see the leaf as sap and not the leaf. I am trying to get nearest ...

Maharishi: No. The leaf will be seen in terms of the sap.

VK: Now, in some way you are taking away the ground from under one's feet.

Maharishi: Now this is a different state of consciousness. Red glass — we see through red glass and everything is of that quality. The glass is changed — that is what the change in consciousness is like — waking state of consciousness, Cosmic Consciousness, God Consciousness, and this Unity.

VK: What you say is that one can't say anything about the reality of something independently of one's own state.

Maharishi: Right. The world is as we are.

VK: You are taking the ground away from under one's feet.

Maharishi: But this is the ground of the waking state, the state of ignorance of reality. So it must be taken out. (Laughter)

VK: You can only say something about it depending on your state.

Maharishi: Yes, depending on the level of consciousness.

VK: And we make a value judgment when we say that this state is better than that state ...

Maharishi: We don't say better or what. It is a different state. It is worth living. (Laughter) That is the value of that state — it is worth living. It can't be compared, just as the dreaming state can't be compared with the waking state. It just can't be compared.

The Autonomy of Different States of Consciousness

The following short exchange arose from a sūtra that Maharishi was translating. He illustrates the autonomy of different states of consciousness by expanding the point made at the end of the last conversation, that the dream state cannot be compared with the waking state. When this conversation was read to him, he spoke further on the same subject, and I have appended the longer conversation which then ensued.

Maharishi: 'And creation from non-birth is no longer a subject for inference.'

VK: Creation has not originated?

Maharishi: No, no. It has originated, but it has not originated from birth.

VK: What does that mean?

Maharishi: That means, it is a mirage. The sea is there, but it has no foundation; it is there as a mirage. It has no origin except in the sight of the seer. So, the world is there; we don't deny its being there, only we deny its origin, its having substance. But this is the vision in the state of Unity.

A man sees a mountain in this room, but he is not seeing in the waking state: he is seeing a reality of the dreaming state. Like that, this creation from non-birth is a reality in the state of Unity and *not* in the ordinary waking state. A man sees a mountain in the room, but he sees it in a different state of consciousness. And in that state of consciousness, *that alone is right*. So here we are speaking of the cognition in the state of Unity, and not in any other state of consciousness but that. We'll have to warn the reader to be careful; this is the vision of that state of consciousness and not of any other whatsoever. And this example of the mountain in the room — as an intelligent conclusion, it's absurd; it's maddening to say there is a mountain in a room, but that is the reality in that [dream] state of consciousness.

VK: When that state of consciousness is judged by the waking state of consciousness, the waking state judges it as false.

Maharishi: It'll be absolutely false. So also, the cognition of a realized man is absolutely absurd for an unrealized vision. It's absolutely ridiculous. When someone says, 'Oh, I am everywhere', he speaks from his level of awareness. But people will say, 'What? You are here, and you are everywhere? It's absurd.' But one man is speaking from the level of the sap, which is everywhere; he is speaking from the level of Unity. And the other man is speaking from the level of separateness, division. That is *his* vision and that is *his* vision. Both are right. (Laughter) Both are right.

VK: So there's no absolute truth, then.

Maharishi: No. No. Truth is always relative.

VK: Truth is relative to one's state of …

Maharishi: It depends upon one's level of awareness. Truth is 'absolutely' not absolute. Anyway, this is very beautiful; so refreshing, so refreshing.

Postscript: Arosa, Switzerland, 31 May 1974

Maharishi: In the dream state of consciousness, the dream is as real as waking experience is in waking consciousness. The dream becomes a mirage only when one comes to waking consciousness. Mirage means non-existent. When one goes from one state of consciousness to another, the experiences of the previous state of consciousness seem to be a mirage, because they are no longer applicable to the new state. Like that, the world was a mirage in Cosmic Consciousness. This is the reality of the … No, it's not the reality; it's the evaluation of the experience of Cosmic Consciousness when one is in Unity or in Brahman Consciousness. If one, being in Unity, evaluates the experiences that he had in Cosmic Consciousness, then he finds that this gap between the Self and the non-Self, between the world and the Self — this gap was a mirage. There was no gap because now he finds everything in terms of himself. So, there now being that Unity everywhere, the duality which was an experience in Cosmic Consciousness was just a mirage. The world was just a mirage.

In the state of Unity the world is my Self. So, this uniformity, this homogeneous wholeness of the Self is all that there is in Unity. And when from this level one evaluates the experience in Cosmic Consciousness, where the world was and I was, the Self and the non-Self, each with its own distinct status — waking was and I was, dreaming was and I was, sleep was and I was — then this duality of experience was just a mirage, because it has now blended into one in Unity Consciousness. But as long as one was in Cosmic Consciousness this duality was a reality — just as the experiences of the dream are real. They become illusory, they are evaluated as being illusory, only when one wakes up from the dream, when one is out of the dream. Just like that. It is for this reason the Gītā says that the wise will not delude the ignorant.[209] So, the wise in Unity will not just throw off the experiences of Cosmic Consciousness as being illusory and unreal and nonexistent. It would be a mistake, because it can only create confusion in the listener's awareness.

VK: But I mean, it is still true that the world has not originated, isn't it? It is there but it has not originated — that is an

---

209 3.26, see MBG, p. 218.

experience. Where does that experience come from?

Maharishi: No, the Vedas explain the origin of the world. There is an origin, there is an origin; and the origin is in the source, that big, huge, great source, that great Brahman, the source from which everything could originate, the big, huge, unlimited reservoir of energy and intelligence from which all this could spring.

VK: That's from one point of view …

Maharishi: Right. Right.

VK: But if you take it from another point of view, from the paramārthika (highest truth) point of view, then, for the Vedānta, there is no origin …

Maharishi: Because Vedānta is concerned with that level of supreme awareness which is the source of all creation. In that source there is nothing other than wholeness — everything is unmanifest. A study which is dedicated to exposing the structure and character of a particular state of consciousness cannot talk of other levels of consciousness. Physics hesitates to talk of chemistry and biology; physicists are only dedicated to physics. Just like that, there are channels of knowledge. A knowledge which is dedicated to exposing one state of consciousness can only talk of that one state of consciousness. And knowledge which is dedicated to bring out the reality of another state of consciousness will talk only of that state of consciousness. And if we try to mix them up or compare the two, they won't compare; they will contradict each other. It is very natural. The description of a hut will not fit in the description of a palace, nor the palace in the hut. They contradict each other. Enormous hugeness of the palace and small tinyness of the cottage — they are different structures. Each has specific characteristics. One may compare them — there is no harm in comparing — but one must know that this belongs to this area, that belongs to that area. As long as one is clear about it, fine. If not, one will make a muddle of the whole thing.

VK: Once again, the autonomy of different states of consciousness.

Maharishi: Autonomy of different states of consciousness. On one level of consciousness there will be unity prevailing, on the other level of consciousness differences will dominate.

Only the Liberated Know Bondage

In this further short exchange, the truth that knowledge is different in different states of consciousness is illustrated with reference to bondage and liberation.

Maharishi: According to this sūtra the jīva (individual soul) is not Brahman. He [the jīva] is Brahman only due to 'svā-pyayāt',[210] due to coming into his own. If he has not brought

---

210 BS 1.1.9.

255

his own Self to his awareness, if he has not enlivened all his potentialities of body, mind, and being, then jīva is jīva; he is not Brahman. If the jīva has not brought harmony between all aspects of his outer and his inner existence, then he is not Brahman, he is jīva.

This means that Brahman is a state of consciousness. If all-harmonizing awareness is there, then that is consciousness of Brahman. And if all-harmonizing awareness is missing, then it is not consciousness of Brahman; it is some other state of consciousness, and that is bondage. Bondage is bondage in comparison to liberation. Otherwise it is just a state of life. Only when compared to that laudable state of Unity is it bondage. If a ten-watt bulb is giving light, it is light. It is dim only when compared with a hundred-watt bulb.

VK: So it is really only the knowers of Brahman who should call it bondage. The others are always shouting about bondage, but it is only bondage as compared to that knowledge. Otherwise it is a beautiful state of life, much better than the animal state.

Maharishi: Very good point. Only the realized should call it bondage.

VK: And these other people go about in misery saying, 'We're in bondage.' I suppose this has come about because their thinking has been so much permeated by the philosophy of the realized.

Maharishi: So much enamoured by it. It is captivating; it is all attraction.

The Philosophy of Action and the Five Components of Action

Maharishi here shows that action must have a different basis in different states of consciousness — a variation on the theme that knowledge is different in different states of consciousness. The basis of action is one of the five components of action mentioned in the Bhagavad Gītā. Maharishi has just begun to speak of these five when the conversation ends rather abruptly. I have therefore added an extract from an earlier conversation where the same five factors are discussed, but in a rather different context, namely, as providing a scheme for examining the nature of Brahman.

Maharishi: Action is no longer baseless in the state of Unity. As long as Unity has not been gained action is baseless.

VK: Action is baseless even in the state of Cosmic Consciousness?

Maharishi: Action is very baseless in Cosmic Consciousness because it is thrown out [from the Self]. The Self is separate; action has not even the Self to support it. In Cosmic Consciousness or in God Consciousness action is baseless. Unity

257

provides the basis of action. We should develop the philosophy of action from here. Whatever illusory basis action had in the ordinary waking state, that basis is taken away in Cosmic Consciousness and action becomes completely baseless. (Laughter) And then it starts to gain its basis, gradually, gradually, until it has a full basis in Unity. It's very beautiful.

VK: You are so far in advance, working on the level of Unity when all your students are hoping to gain Cosmic Consciousness.[211] (Laughter)

Maharishi: They are trying to lose the illusory basis of action.

VK: You are five steps in advance, always.

Maharishi: Lose the illusory basis … The philosophy will be validated by the experiences during meditation and after meditation in daily life. We must write a book on the philosophy of action and bring out everything on a practical level. This is such a brilliant point that came out in the sūtra today — the basis of action came out of that sūtra about intellect.[212]

VK: The sūtras are a sort of peg on which to hang your inspiration.

---

211 As mentioned in the Introduction, the pace of progress since that time has been very rapid. At the Age of Enlightenment Courses, prolonged periods of witness consciousness, which culminate in Cosmic Consciousness, were more frequently reported. *Editor's note:* At the time of publication, the Invincible America Assembly, inaugurated by Maharishi in 2006, is giving rise to frequent experiences of the full range of higher states of consciousness.
212 BS 3.2.33.

Maharishi: The philosophy of action ... it's very beautiful. See, in the eighteenth chapter ... (In Hindi) Bring the Gītā.

VK: You mean these five factors of action.[213]

Maharishi: (Quotes the verses in Sanskrit and continues) Adhishthānam (basis of action), karaṇam (means of action), kartā (actor), cheshtā (mechanics of action), and daivam (support from nature). This is the division of action. Adhishthānam — basis. Now you have a vision of what the basis of action is. You start from deep sleep and then ...

VK: In the ordinary waking state the basis of action is ignorance — identification [with the objects of experience].

Maharishi: Not identification but lack of ability to maintain one's Self, one's own universality — getting bogged down in the boundaries of the object. The body is the physiological basis of action, but in explaining this basis we have to take the body through its different states — in sleep, in dreaming, in waking, in Transcendental, Cosmic, and God Consciousness to Unity, and there [in Unity] establish: 'Now, *this* is the basis of action — real action.'

VK: You've had that in mind for some time. Even last year you were talking about a book on the philosophy of action.

Maharishi: It will be a very profound work, much needed, because from that angle people will see the need for meditation.

---

213 See BG 18.13–14.

VK: All the active people in the world will see the need ...

Maharishi: And it will really be a great awakening — and the means of action are the senses.

VK: And at each level of consciousness all these five factors of action would be different.

Maharishi: Something different ...

* * *

Maharishi: See, there is a verse in the Gītā, in the eighteenth chapter, which says that five factors have to be considered for a thorough consideration of anything.

VK: Of action.

Maharishi: Yes, action. The basis, the doer, and so on. Here [in the Brahma Sūtras] also we will do the same thing. I was considering if it is possible to divide the whole thing in terms of five, and it is possible. (Maharishi quotes Bhagavad-Gītā, 18.14 in Sanskrit.) See, [first] what is the basis? Give the basis to Brahman. [Second] what is Brahman? This is considered under 'kartā' (the doer). [Third] 'karaṇa' — means to the realization of Brahman. We have to see what are the means — prāṇa (breath), and light, and ...

VK: Sound.

Maharishi: Sound. Ākāsha,[214] prāṇa, light. And then [fourth]

---

214 Space, the medium of sound. What Maharishi calls 'means' are

'cheshtā', the actual mechanics — what to do in order to realize Brahman. Absorption of the mind — that will be the cheshtā. And [fifth] the fact that realization is natural, that anyone can realize Brahman — this universality will be 'daivam'.

VK: Isn't 'daivam' karma, past karma?

Maharishi: I was just thinking on that. Daivam must be somewhere here — in this area of how the experience becomes permanent; support from nature. (Maharishi pauses) Daivam is the force of evolution. The force of evolution pushes the mind; it motivates the mind to go to That [Brahman], so that the mind gets absorbed into it.

VK: It might be very good to try and put that classification into every chapter.

Maharishi: Into every chapter, if possible. Now we'll read and see. It might be a very good mirror to the whole teaching: What is Brahman? How is it realized? The practical method, the principle of it — all these.

VK: But the Gītā is really describing the five components of every *action*.

Maharishi: So the action of realization. (Laughter) This makes it intelligible.

VK: And when you've done the second pāda (section), you'll

the steps, or experiences, by which Brahman is attained, as distinct from the mechanics, or methods of attaining it.

see still better how it flows.

Maharishi: How it flows into this thought. And if it flows, then this will be all right. The whole subject is jumbled in the other commentaries.

VK: No, it's not jumbled. The other commentators also have their theme, only it's a different theme. (Laughter)

Maharishi: Basis of the knowledge of Brahman; at what level can one comprehend, or cognize Brahman? And what is Brahman? What are the means to realize it? And then the practical method to realize it; and then support from nature. These are the main things. The main theme of each chapter may be one of these, yet covering the others also.

VK: I can see you getting an idea for fifteen commentaries on the Brahma Sūtras, each one from a different point of view.

Maharishi: Yes, yes, because if it is a reality then it should be supported by all the six systems [of Indian philosophy].

VK: The six systems and the five components of action — that would make thirty commentaries.

Maharishi: Each [component] to be supported by each of the six.

VK: The reviewers would be terrified again when they read it.

Maharishi: A big [important] statement has gone into that

... the twenty-four commentaries in the Gītā. (There is much laughter throughout the last part of the conversation, which recalls Maharishi's suggestion, in the introduction to his commentary, that twenty-four commentaries would have to be written to do justice to the Bhagavad-Gītā, and the reviewers' reactions to this.)

The Gap

The gap in question is that between Self and non-Self, Absolute and relative, which is appreciated in Cosmic Consciousness and is bridged in Unity Consciousness.[215] I must have been reading to Maharishi from some commentary — I cannot recall which, and the reading is not on tape — where a gap is mentioned. There is some teasing and laughter, after which Maharishi gives an account of the development from Cosmic Consciousness, via God Consciousness, to Unity Consciousness. I insist that in principle the gap between relative and Absolute is unbridgeable; Maharishi is more concerned to show that in practice it is bridged. In this connection he mentions the concept of 'leshāvidyā', the faint remains of ignorance that make activity possible in the state of Unity — otherwise one might be completely overwhelmed by the oneness of things. I have

215 *Editor's note:* As mentioned in footnote 38, the word 'gap' is used here in a context different from Maharishi's later discussion of the gap between two syllables of the Vedic text (for example in *Celebrating Perfection in Education*).

included an interesting footnote on this concept, containing Maharishi's answer to a question I put to him after reading him this section of the conversation in Switzerland in January 1974.

The conversation continues with two questions from Jemima Pitman, both concerned with the development of Cosmic Consciousness. The first deals with the process of the infusion of Being, the second with a feeling of dryness, or non-involvement, which may arise when this process has reached a certain stage. They enable Maharishi to show in some detail how the appreciation of the gap, or separateness of Self and non-Self, begins and then grows to its full measure in Cosmic Consciousness.

When the section dealing with the feeling of dryness had been read to him in June 1974, Maharishi, using a child's development as an example, brought out even more clearly than he did in Kashmir the reasons for this feeling. And he ended by emphasizing the need for a balanced development, and showed how the Transcendental Meditation programme satisfies this need. I have added these remarks as a postscript.

The theme of the last few conversations has been the autonomy of different states of consciousness. The present conversation and those that follow it examine the growth and character of higher states of consciousness in greater detail. More than once, as in the present conversation, Maharishi reminds us that every state of consciousness has a physiological basis, and that in the end everything comes back to 'this blesséd human nervous system'. If 'knowledge is structured in consciousness', consciousness is most surely structured in the nerve cells.

VK: ... you mean the gap.

JP: Hold on, this is something I want very much to know about.

VK: Maharishi is always talking about the gap.

Maharishi: This is our copyright. He [the commentator] got the glimpse of the gap. (Laughter)

VK: He doesn't mean by 'gap' what you mean.

Maharishi: But even a faint glimpse of it.

VK: I could see Maharishi starting up when the word 'gap' was mentioned, as if somebody had taken something from him. (Laughter)

Maharishi: (Speaking through his laughter) He found the gap.

VK: Tell us a little bit. You mention the gap so often. It's the gap between the relative and the Absolute, but explain a little more what you mean by this gap.

Maharishi: See, the gap means non-connectedness, un-connectedness — the Self, Absolute, unconnected with the relative. This is Cosmic Consciousness. All activity — the movement of the hands, and the activity of the mind and intellect and ego — and then the Self, Absolute, being a witness to the whole thing. So there is a gap; there is a nonconnection between this [activity] and this [Self], and that is the gap. Now in God Consciousness the gap is there, but it is so beautiful; it is celestial.

VK: That's what he said — the gap is filled by light.

Maharishi: That is what interested me. This gap is filled by light and then, further on, the light gains the state of pure awareness. So [in God Consciousness] there is the celestial and the Self — whatever the gap, that gap becomes celestial. And then eventually the celestial merges into pure awareness, pure consciousness, and then the Unity results.

VK: Ah, so the gap comes from Cosmic Consciousness. I thought you meant a gap in the sense of there being a gap between the relative and the Absolute.

Maharishi: Yes, same thing.

VK: But I meant there being a gap at the finest stage.

Maharishi: Yes, at the finest stage. In God Consciousness there is a gap.

VK: Because there is no connection between relative and Absolute really. Although one merges into the other in point of time, of realization, there is in fact no connection between them. So there is that gap; it continues.

Maharishi: No, no. It doesn't later on. What continues then

266

is the shadow of the gap, the remainder, 'leshāvidyā', the remains of it. And due to that remainder the waves of Unity in the form of activity and behaviour and experience are possible. But [to return to] the gap. The gap is there, but it is so very small in the sense of the difference in character between the Absolute and the celestial.

JP: That is, in God Consciousness.

Maharishi: In God Consciousness.

VK: Small in the relative sense of experience, but unbridgeable in principle.

Maharishi: Yes, unbridgeable in principle, but it then gets bridged. (Laughter)

JP: What, in Unity?

Maharishi: In Unity it gets bridged. But it's not the total thing, because [there is still] behaviour. That's why behaviour is not a murder to Brahman, activity is not a murder to Unity, just as the rising and falling of the waves are not a murder to the character of the ocean. So activity can be there, on that level of pure awareness, or Unity. Activity is no barrier. The state of Brahman is inclusive of both [the activity of the relative and the silence of the Absolute].[216]

---

216 Hertenstein, Switzerland, 8 January 1974. When I had read this part of the conversation to Maharishi, I said that it seemed to me that he had explained how it was possible to live life in Unity: first, because there was still a remaining particle of ignorance (leshāvidyā), and secondly, because the nature of Brahman was such as to be inclusive of the relative

JP: Maharishi, in that case, when you say that in Cosmic Consciousness Being is infused into the relative, that is not really an accurate statement because if there is a gap between the Self and one's activity, this is not infusion. This is two separate things being lived simultaneously but separately, so that this term that we have, infusion of Being, is not accurate.

Maharishi: No, it is accurate. Before Being gets infused, the mind is involved with activity; one doesn't know oneself as separate from activity and so the mind is completely involved. And as the infusion of Being grows into the nature of the mind, the mind finds itself to be non-changing more and more and more. And this finding by the mind of its own nature as non-changing means that one is starting to separate from the identification.

JP: So infusion comes at the beginning.

---

as well as the Absolute. How could these two explanations be reconciled? Maharishi, who had only the previous night come out of his seven days of silence, asked me to put the microphone of the tape-recorder very near him and softly spoke the following: 'What leshāvidyā does is to create a separation in the state of Unity, and it is this separation that is responsible for the emergence of Brahman — Brahman being the whole which is more than the collection of parts. So, unless Unity is in parts, that wholeness of Brahman will not be created. Therefore Brahman is born of leshāvidyā. It is cruel to say that Brahman is born of leshāvidyā, but in the analysis of the situation which actually gives rise to that situation in which Brahman can grow, [we have to admit that] this whole [that is, Brahman] will not *be* without the collecting together of the parts. So parts there must be and they must come together [if Brahman is to be born]. There must be unity *and* unity — the breaking up of unity is the only way to live Unity in life because life must be a kind of relative [existence]. Leshāvidyā does that, and therefore brāhmī-sthiti [the state of Brahman] is based on leshāvidyā. It's so beautiful.'

268

Maharishi: Right from the beginning it starts — one dive into the Transcendent.

JP: And then it becomes less and less infusion; it becomes more and more separation.

Maharishi: No. As the infusion grows, so the separation grows. Infusion brings the mind to its own nature, more and more and more and more. And then the nature of the mind is full awareness, and when it has become full awareness, the gap is maximum. Now when the process of evolution continues, nothing can happen to this infusion of Being because it is already full — Self [is established] — nothing more can happen to the Self.

VK: And this gap is also between the true nature of the mind and the functional nature of the mind — the gap between the mind as Being and the mind as it is functioning in perception.

Maharishi: Yes, yes. The mind gets divided. (Laughter)

VK: So Maharishi is teaching divided mind. (Laughter)

Maharishi: Finding the divided state of mind [in Cosmic Consciousness] is liberation.[217] And when [for someone who has attained Cosmic Consciousness] progress increases, evolution increases, then nothing can happen to the Absolute

---

217 This is itself a state of great fullness; see Introduction, section, 'Cosmic Consciousness'.

any more, nothing can happen to the Self [because it is full]. But the relative can still evolve further. The relative starts to be celestial, more and more celestial. And then the celestial is full and [at the same time] the Self is Absolute. And then the celestial continues to grow into the light, and then the celestial gains the state of infinity. It's so systematic. And all by virtue of the body — all by virtue of the body, that blesséd human nervous system. It all comes back to that.

JP: One realizes one is going to have to have a different nervous system to get to the end. One's present one is not good enough.

Maharishi: One's present one is good enough. It is this present goal which is going to shine through polishing. No other goal is going to come. Just the present — just through polishing, it will shine, that's all.

VK: It needs a very hard brush to polish it.

JP: I know it does.

Maharishi: No, even if one uses light brushes. But only the brushing should continue, continue, continue. That's it.

JP: Maharishi, maybe you wouldn't want to say anything about this just now, but one of the things I wanted to ask you for some time is about that feeling of dryness, a sort of hard, dry phase that one goes through, and I wondered if you could say a little about that?

Maharishi: See, as the separation grows …

JP: That's in connection with the separation?

Maharishi: In connection with the growth, the infusion of Being into the mind. As Being grows into the mind, the separation starts. Now, a time comes when the separation becomes more evident. Before that one was completely *with* what one experienced, completely one with experience, fully identified with it; and that means, fully localized within the boundaries of every experience. And now one is cut off. This loss of bondage …

JP: Of involvement.

Maharishi: Yes, loss of involvement.

VK: Without being completely established in the other yet.

Maharishi: When Being is infused to the extent of fifty per cent, sixty per cent — something like that — there is a sudden sort of awakening of Being, and because it is so fulfilling, it starts to occupy one's awareness more. This awakening, in one sense, is loss of involvement because now one's usual association with objects of perception naturally begins to create a kind of gulf, a kind of separation — a sort of unmindfulness, or gap. And then one may feel as if I have lost this and I have lost this, and what does this mean? So, at this time the teacher is needed to say, 'Go ahead, it's a good sign.'[218]

---

218 'In the ordinary case perception is in terms of involving the mind in it. So every perception so far was involving the mind. And now, when

JP: You may be feeling a loss of involvement outwardly, but you should be gaining inner bliss to a greater extent, and this should make you not feel any sense of loss.

Maharishi: But at that particular moment — complete involvement before and now loss of involvement. With time, as the infusion of Being grows in the nature of the mind, the mind becomes more contented, more contented. Contentment grows, but there is also that aspect of the loss of association. By nature it has been that throughout all these many years one was involved; so one is used to that condition of life, that particular condition of involvement. And now, when one sees oneself apart, one asks 'What is this?' But with the explanation being given, one knows that something good is happening. The hut is being dismantled and the palace is coming up.

VK: Once one knows what is happening ...

Maharishi: Yes. [Before, one asked oneself] 'I am shaking and what is happening?' See, you take off the anchor from the ship and the ship begins to do like that [sway] till the

---

the unboundedness is growing, the experiencer is becoming more stable in himself, so that involvement becomes less. And because so far the habit has been one of involvement and of enjoyment from involvement, when the involvement becomes less, the joy seems to become less. And owing to that, in the beginning days of this experience, one would feel a little dry. But as the self-sufficiency of unbounded awareness is more clearly comprehended, one begins to feel more self-sufficient; and then there is no more dryness.' Conversation, Courchevel, France, 18 August, 1975.

anchor is really put on the ground, put on the bottom, and then the ship will stay. It's just like that.

VK: But of course one must really be sure that this loss of involvement is due to growth of Being and not to something else. It might be due just to lack of ...

Maharishi: Some mineral or something, in the body.

MG: Even lack of responsibility — all sorts of things.

Maharishi: The context will show. [In the genuine case] life has been good up till now and suddenly it begins to rock. And this rocking — as if losing ground, or what — loss of interest ...

JP: Yes, but I still feel that one ought to have more feeling of something more precious growing in one, and if one had that feeling, it would more than compensate for the loss of a lower level.

Maharishi: It's going to, but on ...

JP: Then why is there this discrepancy?

Maharishi: There may be that period of discrepancy until the other grows more fully ...

VK: I can understand this. The other aspect, Being, has been growing and that has given some fulfilment. That has been the positive side; that has given some stability. And then comes the negative side of loss of involvement with the world, which also has to be experienced. And it may start to be experienced before Being is so strong that it can compensate for this. The hut has been dismantled before the palace has been completed.

Maharishi: The thing is that physiology is involved with every level of awareness, and it takes some time for the brain to adapt itself permanently [to the changing requirements]. It takes some time.

VK: But what do you ask someone who reports this feeling? Because you must ask about his meditation too.

Maharishi: You ask if there are some flashes of waking and sleeping [inner wakefulness while asleep] in the night — some flashes, something. It may not exactly be [that], but something [like that].

JP: And anything else? Can you give any other signposts of whether it is right or not?

VK: And during the day?

Maharishi: That [experience where one is] working and suddenly starting to feel that the work is being done automatically without any doing on my part. Maybe for a moment, but it's an experience which we can't miss.

VK: And then you give him that security. Once he knows, he feels secure.

Maharishi: Once one knows. It's a matter of knowing, but even more so it's a matter of *being*. A powerful arm will lift a weight easily; broadened awareness, Cosmic Consciousness, will naturally perform a task without such involvement. This is the secret of feeling uninvolved with activity as pure consciousness grows.

Postscript: Arosa, Switzerland, 1 June 1974

Maharishi: See, one was completely identified before. That identification was with the gross, concrete, and now there is more identification with the abstract. As identification with the abstract increases, identification with the concrete naturally begins to suffer. And up till now this identification with the things around has been a means of joy. It is through identification that one extends one's territory of influence. And this expansion of life is a joy. But now it is the association with unboundedness, which has a greater value, and that is why the seat of enjoyment is shifting.

VK: That's a beautiful explanation.

Maharishi: And when the seat of enjoyment is shifting — this seat being abstract, and the previous seat of enjoyment being concrete — one begins to feel as if dryness, compared to the seat of outside enjoyment. One asks 'What is this?' One begins to feel as if the greenness, the charm in the world, is drying out. This can happen, particularly when the pace of progress of the association with the abstract unbounded is fast. If the pace of progress is fast, then some

275

kind of contrast would be witnessed. If the pace is slow, one would naturally get used to it, and the contrast will not be there. So the experience of dryness along with the growth of inner satisfaction — experience of dryness in the outside association along with the growth of some kind of inner fulfilment — this will be noticed if the pace of progress is fast. It will not be noticed if the pace of progress is not fast.

See, the child takes all delight in his toys. Gradually, day after day, day after day, very slowly, he moves on to an interest in books. He doesn't feel the dryness in the toys; only, he is no longer interested in them. This is slow transition. But if a child whose awareness is in the toys is suddenly put in the library, he feels the loss of the toys. He feels the library is dry. Just that. Just that example. The library is not dry — it is a great inspiration, great interest, great charm, great enjoyment — if the transition from the toys to the library is gradual. But if it's sudden, if it's fast, then the library will seem to be a dry kind of thing. That loss of the charm will be noticed more vividly.

MG: Maharishi, when does the charm return again? You've reached the library and have this dryness. There is the growth of Being, and then this dryness. When does the charm return?

Maharishi: It may take a little while. And as the charm of knowledge grows — it is just a matter of a little bit more growth. Association with the abstract field of knowledge grows, and with that growth, this association with the concrete attachment to the toys falls off, it just slips off.

MG: It falls away.

Maharishi: It falls away. The example is: the snake develops a skin around it, and the time comes when the skin is dry and falls away, and the snake doesn't even notice it. He has grown out of it. The skin is gone. Like that. So, the experience of dryness depends on the fast pace of association with that unbounded, which is abstract, while all the charm so far has been in the concrete. Just the charm of the abstract knowledge and the charm in the concrete toys — just that example. It is very beautiful.

Now, talking in the same context, taking this thing to the range of physiology ... The concrete association with the toys has all to do with the sound of the toys, the vision of the toys, the touch of the toys; so, that part of the brain which is involved with these — eyes and ears and so on — that is very active. What is not active is that part of the brain which is concerned with abstract thinking. The part of the brain which is associated with concrete perceptions is active. The part of the brain which is associated with abstract thinking, logical thinking, intuition — that part of the brain is not so much involved in the play of the toys. Now, with the shift of interest, the other part of the brain begins to be lively. Now, if suddenly, or speedily, that part of the brain is put to function, then it will take some little time; it can't function very suddenly. And this inability of the brain tissue or the brain material to adapt itself so suddenly to such a great contrast in situation, creates a kind of rough awareness. This sudden shift of physiology would create not smooth awareness, but a kind of ruffled awareness — some roughness. And this rough awareness manifests as some dry experience in one's own consciousness.

VK: All transitions are like that.

Maharishi: They have to be like that, because they suddenly shift around. The very active part of the brain now has to learn how to stop, and those sleeping parts of the brain have to learn how to be active. And the feeling of roughness that one experiences belongs to the time when this part of the brain has to learn how to stop functioning and this part of the brain has to learn how to start functioning — till the time comes when this part of the brain is functioning at the same time as this part of the brain. And then that will be a very beautiful, harmonious feeling of fulfilment: all parts of the brain are functioning in a very smooth manner, each without challenging the validity of the other parts.

MG: Maharishi, which side is which? The abstract side — is it the left or the right hemisphere of the brain?

Maharishi: Both must have both values, but even so there will be some more in one and less in the other. See, even the part which is concerned with any one sense — the sense of sight, the sense of hearing — that part has the total value of perception: gross perception, subtle perception, subtlest perception, and transcendental perception. So, each part has a whole range of activity; it is structured in this way.

MG: But it's not active.

Maharishi: The inner is not active, the outer alone is active; and if, suddenly, we put someone to this abstract kind of awareness — unbounded awareness is so concrete, yet so abstract — some different part of the brain has to come into function. This explanation of the underlying physiology makes that experience of roughness, of dryness, so tangible.

VK: Is it because there should be this smooth transition that we are asked not to meditate too long at any one time, except on courses?

Maharishi: Fifteen to twenty minutes morning and evening,[219] and then forget about it during the day — this is the instruction. See, salt is very healthy for the body, sugar is very healthy for the body, but too much salt, too much sugar … It should be in proportion. If in twenty-four hours we give the brain this exercise of two periods of fifteen to twenty minutes, it's going to get enlivened; the full value of the brain will get enlivened. But if we put it to continuous, long-time

---

219 This was said before the Age of Enlightenment Courses. The advent of the Transcendental Meditation-Sidhi programme, which involves activating the silence gained through Transcendental Meditation, made it possible to do a longer but still carefully balanced programme even at home (see footnote 290 in the appendix).

[meditation], then the proportion will be lost. So, whereas Transcendental Meditation is the fastest way to get to the Transcendent, unbounded awareness, in order to *stabilize* that awareness there is a procedure: fifteen minutes, twenty minutes, and then work during the day.

VK: Alternation with activity.

Maharishi: Long period of activity — fifteen minutes meditation, twelve hours activity.

VK: So that Being gets absorbed.

Maharishi: Diluted. In this way it becomes sumptuous. Just as diluted salt makes the vegetable delicious, so diluted Being makes life delicious, charming. And if it's too much … The whole of it is absolutely charming, absolutely delicious, but it must come in a way so that one doesn't feel great contrasts. See, in the life of saints — those who led a life of long-time contemplation, meditation, they got these flashes of awakening, and they were so terrific as to put them out of consciousness.

VK: Following that they had their 'dark night of the soul'.

Maharishi: Immediately, suddenly [they had these experiences], just because the physiology was not trained in a systematic way, in a gradual way. So, Transcendental Meditation provides a gradual way, which is fast enough to be fast — gradual and fast, gradual and not slow. Because it is the physiology that is the basis of the level of consciousness, the physiology must be … To culture the blood and the flesh and the bone must take time.

VK: What about individuals who don't suffer from such fast progress, for whom fifteen or twenty minutes does not make much difference? It may give them some rest and relaxation, but owing to the stresses in their nervous system, there is very little, if any, actual infusion of Being in so short a time? You've told us what happens to people who make fast progress — they should alternate meditation with several hours of activity. Now, what about the people who make very slow progress? How can their rate of progress be increased so that there is any infusion of Being at all for activity to dilute?[220] (Laughter)

Maharishi: For them there is a provision in the teaching: these residence courses, weekend courses, seven-day courses — these are very useful for fostering growth. So the teaching has a procedure for them also. What the world needs is just for this World Plan[221] to be implemented in every part of the globe. The Teachers are there and they know everything. The Teachers know how to cultivate the nervous system.

---

220 *Editor's note:* As well as the courses mentioned in the response here, Maharishi also emphasized the importance of checking the correctness of practice with a Teacher of Transcendental Meditation, and clarifying experiences and understanding of the mechanics of the technique. For example, the infusion of Being is natural and gentle and may be noticed clearly only as some time passes.

221 Formulated by Maharishi in January 1972 'to solve the age-old problems of mankind in this generation'.

The World Becomes More Real
as Unity Is Gained

Here Maharishi illustrates an important consequence of the principle of the autonomy of different states of consciousness. Because in each state of consciousness our experience is different — we change the glasses through which we view the world — the teaching which provides the framework for understanding that experience must also be different. When a new state of consciousness is dawning, to hang on to the framework of the old state from which one is emerging can become a barrier to progress. The case in point is the sense — it is not so much a precise intellectual concept as an overall 'sense' — that the unchanging inner Self alone is real, whereas the ever-changing world of objects, which is separate from the Self, lacks reality. This sense, appropriate to Cosmic Consciousness, becomes an impediment as one is proceeding towards Unity.

My own failure to understand this principle was displayed when I read Maharishi the present conversation. I said it seemed to me that he was contradicting his statement in the postscript to the conversation on 'The Autonomy of Different States of Consciousness'. There he had said that seen from the point of view of Unity, 'the duality which was an experience in Cosmic Consciousness was just a mirage. The world was just a mirage.' Now he was saying that in Unity the world became more real. Maharishi replied: 'The world becomes more real as Unity dawns; it becomes as real as one's own Self. The world was a mirage only in so far as it was experienced as different from one's Self.'[222]

It is clear that the explanations and instructions which go with Unity Consciousness are quite different from, even opposite to, those needed for Cosmic Consciousness — which just goes to show that only a teacher who knows the whole, who is at home in all the different states of consciousness, can take one all the way. With Maharishi there to answer, I could allow myself the luxury of introducing a favourite verse from the Bhagavad-Gītā that seems to point very far along the road to perfection. Lord Kṛishṇa tells Arjuna: '. . . you will see all beings in your Self and also in Me.'[223] Maharishi, responding, gives some tantalizing glimpses of the play of the Absolute as exemplified by the life of Lord Kṛishṇa.

VK: Why does Vyāsa say, 'From casting off what has been heard for the sake of study'?[224]

Maharishi: Now, what has been heard for the sake of study is, 'brahma satyaṁ jagan mithyā'.[225] The mithyātva (unreality) of the jagat (world) and the nityatva (eternity), the reality, of Brahman — this has been heard. If a man remains established

---

222 See Introduction, p. 22 and p. 29.
223 4.35, see MBG, p. 305.
224 A reference to BS 1.3.38.
225 Maharishi is referring to a famous saying of Vedānta: 'brahma satyaṁ jagan mithyā jīvo brahmaiva nāparaḥ' — Brahman is real, the world is unreal; the individual soul is not different from Brahman.

in the sense of 'jagan mithyā' (the world is unreal), then he will never see the jagat in terms of himself, and will never get into Unity. And then again, he has to forget even the distinction between jagat and Brahman: that the two are different — that one is satya (real) and one is mithyā (unreal), and that I-am-this-satya and I-am-not-this-mithyā. If one has that division established in the mind, then this in itself will become a resistance to the dawn of Unity. And therefore, he must cast off what he has heard for the sake of study. It's beautiful.

VK: But that earlier teaching has been useful for the sake of study.

Maharishi: For the sake of study, because that study will give him an insight into his experience of separation in Cosmic Consciousness. When he experiences that separation, then that study is useful. But now he is too far ahead; he is getting into Unity. So, in this state all that study will be a barrier and a resistance to the dawn of Unity. In Cosmic Consciousness that study was necessary to understand what the separation was: that he was feeling active and non-active at the same time.

VK: But on the other hand, in Cosmic Consciousness as you define it, there is no idea of 'jagan mithyā'. There is the experience 'I am here and the world is there', but the world is not unreal; only, it is not me.

Maharishi: Yes, it's not me, and it is changing and has nothing to do with the non-changing, which I am. And that which is changing is just a mirage without a reality. It is changing from moment to moment. That means, it has no existence, and if it has no existence it is mithyā.[226]

VK: Some people do get that idea, yes.

Maharishi: Yes, mithyā, because that is the reality of the situation.

VK: Yes. It's so far away from one …

Maharishi: Yes, it's not part of oneself. That's why he must cast off [what he has learnt about the unreality of the world]. See, these are the two beautiful steps of evolution: one, where the world is completely separate, and the other, where that thing [the unreality of the world] has to be forsaken, has to be abandoned, has to be cast off, in order to come out of this …

VK: The idea that the world is not there?

Maharishi: That it's not there. The 'mithyātva' has to be cast off, otherwise that will become [an obstacle to progress].

VK: And you only cast it off by getting yourself absorbed in the celestial — through the attraction of the celestial?

---

226 The world has no existence because it is experienced as different from the unchanging Self, not because it is not there at all. When one sees a mirage one is seeing something, but seeing it improperly. It is in this sense that the word 'mithyā' has to be understood.

Maharishi: It gets cast off by itself, if only we don't continue on it when it is slipping off. We don't grab it when it is passing away.

VK: How do you mean?

Maharishi: Up till now, say, for so many years, I was established in 'This world is not part of me; I am this [Self].' And now this difference between the two, this gulf, is becoming less and less. So we don't have to feel perturbed; we welcome it, because we know that that gulf was a thing of the past level — the past state.

VK: So that means, in some way, that the relative is becoming more real.

Maharishi: The relative is becoming as real as myself, and that is the criterion of the coming together, of the Unity.

VK: It's very beautiful.

Maharishi: It's very beautiful. And this is the contrast which distinguishes two teachings as completely separate — teaching of Cosmic Consciousness and teaching of Unity.

VK: In fact, the Vedānta has always had this kind of Sāṁkhya overtone of separation, and the way you teach it, it doesn't have these overtones.

Maharishi: No, it's real Vedānta.

VK: The way Vedānta is taught, it always has …

Maharishi: Yes, Sāṁkhya overtones — separateness, negation, but this negation is of that thing …

VK: It's negation of negation.

Maharishi: Negation of negation. (Laughter) Pratishedha (casting off) is negation of that negation which, in the early stage of Cosmic Consciousness — now Cosmic Consciousness becomes an early stage — was necessary and had to be held on to. (Laughter)

VK: It's beautiful. I don't know the first thing about it in reality, but the scheme is very nice.

Maharishi: But now, one thing — there was nishedha (negation) in Cosmic Consciousness and there is nishedha in Vedānta.[227] Both are nishedha, but they are nishedha of two different things. But the word is common.

VK: Yes. What is the nishedha of Vedānta, then?

Maharishi: Nishedha of the separation. (Laughter)

VK: Of the separation, yes.

Maharishi: Because the word is common, people think 'nishedha, nishedha'. But this is nishedha of one thing here and nishedha of something else there.

VK: It is the seeing of all things in the Self and then in Me, isn't it?

---

227 Vedānta is the teaching of Unity.

Maharishi: Yes.

VK: 'In Me' would be even beyond seeing all things in the Self.

Maharishi: It'll depend on what we mean by 'Me'. If it's the Absolute, then the sequence is right. Otherwise, if it's God, then 'Me' would have to come first [because God Consciousness comes before Unity].

VK: What is the difference between seeing all things in the Self and seeing them 'in Me'? If 'Me' is the Absolute, what is the difference? There are two stages. Seeing all things in the Self means a coming closer together — as you said just now — of things coming into the Self. Instead of being separated from the Self, they come into the Self. That already is Unity, isn't it?

Maharishi: Yes.

VK: And so then 'in Me' must be some stage yet further.

Maharishi: Yes, must be. Because that [seeing all things in the Self] will be man's consciousness in Unity. That Unity is an ocean of the Absolute, ocean of life. And then, the play of the Absolute — the ocean and the play of that ocean. It [the play] is a higher reality than my-own-reality-and-the-world-in-terms-of-me.

VK: You mean the Absolute playing with itself?

Maharishi: Yes, the Absolute playing with itself.

VK: Incredible. It's like what you said about that sūtra, 'On account of abiding and devouring',[228] when the Absolute starts to be active, when it starts to be lived. You didn't interpret the Gītā in this way, but I think this is a better way.

Maharishi: We'll have to interpret Bhāgavatam[229] for that — Krishna's life — life of that which attracts everything to itself — life of the Absolute, which is the source and goal of the whole creation, the be-all and end-all of existence.

VK: Fantastic.

Maharishi: It's overwhelming. It's real.

VK: What it all means to somebody who has never even tasted Transcendental Consciousness (laughter) — it's so fantastic.

Maharishi: But it's so beautiful.

VK: It's a beautiful scheme, even to be appreciated only on an intellectual level.

Maharishi: Yes, even on intellectual level it is beautiful.

VK: How much more beautiful it must be if it is lived.

Maharishi: (Laughter) If one lives, starts to live ... I think once we have a few more years to eliminate the stress and strain in the atmosphere — the basic thing is that, the basic thing is that. Then man's life will be happy on earth.

---

228 BS 1.3.7.
229 The Bhāgavata Purāṇa.

On the Distinction Between Cosmic Consciousness and God Consciousness

The number seven occurs in one of the sūtras being translated. Other interpreters refer it to the seven breaths, Maharishi to the seven states of consciousness. I question whether there are really seven states of consciousness because one could classify Cosmic Consciousness and God Consciousness as a single state. Maharishi puts the case for God Consciousness as a separate state with its own distinct 'glasses' — golden ones.

Maharishi: This is the difference: they [other interpreters] think there are seven senses and seven prāṇas (breaths) — that this is what the sūtra[230] means — and we say there are seven states of consciousness and from the seventh is Brahman. Now you see the difference in the level of thinking?

VK: Yes, but …

Maharishi: They are held up in the field of senses (laughter) and we are in pure awareness.

VK: But Maharishi, your classification of seven states of consciousness is a little arbitrary.

Maharishi: No, that is the level of thinking.

VK: But Cosmic Consciousness and God Consciousness could be one state. So it's a little arbitrary, that classification.

---

230 BS 2.4.5.

Maharishi: No, no, no.

VK: Yes, because there is no definite division between Cosmic Consciousness and God Consciousness.

Maharishi: Oh, there is. Oh, it's very great.

VK: Yes, but gradually one shades into the other, doesn't it?

Maharishi: Ah, then, (laughter) just that is the difference — that shading. Because the vision ... such a change in the vision, and that is what makes a different level of awareness. Celestial perception [of the finest aspects of the object, on the one hand] and perception separate from oneself, yet of the ordinary, gross [aspects of the object, on the other hand]. It's like looking through green glasses and through golden glasses. It's a big difference and it's good to classify as separate — a very big difference.

VK: But it's possible to have glimpses of this state of God Consciousness even when one has just started practising Transcendental Meditation.[231]

Maharishi: Yes, yes.

VK: The subtler is infused into the mind in the same way as the Transcendent. You stay down there, in the subtle field of perception, for some time, and then begin to see through those glasses.

---

231 See Introduction, pp. 30-1.

Maharishi: Yes, stay down there some time and then start to have that — that level of awareness, of vision.

The Role of Devotion in the Transition from God Consciousness to Unity

Here Maharishi makes a rather similar point to that which he made in the last conversation but one, where clinging to the sense that the world is unreal was presented as an obstacle to the dawning of Unity. Now Maharishi says that only through more intense devotion will the climax of God Consciousness, where the difference between celestial and Self falls away, be attained. Therefore 'any sense of [the desirability of] abstaining from devotion to God will prevent a man from reaching to the highest limits in God Consciousness'. The word 'sense' is again used to represent an inappropriate or outdated frame of reference that may delay one's progress to a new state of consciousness. However, when this conversation was read to him, Maharishi, perhaps feeling that the words 'will prevent a man' were too strong, made rather light of the delaying power of an inappropriate way of thinking. He chose instead to emphasize the irresistible forward momentum of the force of evolution, which would automatically change one's attitudes. (I have added these remarks as a postscript.)

But to say that they represent a comparatively weak factor does not mean that wrong attitudes cannot delay progress. It is a question of emphasis.

At the end of the short original discussion, I point out that Maharishi's great contribution is to place each stage of development in its proper context — the 'systematic procedure', as he calls it. Thus devotion is firmly based on knowledge of one's own Self, or Being — God Consciousness is built on the foundation of Cosmic Consciousness.

Maharishi: [It is not possible for one] to go out of the realm of the celestial and reach Unity by [mere] thinking, because so long as the natural state of Unity has not arisen, so long the fascination of the celestial is spontaneously gripping him to the fullest extent. And the more he gets gripped by the glory of the celestial, the greater his chance of slipping out of it and getting to Unity. So any sense of [the desirability of] abstaining from devotion to God will prevent a man from reaching to the highest limits in God Consciousness.[232]

VK: This is your interpretation, but a lot of other interpreters say that one has to rise above devotion to God, for that is merely a preparation. In fact, they say it's bondage.

Maharishi: Only in comparison to Unity. But the technique of coming out of that bondage is ...[233]

---

232 See postscript to this conversation.

233 When this was read to him, Maharishi completed the sentence and then added something further: 'The technique of coming out of that bondage is to get properly bound, and so intimately identified with it that you just don't feel it's a bondage. The two become one. It's the glorification of the boundaries, the glorification of the means of bondage.

VK: Through that devotion.

Maharishi: Yes.

VK: But this they don't say. They regard devotion to God as another path, suitable for those who cannot attain to Vedānta.

Maharishi: Vedānta cannot come unless the climax of Pūrva Mīmāṁsā[234] has been reached. Slipping into Vedānta [that is, into Unity] is an automatic thing when one has reached the climax, the top level, of Pūrva Mīmāṁsā [that is, God Consciousness]. That means, having enjoyed celestial awareness in God Consciousness to the extent of actually being it ...

VK: This is your great contribution.

Maharishi: Systematic procedure.

VK: Yes. You base devotion on steadiness in Being. If devotion were not based on Being, then perhaps it [devotion] would not be the right path. In your scheme it is. It's very logical and very beautiful.

Maharishi: It's so systematic. It has given the whole meta-

That is the gift of God Consciousness: it glorifies and raises it [bondage] to infinite freedom, because if one wants to be eternally free one has to bind himself to freedom. So it's through bondage that the path to freedom grows.'

234 Pūrva Mīmāṁsā is the fifth of the six classical systems of Indian philosophy, which deals with action from its grossest to its subtlest levels.

physical field a systematic character. It's so profound and perfect, and this is beautiful.

Postscript: Vitznau, Switzerland, 25 February 1975

Maharishi: It [growth towards Unity] is inevitable once Cosmic Consciousness is reached. It's not a matter of choice. It just flows into that growth naturally because, more than ever before, the natural evolution is fastest from the level of Cosmic Consciousness — because there are no obstacles, no stresses. A man may think anything, but his thinking will not have any bearing. In the path of evolution these attitudes will change. It just doesn't matter what a man thinks. (Laughter) This is the Age of Enlightenment. Everyone will be inevitably drawn to enlightenment — it doesn't matter what he thinks.

VK: Thought is on such a superficial level.

Maharishi: It changes from time to time.

VK: From moment to moment.

Maharishi: So on *that* the passage of evolution can't be based. This is the reality of the Age of Enlightenment; no matter what you think, you are on that [path of evolution]. That's why it has a name, 'age' — it's the time, the character of the time.

The Transition from God Consciousness to Unity

The present discussion, which dates from near the end of my stay in Kashmir, arises from Maharishi's interpretation of three consecutive sūtras in the third chapter. These enable him to explain in some detail the stage where God Consciousness gives way to Unity and, in the process, to elucidate the most famous of the Mahāvākyas (great sayings)[235] of the Upanishads — 'That thou art.' The first sūtra declares that as the 'thou' — that is, the Self — diminishes, the teacher says something more. What he says is related by the second sūtra, which declares 'That' to be unmanifest, while the third adds that this is known to be so in the fulfilment of devotion. The climax of devotion, as Maharishi makes clear in this conversation, is Unity Consciousness; the knowledge of Brahman, as he was to make clear in later years, is the climax of Unity Consciousness.

While excluding all the detailed discussion about grammar and word meanings, I have left in, for light relief, the banter that so often accompanied the translation. It shows the total absence of solemnity and pomposity that made it such a joy to work with Maharishi.

Maharishi: When the 'thou' is being diminished, the teacher says something more. He says 'That' — 'That thou art.'

---

235 See Introduction, p. 54; also the conversation 'The Mahāvākyas'.

JP: What do you mean by being diminished?

Maharishi: In God Consciousness there is Self and non-Self. Now when the Self [the 'thou'] starts to diminish, then the teacher says: 'Oh, you are losing your identity, but you are That.' The teacher says something more than the Self. He tells him: 'You are That Unbounded.' He [the aspirant] experiences the dissolution of the Self, of Self-awareness, which was the most dominating factor so far [that is, from Cosmic Consciousness onwards] and on the basis of which he was experiencing God Consciousness. This awareness starts to dissolve. 'So long as the "thou" is manifest in your awareness, so long as you are aware of your Self and of the celestial world as different from you, so long you are not That because That is avyakta (unmanifest). So when you get to the state of losing the awareness of the Self you will know that That is Brahman and that [Brahman] is unmanifest.' Now we should adjust the grammar of this beautiful sūtra. (Laughter)

VK: Do a little manipulation.

Maharishi: It won't be difficult.

VK: It is easier to manipulate in the realm of the subtle than in the gross written language. That is the trouble.

JP: There is no doubt about that.

Maharishi: It will come round. (Continued laughter) But what a beautiful thing comes out of this translation. This sūtra tells of the particular experience when the awareness of the Self begins to dissolve. The teacher tells him that it dissolves into That Unmanifest. (There follows a discussion about the meaning of a particular word.)

VK: Maharishi has got his meaning [confirmed by the dictionary].

JP: Foiled again, Vernon.

VK: Yes [Maharishi got his meaning], despite obstructions.

Maharishi: The sūtra says, 'In the fulfilment of devotion', because that Unity dawns as the fulfilment of devotion. This gives the essence of the sense, not the exact …

JP: It's a very novel interpretation of a dictionary, Maharishi.

VK: A dictionary is supposed to have precision, Maharishi. That's the whole point of it.

Maharishi: But in such cases, when the whole thing is so far removed from the intellect of all [those whose] mottos [govern the] manufacturing [of] dictionaries! This word refers to a particular state. It is not the delightful state of devotion, because the delightful state of devotion will be when one feels the breath of the Lord everywhere and hears his whisper in everything, from everything. Rather, it is the fulfilment of devotion, when devotion is coming to its state of fulfilment — a state when devotion has ceased to be.

VK: So it's beyond meditation, Maharishi.

Maharishi: Oh, far beyond anything. It is the fulfilment of devotion. The home is always beyond the path, at the end of the path.

VK: But doesn't Unity come through transcending, whereas in devotion …

Maharishi: Unity comes through transcending the separateness of the Self and the celestial.

VK: And this is done only through devotion?

Maharishi: It's the *climax* of devotion. Because in that state [before Unity has dawned], when the Lord is there and the celestial field is there — even with closed eyes it [the celestial] is there, even with open eyes it's there — one is completely absorbed in the richness of the vision and the celestial behaviour and all that.

VK: So one becomes that [celestial].

Maharishi: One becomes That [Brahman]. In the oneness of devotion is Unity.

VK: One becomes That, but then what happens? You become that divine celestial, and then the divine has to become Brahman?

Maharishi: The waves of the divine [are experienced] in the whole field of perception and action.

VK: But that is only the stage where you become the divine. It's not yet that stage where the divine becomes Brahman.

Maharishi: No, the divine is Brahman. Once the 'thou' is gone, 'That' alone remains. That thou art.

VK: But couldn't it be just absorption in the personal [as a preliminary stage]. 'He and his God are one', you said once.

Maharishi: He and his God — that kind of absorption will be on the level of appreciation, but this will not eliminate the gap [between celestial and Self]. The absorption in the glamour of the celestial vision is another kind of absorption, but [it is different from] this expansion, this becoming more and more and more and more [as one passes to Unity].

VK: But the absorption in the celestial must come through devotion, while this fact of becoming Brahman must come through knowledge. Through devotion you get more absorbed in the celestial, but then the point comes where you realize that the celestial is nothing but Brahman.

Maharishi: Now that is why the teacher says, 'That is unmanifest.' When he [the aspirant] starts to lose his identity of the Self as separate from this celestial, then [is given] the instruction, then [is given] the Mahāvākya, 'That thou art.' And That is unmanifest.

VK: But how does devotion come in? Devotion can only bring you to the highest celestial. Ah, it's not devotion — it's the *fulfilment* of devotion.

Maharishi: It's the fulfilment of devotion, it's the climax of devotion. Devotion is the result of the cognition of God; you get attached to him, devoted to him. But when that state is fulfilled, then the Self starts to go, 'thou' starts to go, and only 'That' remains — 'That thou art.' And Vyāsa is so beautiful. He says, 'Listen, just this expression, "That is unmanifest." ' When he [the teacher] sees that the Self is dissolving, then it is time to say, 'Yes, it is dissolving, but it's all right, because only after the dissolution of "thou" will dawn this Brahman, because That [Brahman] is unmanifest.'

This word 'unmanifest' is so beautiful. It's much more beautiful than the shruti [Upanishad], which says, 'That thou art.' Here Vyāsa says, 'That is unmanifest'; shruti only says, 'That thou art.' But it is necessary to save the aspirant from drowning into nothingness, [and this needs] just the wisdom to come and say, 'Oh, That is unmanifest.'

VK: One has to be a little more explicit about the 'That', you mean.

Maharishi: More explicit. And when he [the aspirant] has found the 'thou' dissolving and coming to 'That', then comes the significance of the shruti, 'That thou art.' When the 'thou' has dissolved, and 'That' alone remains, then the shruti comes to say, 'That thou art' — not when the awareness of 'thou' remains, awareness of the Self remains; it's meaningless then. But become 'That' and then he [the teacher] comes to say, 'That thou art.' It's so beautiful.

VK: When Maharishi's attention is on it, then we do all right [with the translation].

301

Maharishi: No, when the sūtra comes which has been wrongly interpreted so far.

VK: When the sūtra comes which suits …

Maharishi: Which suits, yes. (Laughter)

VK: (Speaking to the others present) It's funny. One feels tired like anything and then Maharishi pulls one up. Now I don't feel at all tired. It's so strange.

Maharishi: (Laughs) No, it's the sūtra — the junction of the grammar and the meaning.

Postscript: Vitznau, Switzerland, 25 February 1975

VK: Maharishi, you talk about the cognition of God, but the experiences that people report are experiences of light, and so on. When people report their experiences on courses they speak of light, so it doesn't seem correct to call this God Consciousness.

Maharishi: Just flashes, here and there.

VK: Just because they are flashes, they are not complete? Later, the whole nature of God manifests itself, and not just his light? They say 'God is light', but you can't be devoted just to light.

Maharishi: You can be devoted to the thrills of emotions that get generated in the finer levels of perception. God

Consciousness is enjoyed in the ability to overflow in love for the supreme relative reality of everything. So it's one's own — just as Unity is one's own status, so God Consciousness is one's own status, to be comprehended and enjoyed in oneself — supreme relative [status].

VK: In some ways Unity is more oneself than the supreme relative, which is the level of the Creator.

Maharishi: It's the appreciation of the finest creation, that from where creation began, and that attunement is on the level of one's own Self. And that is why God Consciousness is one's own, it is on the level of one's own existence. The one who is in God Consciousness — he is like that, not because of the status of God or creation, but because of his own status. He just overflows. That is his life.

VK: Why does one call it God Consciousness if it is one's own status?

Maharishi: Because it is the appreciation of that value of creation from where creation begins — the source of relative creation. That is why it gets a name: God Consciousness. Otherwise, it is his own consciousness. In this we distinguish between man's consciousness and God's consciousness. So man's consciousness is his own, only it gets a name due to that character of being associated with that level of creation which is the source of creation.

VK: It is difficult to explain this concept of a source of creation. We can say it's the source of thought, in the sense that when you come out from the Transcendent you come out on the finest thought. That is a matter of experience.

Maharishi: Source of creation means finest relative creation.

VK: Yes, but it's difficult to explain how that evolves into the gross creation. We can say that finest relative creation would be on the finest level of thinking.

Maharishi: Right.

VK: We can explain it in our own terminology, but it's a very difficult thing to put over in a scientific way.

Maharishi: State of least excitation, the level of all possibilities and the level of perfect order.

VK: But to make that transition from thought to physics.

Maharishi: Yes, that is that state of least excitation of consciousness. Consciousness — waking, dreaming, sleeping — gross levels of consciousness, and then consciousness settles down and reaches a level of least excitation — no movement.

VK: And we posit that this is the same as the least excited state of physics.

Maharishi: Yes, as known to physics, as known to modern quantum physics. The state of least excitation, the vacuum state.

VK: Yes, we posit that the scale known to physics is the same as the state of least excitation on the level of consciousness.

Maharishi: Least excitation is one characteristic. It is a characteristic of the field level of existence — physical existence. But that state of least excitation which is the state of least activity, that has the same characteristic on the level of consciousness. When consciousness settles down and has no reference point, it is on its own. Consciousness is then in the state of least excitation. Now, physics doesn't talk of consciousness — it talks of particles or waves, of the ground state or vacuum state where existence becomes unmanifest. Here we talk of consciousness. Now, for consciousness to experience itself, there has to be a nervous system. In the case of physics, that vacuum state *is* the ultimate of everything that is there. Whether someone experiences it or does not experience it, it is the basis of all creation. But when the activity of consciousness — mind, thinking — when that settles down and gains the character of least excitation, then this level is lively as opposed to the dead level of the vacuum state which is permeating everything. When consciousness settles down to that level of least excitation, then it's lively. So, the vacuum state of physics is dead, and the state of the least excitation of consciousness of the Science of Creative Intelligence is lively. They have one characteristic which is similar — both of them are not active.

VK: But you can't go beyond that similarity, really.

Maharishi: It's the same word. That is why we use the same word — state of least excitation. It makes it easier to comprehend. Just like 'Absolute' and 'Unity Consciousness'. The Absolute is omnipresent; it's the basis of everything. But it's dead. But Unity Consciousness is the consciousness on the same dead level, but because it's consciousness, it's lively.

VK: But the conclusion to draw from that is that it's consciousness which enlivens the vacuum state, which makes the vacuum state lively so that particles appear on the physical level. It would mean that owing to consciousness it starts to …

Maharishi: It starts to get to higher levels of excitation.

VK: To vibrate and produce the physical world. That's the conclusion you would draw from that kind of argument.

Maharishi: That kind of parallelism.

VK: Yes. But in physics it's not consciousness which actually makes it vibrant, is it?

Maharishi: All possibilities exist there.

VK: The state somehow gets excited. I don't know how, but it gets excited. You called it a dead state, so perhaps it's only through consciousness that it gets excited. In physics there must in some way be a parallel to consciousness which makes that dead state of physics excited. Maybe that is the far-out universe of which they speak.

Maharishi: That's what we'll come out with in these two parallels.

VK: You can never really go beyond the analogy, but still, it's good to make it.

Maharishi: Because then it makes at least one point of steadiness of the mind. Because there physics ends.

VK: Physics would end where?

Maharishi: In the vacuum state. But it's marvellous for physics to have located it, calculated it, found that all possibilities are there, that everything arises from there, and given equations for that — tremendous credit.

VK: The abstraction which has taken place in physics, from atoms as little balls to its present completely abstract character.

Maharishi: It's highly creditable.

VK: But I'm sure it can't really go to the level of consciousness ... If it's physics, it must be on the level of Prakṛiti (nature), not Purusha (pure consciousness).

Maharishi: Prakṛiti — settled state of Prakṛiti.

VK: Settled state, yes. And that needs the light of Purusha to activate it. May be that far-out factor will turn out to be consciousness.

Maharishi: Yes, I think we are all right.

VK: If you say so.

A Criterion of the State of Brahman: How the World Is Cognized

The sūtra discussed here echoes the famous saying of the Ṛig Veda: 'All beings are one-fourth of him; three-fourths immortal in the sky.'[236] Maharishi gives a unique and beautiful interpretation. He says that the criterion of the established state of Brahman — here identified with Unity Consciousness — is that only one-fourth of one's awareness engages in multiplicity. This fourth can perhaps be identified with 'leshāvidyā', the remains of ignorance, mentioned in the conversation on 'The Gap'. The other three-fourths of awareness are held in Unity.

Maharishi: What does it say?

VK: 'And because That rises up in this way, there is the statement that beings and the rest form one-quarter of It.'[237]

Maharishi: This sūtra qualifies the darshana (cognition) mentioned in the previous sūtra. What kind of darshana? That kind of darshana which leaves 'beings and the rest' to be dealt with by one-fourth of awareness. And by virtue of the fact that beings and the rest are cognized, by virtue of only one-fourth of awareness, the state of Brahman is established. The previous sūtra said, 'In that way, indeed, lies

---

236 Ṛig Veda 10.90.3. Compare CU 3.12.6.
237 BS 1.1.26, as translated at that time.

cognition.'[238] Now what is the criterion of cognition? The criterion of cognition does not lie in cognizing Brahman, but in cognizing the manifest creation with one-fourth of awareness. So, it's just the other way round. Vyāsa establishes the criterion of the cognition of Brahman from the cognition of the world. When the world is cognized, engaging only one-fourth of one's awareness, then is the state of Brahman realized. He lays out a standard of cognition. Brahman as such is not to be cognized [as an object]; it is just lived because it is in terms of oneself. Then what else is the criterion of cognition? That which has been absorbing fullness of awareness now absorbs only one-quarter of awareness — that is the criterion. It's beautiful, very beautiful.

VK: And this refers to the realized man? It's not something said about Brahman, as when the Ṛig Veda says that all beings form one pāda (quarter) of it?

Maharishi: That is the state of Brahman in which the cognition is that the world is just one-quarter, the universe is just a quarter of it. 'Quarter of it' means, three-fourths of awareness are held in that Unity; one-quarter engages in multiplicity. This is the standard criterion of cognition. In the previous sūtra Vyāsa established how the cognition comes: it comes by mind getting absorbed in it [Unity]. Now the question is, how much could the mind be absorbed? It is absorbed to the extent

---

238 See conversation, 'Ways of Transcending in Indian Thought'.

that only one quarter of awareness is enough to handle the situation of life. That is the state of Brahman. This sūtra sets such a beautiful, absolute criterion for all time.

VK: Yes, but how do you reconcile that with 'sākshī' consciousness, witness consciousness, which means that there is no involvement, no absorption whatsoever. The awareness is there and the world is separate from it.

Maharishi: Right. It's beautiful. See, this full sākshītva (state of being a witness) has already been lived by him from the time he has gained Cosmic Consciousness and God Consciousness. What speciality takes place now when Unity gets established? The sākshītva was full; the Self-awareness was one hundred per cent. But one hundred per cent also was the awareness of the multiple creation; the non-Self was one hundred per cent. Now he says the non-Self should get reduced to one quarter of its value, of its intensity.

JP: It goes to twenty-five per cent from one hundred per cent.

Maharishi: One hundred per cent Self and one hundred per cent non-Self in Cosmic Consciousness. Now, in this state [Unity], one hundred per cent Self is there, but the non-Self is reduced down to twenty-five per cent only. Seventy-five per cent has been dropped.

VK: But you said before that the non-Self becomes more glorious and more glorious through God Consciousness.

Maharishi: Right. More glorious.

VK: It becomes more glorious, so in that sense it can't become less. It would become more fascinating in God Consciousness.

Maharishi: In God Consciousness this [Self] is full. But the ordinary worldly, I mean earthly [world of objects], becomes celestial. So the celestial also is non-Self.

VK: One hundred per cent.

Maharishi: One hundred per cent non-Self. Now, this one hundred per cent non-Self is dissolving. [On the level of the Self] there can't be anything more than the one hundred per cent Self which has already been established. So the only criterion [of evolution] which has to be established is on the level of the non-Self. What happens here? He says that only one-fourth remains.

VK: Just the minimum for a man to be able to engage in activity.

Maharishi: To be able to engage in activity. That means, now any cognition which needed ... Even for sākshītva something is needed.

VK: If there's nothing to witness, there's no need for witnessing.

Maharishi: Now, that sākshītva establishes only duality. So now duality drops off seventy-five per cent and that is called Unity, that is called Unity.

311

VK: But this idea that beings only form one-quarter of it is usually interpreted to mean that Brahman is Brahman independently of what happens to the world. It is transcendent, in that sense in which you say that although water changes into ice and so on, this does not affect the real nature of H_2O. That is the idea.

Maharishi: Right.

VK: They interpret it more from this ontological point of view — the being of Brahman — rather than from the point of view of experience. But I suppose these two points of view could be combined.

Maharishi: Could be combined, yes. One quarter of That is this.

VK: What you say in the *Science of Being*[239] about the integrity of Being — that whatever happens, whatever changes occur, Being is not affected.

Maharishi: It is not affected. Unity is established. It's a very beautiful criterion. He establishes the criterion on the level of cognition.

VK: It's a marvellous interpretation. Nobody has ever interpreted it like this. It's a famous saying, this, that three-quarters of That are in the sky and one-quarter down here. It's a theme that runs right through the Vedas and the Upa-

---

239 *Science of Being*, pp. 38–9.

nishads, but no one has ever interpreted it in this way.

Maharishi: Because that is the state of Brahman. It's the teaching of Unity from the angle of the cognition of the world.

A Criterion of the State of Brahman: How One Behaves in the World

In the previous conversation, cognition of the world provided a criterion of the established state of Brahman. Here the criterion is found in the field of behaviour.

Maharishi: If life is in accordance with the smṛitis (codes of conduct)[240] in the most spontaneous manner, then that will be the criterion that Brahman has been established. In the most natural way, without any effort towards that, life has to be established in accordance with dharma,[241] and then only is Brahman established. Life in the state of Brahman is naturally in accordance with the smṛitis. So a life lived according to the smṛitis is a criterion of the establishment of full Brahman.

Now, the thing is that the injunctions of the smṛitis are

---

240 See conversation, 'Shruti and Smṛiti'. Smṛiti also has the meaning of memory (footnote 181).

241 Dharma 'is that invincible power of nature which upholds existence … It supports all that is helpful for evolution and discourages all that is opposed to it.' MBG 1.1, p. 26; compare 4.7, pp. 262-3. The smṛitis lay down the rules by which dharma is maintained. There are some general rules which apply to everyone, but individuals also have their own dharma (svadharma).

for the unrealized. 'Do this, and don't do this' — all the pro-
hibitions and injunctions are there to give a standard of good
life for a rapid pace of evolution. But here [in the sūtra under consideration] the smṛitis are brought onto the level of
enlightenment. It is the life in accordance with the smṛitis
in a natural way that is set as a criterion for measuring the
state of Brahman. This means that while the teaching of the
smṛitis is a lighthouse for the unrealized, it is also a gauge to
measure the strength of realization of Brahman.

VK: But a lot of people behave in accordance with the smṛitis
in an external way, and they've got no realization whatsoever.
Some religious people are like that.

Maharishi: No, no, no. The behaviour will not be absolutely
in accordance with dharma unless the level of consciousness
is established in Unity.

VK: But really you find that much behaviour is strictly in accord
with the injunctions of the smṛitis, but in a purely external way.

Maharishi: No. A man fearing to do wrong cannot possibly
do right spontaneously. His spontaneous action will not be
right, because he who fears to do wrong won't spontaneously
be right.

VK: But he will see what smṛiti says and his actions may be
much nearer to it, in some way, than those of somebody who
is on the path to realization.

Maharishi: Say that fifty per cent of smṛiti is lived in life:

according to his level of consciousness, a man will think, 'Oh, this injunction means this', and he will go that way. But it may not mean the same to him when he is in the state of enlightenment. Whichever way he walks in the state of enlightenment, that is the way of smṛiti. So whereas smṛiti guides the action of an unrealized man, smṛiti is lived spontaneously by the realized.

VK: Oh, you mean the realized man makes his own smṛiti.

Maharishi: He just lives spontaneously and that corresponds with smṛiti. In the other case he has to *try* and in trying he will always miss some valuable aspects. The perfect smarta life [life in accordance with the smṛitis] is that of an enlightened man, a fulfilled man, one who lives Brahman.

The Mahāvākyas

The term 'Mahāvākya' (great saying) is usually bestowed on four well-known sayings of the Upanishads. In the two conversations that are included under this heading — the first of them very short — Maharishi explains the role of the Mahāvākyas in setting the seal on a particular state of consciousness. At the start of the second conversation he quotes all four Mahāvākyas and later uses the most famous, 'tat tvam asi' (That thou art), as an example. It was thought at the time of this conversation that the Mahāvākyas might help to explain the theme of each of the Brahma Sūtra's four chapters.

At the end of the conversation I ask Maharishi a question about the source of his inspiration. But Maharishi never dwells long on anything that concerns his own person, and although he answers very sweetly and simply, he takes an early opportunity to change the subject.

There is also a postscript in which Maharishi develops two themes. The first is that each Mahāvākya goes with one particular state of consciousness — Transcendental, Cosmic, Unity, and Brahman Consciousness. The second theme is that all four Mahāvākyas can be applied to each of these states of consciousness. Maharishi develops these themes with great brilliance.

Maharishi: Brahman becomes an all-time reality through the Mahāvākyas. See, through experience everything is recognized in terms of the Self, but that experience of everything in terms of the Self becomes significant through the teaching, because through the teaching it comes onto the level of understanding. Experience is one thing, understanding another, and only when it [the experience of everything in terms of the Self] comes onto the level of understanding does it become established everywhere. Then its all-pervadingness becomes a living reality. [Otherwise Unity is dependent on, and limited to, particular experiences.][242]

---

242 See conversation, 'The Aggregate'.

VK: It becomes established in the buddhi (intellect) when it is understood, but even before that you already live it everywhere.

Maharishi: One lives it, but in order to fully appreciate it one has to know intellectually. You see, it's like a diamond — wearing it is fine, beautiful, but the full joy of it comes when ...

VK: When you know its value.

Maharishi: This is the significance of gyāna, of knowledge — the joy is multiplied.

* * *

Maharishi: Brāhmī-sthiti (the state of Brahman) comes from the Mahāvākyas. So the Brahma Sūtra is there to explain the Mahāvākyas: 'aham brahmāsmi' (I am Brahman),[243] 'tat tvam asi' (That thou art),[244] 'pragyānam brahma' (Brahman is consciousness, or intelligence),[245] and 'ayam ātmā brahma' (this Self is Brahman).[246]

VK: You mean, the perfection of brāhmī-sthiti is reached only when you've reached that state on the level of experience and then the teacher tells you ...

Maharishi: Yes, yes.

---

243 BU 1.4.10.
244 CU 6.8.7.
245 Aitareya Upanishad 3.1.3.
246 BU 2.5.19.

317

VK: Through living in God Consciousness for a long time you come to live this Unity on the level of experience, and then the teacher gives you the intellectual …

Maharishi: Full stop.

VK: When he feels that your experience of Unity has come to fruition, then he gives you the Mahāvākyas and then it becomes clear to you …

Maharishi: Yes.

VK: What I can never understand is that the Indians must all have known the Mahāvākyas since their childhood, so what difference can it make when the teacher now gives them to you? I suppose it's just more clear …

Maharishi: But when the experience is *ripe* and the teacher says 'tat tvam asi — really you are That', (and Maharishi adds this in a very soft voice) it's a *revelation*. He may have known [the expression] 'tat tvam asi' before, but that 'tat tvam asi' did not pinpoint that experience.

VK: It's just when he's ready for it that it has this effect.

Maharishi: Even when he has experienced and even when he has known 'tat tvam asi' [earlier on], the preciseness of conviction and the exactness of appreciation come only when the teacher says 'That is yours', and he [the aspirant] says 'Oh — right — yes'; immediately [it connects with his experience].

VK: But these Mahāvākyas must be given each at a different time, mustn't they?

Maharishi: They are. They are given at the time of initiation. It's an initiation, a process of initiation. It's a very beautiful system — so perfect.

VK: So the 'tat tvam asi' must come earlier than the 'sarvaṁ khalvidaṁ brahma'.[247]

Maharishi: Yes, yes. 'Tat tvam asi' can even come in the experience of Transcendental Consciousness because one has to be told 'That you are, unbounded, unlimited, and that is your [nature]. That you are.'

VK: So really one would be given the appropriate Mahāvākya when the experience was fairly full and one was already familiar with the experience pinpointed by the Mahāvākya. Maybe you yourself have done something similar when you have checked people's meditation. This checking may be similar to the giving of the Mahāvākyas. It means explaining a state that is already being lived. That would be like giving them the Mahāvākyas.

(Maharishi does not respond to this point but goes on to speak about the Brahma Sūtras and the possibility of associating each chapter with a particular Mahāvākya.)

Maharishi: With one Mahāvākya predominating in each adhyāya (chapter).

---

247 'Truly, all this is Brahman', CU 3.14.1. This is sometimes, though not generally, included among the Mahāvākyas. See Introduction, p. 54.

VK: This you can check only when you have done all the translations and you read through them and see the general …

Maharishi: The general trend.

VK: This structure was lacking and this is what we need to have.

Maharishi: And once we have this the commentary will be much more lively.

VK: It will fall into line.

Maharishi: It will be livelier because the thread will be there.

VK: I think if you had waited to do the commentary on the Gītā, too, it might have been even better.

Maharishi: Because the thoughts that come now are not contained in the Gītā commentary.

VK: Yes, exactly. But now we can include them in this commentary.

Maharishi: It [the teaching] is progressive.

VK: Yes, exactly, this makes it exciting. It's not just something …

Maharishi: Static.

VK: Yes, living and growing, not static and dead. I would like to know how you get these inspirations. (Laughter)

Maharishi: (Very sweetly) I just think, sit on that [subject] and think, and something comes out. It doesn't need any stimulant. The atmosphere is the stimulant. Once we have the right type of people — not jarring — that is the stimulant. It's just conducive and things come out.

VK: I suppose it's really in some way clarifying your own experiences.

Maharishi: Right, right. That is what it means.

VK: The experience comes but it takes time for the intellectual realization to be there.

Maharishi: Hm.

(There is a long pause, after which Maharishi returns to some notes on the Brahma Sūtras that he had prepared.)

Postscript: Courchevel, France, 18 August 1975

Maharishi: All these four Mahāvākyas are in good sequence of development of brāhmī chetanā (Brahman Consciousness). In this theme of the Mahāvākyas, 'tat tvam asi' — 'That thou art' — could be for Transcendental Consciousness. That thou art: your real nature is that Transcendental Consciousness.

VK: Excuse me, Maharishi, but we've already used 'tat tvam asi' for Unity Consciousness — when the 'thou' is being diminished and 'That' alone remains.[248]

Maharishi: That also is not wrong, because it is Transcendental Consciousness which, having become a practical reality of daily life, becomes Unity Consciousness. So it will be applicable. All the four Mahāvākyas will be applicable to each of these four states of consciousness — Transcendental, Cosmic, Unity, and Brahman; this will also be all right. Or, if we go deep into the fabric, we will find that we can really have them in a growing sequence, one from the other — that also will be right. Because Brahman will be right everywhere. So no matter which way we look at it, it will come out right. (Laughter)

VK: That's a great safeguard.

Maharishi: So if we say each Mahāvākya reveals the ultimate Brahman — fine, it does. And if we want to find a sequential progression in these four we can find it. So, in the first stage it is realized, 'That thou art' — not this, but That, because it is transcendental, it is unbounded. Now what is that aspect of 'thou' which is 'That'? The Ātman (Self) aspect of thou: 'ayam ātmā brahma'.[249] This Ātman, your Self aspect, not your body, is That. That unboundedness which is separate from this. So 'ayam ātmā brahma' is the clarification of 'That' in 'That thou art.'

---

248 See conversation, 'The Transition from God Consciousness to Unity'.
249 'Ātmā' is the nominative singular of 'Ātman'.

VK: Are we still talking about Transcendental Consciousness?

Maharishi: 'Ayam ātmā brahma' is the clarification of Transcendental Consciousness, but it's applicable to Cosmic Consciousness as well, because there is 'ayam ātmā' (this Self) and then there is 'jagad-anātmā' (the world is non-Self) separate from this Self.

VK: And what comes then?

Maharishi: And then 'ahaṁ brahmāsmi'. The word 'aham' (I) — 'aham' [is equivalent to] individuality — joins together Self and body: together [they] become 'aham'. In 'ayam ātmā brahma' only the Ātmā (Self) was considered Brahman. But when the gap between Ātmā and anātmā (non-Self), between soul and body, is bridged, then is the total 'aham'. 'Aham' takes into account body and soul — both together.

So in 'ahaṁ brahmāsmi' Unity has been reached: this in terms of my Self, this in terms of my Self, this in terms of my Self. 'Ahaṁ brahmāsmi' bridges the gulf that 'ayam ātmā brahma' has created between Ātmā (Self) and anātmā (non-Self).

Now 'aham' is something individual. 'Ahaṁ brahmāsmi': 'the individual is Brahman.' What is that individual in his ultimate value? 'Pragyānam' (intelligence), that is, the 'pra' (foremost) value of 'gyānam' (knowledge). The individual, 'aham', is vibrant knowledge — pure knowledge vibrant. Therefore 'pragyānam brahma': 'vibrant knowledge is Brahman.'

VK: So that is Brahman Consciousness.

Maharishi: That is Brahman Consciousness: 'pragyānam brahma'.

VK: So here you have the Mahāvākyas in sequence: one for Transcendental Consciousness, one for Cosmic, one for Unity, one for Brahman Consciousness.

Maharishi: As one rises to different states of consciousness each Mahāvākya becomes significant, comes to be true to his life. Each Mahāvākya has to be realized by him.

VK: But you also said that all four Mahāvākyas were needed for each state of consciousness — all four applicable to Transcendental Consciousness, all four applicable to Cosmic Consciousness, and so on.

Maharishi: Fine then let's discuss. Even this should be all right. Because, you see, Brahman is that wholeness, and all these four expressions delineate the character of Brahman in some specific way. Each in one specific way. So for Transcendental Consciousness, 'That thou art.' When the aspirant explains that he has transcended everything and has got to that unbounded awareness, then the teacher says, 'Oh, That thou art. That unbounded awareness is what you really are in your ultimate ... '

VK: Constituent.

Maharishi: 'Constituent of yourself.' And then he [the aspirant] asks, 'How do you classify that, what do you classify that to be?' Then he [the teacher] says, 'That is Ātman. That ultimate constituent of yours is Ātman. And this Ātman is Brahman: "ayam ātmā brahma".' And that is not only Ātman, because Ātman is associated with the individual, the individual soul. That individual soul in its character is 'bṛihat' (great), is Brahman, is great. That raises the point, if Ātman is Brahman, then what is the body? Then he says, 'Body and Ātman, both, are talked about as "aham". So this "aham", the totality of the individual personality — body and Ātman included — is Brahman. And what is that which is body and Ātman together? What is that?' Then he says, 'It is the vibrant nature of pure knowledge: "pragyānam".'

VK: The vibrant nature of pure knowledge?

Maharishi: The vibrant nature of pure knowledge is 'aham', and 'aham' is body and soul included. And that soul is Brahman, is great: 'ayam ātmā brahma'. And what is that soul, where is that soul? It is 'That'— transcendental. Go beyond, and then you have that soul.

VK: So all that would just refer to Transcendental Consciousness. A clarification of Transcendental Consciousness.

Maharishi: Yes. Now, when he is in Cosmic Consciousness, then the aspirant says, 'I feel uninvolved. I am a witness to this thing — witness to sleep, witness to waking.' Then the teacher says, 'Oh, That thou art. That which is not this, which is separate from this. Really you are That.' And then 'What is That?' All the same …

VK: The same sequence.

Maharishi: The same logic again.

VK: And Unity Consciousness?

Maharishi: Now, when one says, 'Oh, it is no longer true that I am a witness to this. I am so close to it that I see it as myself', then the teacher says, 'Ah, yes, this unity of subject and object is that wholeness: That thou art. Your status is that holistic value, that Unity Consciousness.' And then the question comes, 'What is that?' He says, 'That is Ātman and that Ātman is Brahman: ayam ātmā brahma.' We continue the same logic here. And then he says, 'aham brahmasmi'. And what is this 'aham'? It's just the vibrant nature of the Great, which is Brahman: 'pragyānam brahma'.

VK: And how are these Mahāvākyas given?

Maharishi: The sannyāsīs receive them from their guru.

VK: I wonder if you will do the same kind of thing eventually — give the Mahāvākyas?

Maharishi: We will do it on the meaning level; we talk in English.

The Aggregate

This conversation throws further light on the function of the Mahāvākyas, but it is especially remarkable for the way in which it foreshadows Maharishi's later teaching about Brahman Consciousness. The problem is that if one can only see the sap, or Absolute, in one thing at a time, how can one know that it is there in everything? Here Maharishi says that the cognition of the sap has to be deepened, so that one knows Brahman as the 'aggregate'. Maharishi later traced this deepening process in great detail, and in place of the aggregate, spoke of Brahman as 'the whole which is more than the collection of parts'. But the essentials of his teaching are here in this conversation.

Maharishi: Even if awareness of the Self is continuously maintained, and even if form is cognized as non-form, as long as the awareness does not present the aggregate of all the differences, so long Brahman, Unity, is not gained. This means that Unity is 'samudāya' — the collection of all.

VK: You mean all the relative?

Maharishi: Let me [continue]. The thing is, the fourteenth[250] says that the Unity of the Self is continuously maintained. Now this sūtra[251] says that even this situation ...

VK: Is not enough.

---

250 BS 2.2.14.
251 BS 2.2.18. The sūtra is 'samudāya ubhaya-hetuke 'pi tad-aprāptiḥ.'

Maharishi: Is not enough, because this situation is available even in Cosmic Consciousness: awareness–continuum is gained even in Cosmic Consciousness. Now, along with this situation comes the other situation [when Unity starts to be gained], where form is cognized as non-form. Now, this form may be cognized as non-form and that form may be cognized as non-form, but even this will not establish Unity so long as the assembly of all these different forms-as-non-forms is not gained.

VK: That is impossible for one person's consciousness. You can gain the principle but you can't gain the ...

Maharishi: And that is the state of Unity — this is what the sūtra teaches. It's not enough that somewhere you see non-form — that you see unity there, and you see unity there, and you see unity there.

VK: You have to see unity everywhere.

Maharishi: You have to see the congregate, the aggregate of all these unities.

VK: But you can see it only when you look. You can only see one unity at a time. When you look at that tree you can see that tree as unity [that is, in terms of your own Self], but you can't also see New York City as unity at the same time as you are looking at that tree.[252]

---

252 *Editor's note*: In discussing this manuscript, Vernon remarked that it was a great privilege to ask Maharishi questions. Looking back, he thought the question about New York City was perhaps the most impor-

Maharishi: No, but the unity perceived in the tree extends to New York. (Laughter) The aggregate of these experiences …

VK: I don't understand.

Maharishi: Now, in the state of Cosmic Consciousness the Self is maintained, fine; and along with the Self, this and this and this [object of experience] — such a huge diversity of things. Another situation can arise [as Unity starts to be gained] where one sees sap here, sap here; one sees sap here, sap here. But the aggregate of all these visions of the sap spread over here and there, is necessary [for complete Unity] — the collection.

VK: But that is impossible because you can't see all the relative at one and the same time.

Maharishi: See, it's just a matter of the extension of the same situation. That is, one sees the absolute aspect of the object — which is one's own Self — in different objects of perception successively.

VK: A matter of continuing to see the sap — as you see it, you see it in different places. But you can't see everything, you can't see the whole aggregate.

Maharishi: Now, this is gained through the Mahāvākyas.

VK: What is, Maharishi?

---

tant of all the questions he asked.

Maharishi: That the individualized experience gains the status of unboundedness. The experience of non-form in the form is still an individualized cognition. Now, this individualized cognition has to be established on the level of universal awareness. One could gain that awareness of the sap here [in one place], but when he looks here [elsewhere], he may find the situation different. Now, he may get the awareness of the sap here [in the second place] also, but these are two different localized awarenesses of unity — awareness of unity, but in each case localized. So, the same cognition of the sap has to be deepened a little more in order not to require different cognitions here and here. The same thing, but a little more established, will give the aggregate — samudāya.

VK: I can see that the Mahāvākyas will establish the principle in the mind, so that wherever you look you will find Brahman.

Maharishi: Right. When the vision has been gained, what remains to be established is the principle. If the vision is of sap here and the vision is of sap here, what remains to be established is just the principle that the same sap is here and there.

VK: That it applies everywhere.

Maharishi: That it applies everywhere. There is some sūtra in the beginning somewhere which says that through the upadesha [teaching] Brahman is established everywhere.

VK: 'Sarvatra prasiddhopadeshāt.'[253]

Maharishi: That 'sarvatra prasiddhopadeshāt' Vyāsa here expresses as 'samudāya'. But we are trying to establish samudāya as Brahman. This is the real situation in itself.

VK: But 'samudāya' also means 'whole'.

Maharishi: It [Brahman] is whole. But 'aggregate' is better in this case. When we say 'aggregate', people will understand: 'Ah! Picking up small things and putting them together.' It is the aggregate, but the sūtra says that it is such that it is not dependent on any cause. The previous sūtra[254] has established Brahman on the level of absolute non-dependence, and the present sūtra clarifies that the state of Brahman is not dependent on causes. Brahman is not obtained because of this or because of that.

Vyāsa is saying that neither cause nor absence of cause can be attributed to the state of aggregate. It is neither from reasoning nor from absence of reasoning, and it is this which establishes its absolute non-dependence. It is independent of cause. No cause can cause it to be what it is. No cause can cause it to be the aggregate. Vyāsa is negating the validity of cause in establishing Brahman. He just wants to establish it on the level of itself. That means, causality is no basis for Brahman, and if any kind of cause is introduced, Brahman won't be found.

---

253 'It is made effective everywhere because of the teaching', BS 1.2.1.
254 BS 2.2.17.

The beauty is that Vyāsa uses the word 'aggregate' and yet takes it beyond causation. He uses a word which indicates there must be a cause for it to be like that — 'aggregate' implies that everything is coming together, and there should be a cause to stimulate this. And then he refutes causation. It's such a marvellous use of words. He uses a word which should have a place for causation. And then he refutes causation so that absolutely no trace of causation can remain around Brahman and it is proved to be absolutely non-dependent.

The Role of Action in Gaining and Living the State of Brahman

In the preceding conversation the climax of the discussions on higher states of consciousness was reached with Maharishi's description of the aggregate — Brahman Consciousness, the state of full enlightenment. The present conversation and the one that follows it give some fascinating insights into the mechanics of the process of gaining enlightenment.

In this conversation Maharishi is commenting on sūtra 3.1.8, which was translated at that time as: 'From what is seen and from smṛiti, it is clear that on the termination of all that has been done he is possessed of the remainder. Thus is his course and also otherwise.' Even within Maharishi's overall theme that each sūtra displays the nature of Brahman, there is room for more than one interpretation of particular sūtras.[255] Here Maharishi explains 'the remainder' in two different ways. In the first, and longer, interpretation he speaks of the remainder of stress, which brings the awareness out of the state of Unity. This enables him to go into the mechanics of how higher states of consciousness become permanent: by being alternately gained and lost. Stress is identified with the deposit of karma,[256] and in answer to questions by Nikolaus Blücher and myself, Maharishi distinguishes the different types of karma. At the same time he shows that a remainder of karma is necessary not only to gain the state of Unity but to live it.[257]

In the second interpretation, only part of which is on tape, Maharishi explains 'the remainder' as the state of Brahman itself, and the conversation ends with a beautiful description of this state.

Maharishi: This [sūtra] means that whatever stress remains, the awareness comes out of Unity due to that remainder of that stress.

VK: You mean, when one has had some experience of Unity, but the state is not yet full, the stresses that remain bring the awareness out.

---

255 It will be recalled that in his commentary on the Bhagavad-Gītā Maharishi frequently gave more than one interpretation of a verse.

256 The word 'karma' means 'action'. It stands for the cycle of impression, desire, and action. See MBG 2.50, pp. 142–3; 4.19–20, pp. 284–6.

257 Compare the concept of 'leshāvidyā' in the conversation on 'The Gap'.

Maharishi: Yes. One comes out of Unity due to the remainder. And when karma comes to an end, then the awareness goes to Unity. In meditation, when action comes to an end, one gains the awareness of Unity,[258] but due to the remainder the awareness comes out — the remainder of the karma because stress is nothing but the deposit of karma. So one karma ends and Unity is gained, and then due to the remainder the mind [again] comes out of Unity.

Now the gaining of Unity is the field of shruti; the teaching of shruti tells us of gaining Unity. Smṛiti tells us of engaging in action.[259] That is why the sūtra says, 'From what is seen [shruti] and from smṛiti' — both. Going to the state of Unity is by virtue of shruti — the field of karma coming to an end. Coming back from Unity to this awareness of diversity is due to smṛiti, which deals with the process of purification of life. And this remainder of stress being released means purification of life. The coming back from Unity is due to some stress in the nervous system, which explains that coming back is within the domain of smṛiti, while going in is the region of shruti — in and out.

VK: So, it's possible to come out of Unity, is it?

Maharishi: It always happens — going in and coming out.

---

258 Transcendental Consciousness, where there is no division of subject and object, is also a state of unity.

259 See conversation, 'Shruti and Smṛiti', on the distinction between these categories of scripture.

Coming out is due to the remainder. Even some previous sūtra has said that Unity is by virtue of gaining and losing, and gaining and losing. This is how it becomes permanent. If it is to become permanent, the mind has to gain it and then lose it, keep on gaining and losing it. This is how Unity becomes permanent — the same way as Cosmic Consciousness; the same way as God Consciousness with its flashes of celestial [perception] — coming and going, coming and going.

VK: And when the teacher has realized that it is permanent, then he gives you the Mahāvākya.

Maharishi: Then the Mahāvākya.

VK: And then the truth of the Mahāvākya is realized.

Maharishi: Yes.

VK: And karma doesn't come to an end with Cosmic Consciousness? The bondage of karma should come to an end in Cosmic Consciousness.

Maharishi: Karma doesn't come to an end in Cosmic Consciousness. The bondage of karma comes to an end.

VK: So what is that karma which takes one out of Unity? Is it an unbound karma?

Maharishi: The remainder.

VK: Prārabdha karma.[260]

Maharishi: Yes, prārabdha karma. Saṁchita karma[261] is burned, but that [prārabdha] karma remains.

NB: And there is no karma any more when gyāna (knowledge) has been gained?

Maharishi: Karma is there even in the process of gaining it, and having gained it also there is that karma. We had some sūtra yesterday, something about action continuing, about that [the state of Brahman] not being opposed to action. Vyāsa is a perfectionist. By saying that when saṁchita karma, the totality of karma, comes to an end there is still a remainder, he wants to make it clear that the state of Brahman is *lived*. He pictures a situation where the state of Brahman is lived in life on account of the karma that yet remains. Karma remains, but the state of Brahman would not arise if the totality of karma had not come to an end. Thereby, he is distinguishing saṁchita karma and prārabdha karma. Saṁchita karma has to come to an end, and by means of prārabdha the state of Brahman is lived in life. Now, there could be a situation where the totality of karma (saṁchita) has been lost and no more karma (prārabdha) is there — that means, at the time of leaving the body. The situation could be that the totality of karma is lost due to the cognition of

---

260 Karma which has begun to bear fruit.
261 Accumulated karma which has not yet begun to bear fruit.

Brahman, but there is no longer any remainder which would enable the state of Brahman to be lived. In this state also Brahman is realized. Brahman comes if there is a remainder, or if there is no remainder.

VK: What happens if there is no remainder?

Maharishi: If there is no remainder the state of Brahman comes and one loses the body. Brahman doesn't become a living reality, but the ultimate purpose of the realization of Brahman, which is just Being, is gained. So when Vyāsa brings to light one situation, he doesn't lose sight of another possibility, and that possibility he puts in the sūtra. He says that in one situation Brahman comes in a manner where the totality of karma is completely lost and something remains. By virtue of that remainder of karma, one lives the state of Brahman. But in another situation where the totality of karma is lost and no remainder is there, even in that state one is Brahman.

VK: But what does this mean, 'it comes in another situation'? It comes at the time of death?

Maharishi: It comes at the time of death — this is it, in plain words. It has come but it doesn't remain a living reality.

NB: What are these two kinds of karma, saṁchita karma and the other one?

Maharishi: Saṁchita is all the heap of karma that has been done and stored. The mountain of karma.

NB: Saṁchita, yes. And the other one was?

Maharishi: Prārabdha. Prārabdha is that portion which has been taken off from that big heap, to be borne in this lifetime.

VK: There's another kind of karma.

Maharishi: Kriyāmāṇa.

VK: Kriyāmāṇa, yes.

Maharishi: Kriyāmāṇa is that which is being stored as a result of what one is doing now — something coming out of the present action. So, that which comes out of the present action is eliminated, because the separation of the Self from the non-Self [in Cosmic Consciousness] accomplishes that state in which one is only a witness of action, in which one is no longer a doer and an experiencer and the bearer of karma.

VK: Then there's no difference, really, between gaining Cosmic Consciousness at death and gaining realization of Brahman at death.

Maharishi: No difference as far as liberation is concerned. Only the charm of life is a little bit more.

VK: But at death it won't be more.

Maharishi: At death it won't be anything, no.

VK: It'll be the same.

Maharishi: So here the main teaching is that the remain-

der of action is no barrier to living the state of Brahman
— gaining the state of Brahman and living it. And the field
of action is not the field of shruti; so he has also to mention the field of smṛiti — what is seen in daily life. Where
is the smṛiti? In the field of action. Shruti just says 'sarvaṁ
khalvidaṁ brahma neha nānāsti kinchana'[262] — it denies everything. So we can't say that the remainder remains from
the point of view of shruti. But we see the man is active and
one could be active only on account of the remainder of action. Smṛiti will not testify to the state of Brahman; smṛiti
will only testify that action remains.

* * *

(Maharishi now gives another explanation of the sūtra. Unfortunately the beginning of this new line of thought is not
recorded.)

Maharishi: What we say [now] is that karma has ended and
at the end, at the culmination of karma is the state of Unity.
Previously we said that because we see realized people acting
in the state of Brahman, because we see the realized man in
the field of action, therefore even at the end of the karma,
something clings on to him. The sūtra says that. But [we now
say that the] something that clings on to him in this state is
the state of Brahman itself. Before, we said that karma clings
on to him, on the basis of which karma he acts. But I think

---

262 'Truly all this is Brahman; there is nothing else whatsoever':
Nirālamba Upanishad. Compare CU 3.14.1 and BU 4.4.19.

it is better to say that he [Brahman] is the remainder. At the termination of all works, what remains is he — finished.

MG: Maharishi, may I ask, what does Brahman do with all these karmas? You say he takes them. Now, what does he do with them?[263]

Maharishi: Just that which the sap does to all the petals and this and this. Brahman does with the karma just what the sap does to the leaf and the flower and the tree — just that.

MG: Could that be put in the explanation, Maharishi, because somebody like me could ask that and get the answer?

Maharishi: The thing is, Brahman is the state of oneness, and oneness is all-pervading. Like H_2O — water; it's there in ice, in vapour, and so on. The content is the same, hydrogen and oxygen, in all forms of water. Like that, the essential content of all manifested creation is Transcendental Consciousness. Brahman, that unity of life, that unity. Now, as long as one has not risen to that awareness of unity, so long one's awareness is held up in different manifestations, different experiences, different forms and all that. But as the awareness grows to unity more and more and more and eventually is established on the level of Unity, karma and other things are just as superficial as the shape of water and ice and vapour are for H_2O. H_2O, in its structure, has

---

263 Mrs. Gill is referring to a statement by Maharishi that was not recorded.

nothing to do with all these different manifestations, and yet H_2O is homogeneously present everywhere. Actually there is only H_2O, and all these forms and names are only a phenomenal appearance. Just like that, all this multiplicity is a phenomenal appearance on the flat level of unity.

When one wants to see the sap in all its manifestations, then the most practical way is to get rid of the manifested field [during Transcendental Meditation] and cognize the sap in its unmanifested shape. And cognize the sap in its unmanifested shape as clearly, as profoundly as possible, so that that vision of the sap is contained in the vision of the petal. In this way, even when the manifested aspect, gross aspect, is experienced, even then the cognition of the subtle cause is not missed. This is what makes the path to realization of Unity.

Purification of the Nervous System and Growth of Consciousness

This is part of a long talk with Maharishi on 18 August 1969, in which Marjorie Gill, Jemima Pitman, Nikolaus Blücher, and I took part.

The major part of the discussion reproduced here concerns the nature of stress and its release with reference to different states of consciousness. And as in the preceding conversation, stress is related to the concept of karma. In the course of his analysis Maharishi has some interesting things to say about the way in which sleep changes with the growth of consciousness. He emphasizes throughout that the evolution towards higher states of consciousness is based on changes in the physical system — these are, after all, two sides of the same coin. I think it is legitimate to call these physical changes a purification, just because without them higher states of consciousness could not be supported.

Maharishi: Every present desire has its root in some past impression, whatever that may be, and those impressions are stored as stresses here and there — good or bad or whatever. So in that sense every desire is release of stress. Desire is for fulfilment, and stresses are due to obstacles on the way to fulfilment.

VK: Now this is desire. But what about thought?

Maharishi: Thought, if it is significant, is the root of desire. Thought comes out as a desire.

VK: But when you think about problems where genuine reasoning is involved ...

Maharishi: But that reasoning springs from somewhere. It has a root, and from there it develops into this and this — various things — but it is coming from somewhere. Every desire is for enlightenment, for achievement, for fulfilment, and the path to fulfilment is tracked through desires coming out, desires being fulfilled and giving rise to some other desires. Like that, one desire leads to the other and so on, and these are all ways of removing the unfulfilled desires rooted within.

VK: And what is the difference between this kind of everyday desiring and the desiring that comes in what we call release of stress? Is it a difference of degree?

Maharishi: Yes, a difference of degree or … It is difficult to say what kind of desiring will come out from a release of stress because the quality of the desire will be according to the quality of the experience which had caused the stress now being released.

VK: So, all this is a question of difference in the depth of stress, because every experience, in that it leaves some impression, leaves some stress. So, what we call release of stress results from deeper stresses, whereas the ordinary way of thinking and desiring results from comparatively surface stresses.

Maharishi: And when, owing to these stresses gathered during twelve hours of the day, the system can take no more, it falls flat into sleep — the system can't take any more. And then the release of fatigue by sleep, or the release of some deep-rooted stresses by way of dreams, refreshes the whole system.

VK: But often you don't feel so good after the night; you have heavy dreams and it's far from refreshing.

Maharishi: Then that means that the release of stress caused during the period of dreams is not yet ended; it is continuing even till that period of the morning.

VK: Really, the attitude to cultivate, if there is such a thing, is just acceptance.

Maharishi: And nature does it. One doesn't have to make a mood of acceptance; one just accepts. Nature does it naturally. There is nothing that one can do about it.

JP: But Maharishi, there is another type of thinking, which is thinking in response to a situation. For instance, as Vernon brought up, when we were thinking about whether you should go to Switzerland for the September course or whether you should stay in Rishikesh. That kind of thinking is …

Maharishi: All due to the stresses caused in Rishikesh. (Laughter) Must have something to do with it.

* * *

Maharishi: If it [the body] is subjected to this it will respond in one way, if it is subjected to that it will respond in a different way — that is all. Like a computer, whatever we feed it with, it responds. The physical machine and that's all — the whole code of action is for the sake of maintaining the machine in perfect order, to get the best possible reaction from it.

JP: But I asked you a question when I was here last time, Maharishi, about the case of a realized man — a man in Cosmic Consciousness who presumably is free from stress, but still continues to think. And you gave a very good answer to that. You brought in the force of evolution as being the cause for further thinking, so to speak. Could you explain that more?

Maharishi: Once the Self has disassociated itself from the three guṇas,[264] once it is separated, it does not mean that a person does not have stresses, it does not mean that he will not release his stresses, because the waking state is there, sleep state is there, dream state is there. At the same time pure awareness is also there. The stresses gathered in the waking state will naturally be neutralized during sleep, and due to that some dreams are inevitable. This separation [in Cosmic Consciousness] does not stop all this field of relative existence from going on.

VK: But you say that no new karma is being formed? — there are no impressions deep enough to form new karma. But if stress is there at all, it must be deep enough to form new karma; or is it purely physical?

Maharishi: Physical, and mental also. The mind is involved with all the actions and experiences, and the physical is involved. Only the spiritual aspect [the Self], which previously was involved and was not clear in its own structure, now is clear in its own structure. It is free. But this doesn't mean that one will not have stress in the body. If that were so, then one would not fall asleep; but sleep one gets, only it's a different kind of sleep in that now the awareness is not lost during sleep. But sleep is inevitable, as waking is inevitable. When one is in the waking state stresses have to come because, if

---

264 On the guṇas, see later in this conversation. See also MBG 2.45, p. 128; 3.27–8, pp. 220ff.

[for example] the eyes see some big flashes, even the eyes of a man in Cosmic Consciousness — it's a physical thing — the physical system must be hurt and stress must be gained. And that stress must go when the system is resting. It is a natural quality of the system to throw off foreign material. Stress is just that. So, all this continues in Cosmic Consciousness; only, awareness gets maintained.

VK: And this means no new karma, it seems.

Maharishi: This does mean that no new karma is born, because the karma, the impression, in such a case will be, as we say, like a line on water. The line will be there, but it will be there just to give that much experience — and finished. The purpose has been gained. The purpose of gaining birth, which was to free oneself, to have eternal freedom, has been gained. Now, from Cosmic Consciousness to God Consciousness there is a glorification of the system.

JP: Glorification?

Maharishi: The nervous system becomes much more glorified, much more glorified, so that the ordinary vision of today becomes the celestial vision of tomorrow. Celestial: this is just the further glorification of the system. Still further glorification of the system will produce Unity.

JP: So then, Maharishi, that's not related to stress. If you look at it from the side of the ordinary waking state of consciousness you see the coin in one way; if you look at it from the side of Brahman you see it in another way. And surely at some point cosmic intelligence enters into the picture. And cosmic intelligence must lead to thought in the individual without it being anything to do with stress.

Maharishi: In that state of perpetual Unity on the level of awareness, the system is so pure. This is what some of the sūtras of the fourth chapter made clear today. They talk of immortality on the physical level — the possibility of that. Then the system would be so stress-proof that even deep sleep would not be the deep sleep of complete loss of awareness; it would be the deep sleep of awareness of the celestial, so that the pure awareness is a witness, not of the tamas[265] and negation of life in deep sleep, but of the negation of life — [in the sense of] negation of activity — in the celestial. See the difference?

VK: Because the whole level of consciousness has been raised.

Maharishi: The whole level of the physical body has been raised to such great purity that it is not influenced by the rajas[266] or tamas of the guṇas; only sattva[267] prevails. Permanence of celestial awareness, that is, God Consciousness, is on the level of satoguṇa (sattva). So, sattva dominates. And if sattva dominates deep sleep, then deep sleep is unlike the deep sleep

---

265 The guṇa responsible for inertia. The word means 'darkness'.

266 The guṇa responsible for motion and energy. See also MBG 3.37, pp. 236ff.

267 The guṇa responsible for progress, creativity, purity.

in which one feels blank. Even in Cosmic Consciousness that experience of complete loss of awareness during deep sleep is still there; only the Self is a witness to that loss of awareness. With the progress of purity in the system, the deep sleep is the celestial field, and then the pure awareness, or the Self, is a witness to that celestial sleep, witness to that celestial field of dreams, witness to that celestial level of waking consciousness.

NB: There are also these three guṇas in God Consciousness?

Maharishi: There are always the three guṇas as long as there is some duality. Only, in God Consciousness sattva dominates; it is not exclusive of tamas and rajas, but it predominates.

NB: So sleep will not be entirely zero — inactivity.

Maharishi: It will be inactivity; only, it will be inactivity where sattva dominates, and not where tamas dominates — celestial awareness as against loss of awareness when sleep is dominated by tamas. So the system will always be exposed to these variations.

VK: Maharishi, it's loss of awareness. It's just a different loss of awareness, but it's still loss of awareness. So really what it means is, as you said, that the system has become more refined and therefore doesn't sink quite so low as it did in Cosmic Consciousness, but it's still loss of awareness of objects.

Maharishi: Right, loss of awareness with the celestial light [present].

VK: Oh, that continues!

Maharishi: Yes, that continues.

VK: But no details can be perceived in it.

Maharishi: No details. But when the celestial dominates, then the perception, the vision, is coloured in that light of sattva, in that celestial light. And when it is [thus] coloured, whether it is deep sleep or waking or dreaming, that [light of sattva] is dominating.

It [sleep in Cosmic Consciousness] is like diving into black-coloured water where you open the eyes and you don't see anything, and [sleep in God Consciousness is like] diving into clean water where you open the eyes and you are able to see. There is that difference: even if you don't see anything [in the clear water], you have something [some clarity] there.

JP: But the awareness — the diver — is there at all times.

Maharishi: Yes, it's there.

JP: So awareness is not lost. What you see is different, but awareness is not lost, is it?

Maharishi: See, there are two situations. During sleep this pure awareness, Self-awareness, is not lost, but awareness of the waking state gets drowned. Now, awareness of waking is lost into complete inertia during sleep in Cosmic Consciousness; in the other case, in God Consciousness, awareness of

the waking is lost into what we can call celestial awareness.[268]
So [in God Consciousness] the sleep also is much more enjoyable, as are the dreams, as is the waking state — it's only a
matter of increasing the joyfulness of perception.

VK: I seem to remember you saying once that in God Consciousness sleep was the same thing — loss of awareness — as
in Cosmic Consciousness.

Maharishi: No, no. It should be different because in God
Consciousness sattva dominates, while in the beginning days
[at an earlier stage] — in Cosmic Consciousness — sleep is
sleep just as before, dominated by tamas. Because all these
three states of consciousness — waking, dreaming, sleeping
— are the fields dominated by, or reigned over by, the three
guṇas. In God Consciousness sattva dominates — finished:
and once sattva dominates, all three states are dominated by
sattva.

VK: Yes, of course, it's natural. You must witness sleep in Cosmic Consciousness because awareness is never lost, and you
will witness a different kind of sleep in God Consciousness.

Maharishi: Different kind of sleep, but it will be deep sleep.

---

268 When this was read to him on 1 June 1974, Maharishi explained:
'The sleep state itself is loss of awareness — zero awareness. And sleep in
Cosmic Consciousness is awareness of zero awareness. But sleep in God
Consciousness is awareness, not of zero but of celestial zero, just as the
waking state aspect of God Consciousness is the celestial waking state,
while the waking state aspect of Cosmic Consciousness is the ordinary
waking state.'

Just like when you are diving into a very deep ocean, and you go a little and you open the eyes. If the water is black you just can't see anything. And if the water is clear you are able to see. Even if you don't see anything in particular, but you are able to see. It's just like that.

JP: But to come back to my question please, Maharishi, or maybe it's not a relevant question.

Maharishi: What is it?

JP: About thought from the point of view of cosmic intelligence.

Maharishi: Thought always arises out of need.

JP: And cosmic intelligence has a need?

Maharishi: It has a need, and that need is for everything to grow and grow and grow and be united with the Infinite. That's the need.

JP: But is that a stress on the part of cosmic intelligence?

Maharishi: When cosmic intelligence has to fight its way through — a man is not doing right things and cosmic intelligence is pushing him on to the right lines. It's just like the government putting hunters [policemen] on to a man to put him right. They strike him and tell him, 'Don't steal!' The purpose of the government is to free society from fears; and if someone begins to behave badly there is a danger to the whole society, and it has to be put right, for his own sake and for the sake of others also. The whole purpose is evolution, automatic evolution.

JP: So you mean that right from the very lowest end of the scale up to the most evolved, up to Unity, all thought is the release of stress?

Maharishi: And that is a help to growth, because anything that releases stress makes life advance more ahead. It's a natural phenomenon.

JP: Yes, Maharishi, but after a man has reached Cosmic Consciousness and he is relatively free of stress, his thinking is not in answer to his own personal release of stress any more, is it?

Maharishi: The process of evolution does not end with Cosmic Consciousness. So, even when those depths of stress which were binding the Self to the field of the three guṇas, even when they are gone, the system is still not a fully evolved system. It is evolved enough for Self-awareness to be maintained — one is a witness to everything that is going on — for that it is enough, but the system is not, so to say, foolproof. Every day it gains stresses and every night it loses stresses. This is what we mean to say: the experiences after one has gained Cosmic Consciousness are such that they do not leave a deep impression. The impressions are not like lines on stone; they are like a line on water. But the impressions are there and it is these impressions of experiences that leave some stresses that are released during the night. Only, no stress would [any longer] go so deep as to be able to remain stored; no stress would be so deep as to hold the awareness in the state of bondage.

This is what I was saying — let me make it clear. In the state of Cosmic Consciousness the stresses have been released, and they have been released to an extent sufficient for the Self to be forever maintained. But the system has not become foolproof — this is what I said. Foolproof means it has not become completely shielded from the possibility of gaining more stresses. During the day it gains the stresses and in the night they are eliminated. This keeps happening, but the gathering of stress during daily experiences does not bring stresses deep enough to be stored so that the Self could be overshadowed and could remain bound, and the cycle of birth and death could continue. So, that possibility is eliminated with Cosmic Consciousness; experiences in the world will not leave such deep impressions as could overshadow Being. But, sure enough, they will leave some impressions, some stresses, which will be eliminated during the night's rest.

Now, this is the situation in Cosmic Consciousness. As evolution continues, the system becomes more and more cultured, more and more refined, and this greater refinement of the physical nervous system means that it will be gathering a smaller and smaller amount of stress to be neutralized during the night. And as the celestial awareness grows, the system will be more and more pure. And more and more pure means that it will receive less and less stresses to be released during the night — less and less stresses.

And this is just the culture of the physical nervous system and its capability of shielding itself from gaining stresses, even in the activity of daily life. When the perception becomes dominated by celestial vision, the chances of stresses are less and less — increasingly less. When every perception is a joyful wave, then the chances of gaining stresses are naturally less. So, the system gains that quality where the perception will be less taxing, more joyful.

JP: But joy can produce a stress.

Maharishi: Now, joy can produce a stress, of course. See, in order to further improve upon the nervous system's ability to not gain stresses — not even from great joyfulness — the process of evolution continues and one gets to the state of Unity. And when one perceives everything, not in terms of great waves of joyfulness, but in terms of one's Self, then the chance of accumulating stresses is eliminated forever. It will be like a sponge — the sponge when pressed bounces back to its original state. Now, this is just the gradual improvement of the quality of the nervous system with the process of evolution.

The nervous system gets refined as one advances from Cosmic Consciousness to God Consciousness; as the perception becomes more and more celestial, so the possibility of gaining stresses becomes less and less and less and less. Now, in the state of God Consciousness there is absolutely no possibility of gaining stresses from the negative type of experience, but there is surely a chance of gaining stresses from the positive type of experience, from the celestial. The example is: one has cast off the iron chains but now has taken on golden chains. All the joyful experiences of the world in God Consciousness are said to be bondage — not enough bondage to bring one back to the cycle of birth and death, but still bondage from the consideration of unity of life.

VK: In fact those who interpret Indian philosophy do say it's bondage, the bondage of birth and death.

Maharishi: Because they don't make such fine distinctions between what type of …

VK: Because it's desire still, in the sense of desire for celestial bliss, and therefore bondage according to them.

Maharishi: They don't know what a desire is. That desire is binding when one could get lost in it. But when one is a witness to the desire, then one is a witness to the desire. So, right from Cosmic Consciousness there is no chance of getting bondage through action and desire and all that. But because there is no clear vision of these distinct states of Cosmic Consciousness, and God Consciousness, and Unity, that is why people make a muddle of the whole thing. It is just the culture of the nervous system. The system keeps on being built of more and more refined material because the breath is getting finer and finer and finer and finer. Finer breath means that the system is working on more refined fuel. The mechanism, the machinery, is working through more refined fuel, and as the refinement of the fuel increases, the efficiency of the machinery increases. And the increased efficiency of the machinery means, firstly, that it does not receive impressions from the bad things, and then, later on, not even from the good things; and then, still later, one just remains in the evenness of existence on the level of the sap, never to descend to the level of the manifestations of the sap — the leaves and flowers and branches. So, that becomes the all-supporting nature of life in Unity; the sap supports the thorn and the flower alike. And that is the evenness, that is the grandeur of life.

The Bondage and Release of Brahman

I am ending this volume with some rather intimate exchanges, of which this delightful interlude is the first. We must have been working on the Brahma Sūtra in the garden, as we sometimes did in the mornings before the sun became too hot. Tables were arranged for the books and, to give Maharishi extra protection, an ancient umbrella was hung in the tree under which we were sitting. It was a peaceful scene with grass and bright-coloured flowers all around us. The birds chattered away, almost drowning the rumble of the occasional car passing in the distance.

VK: 'But that is the hidden one on account of transcendental absorption in meditation. From there, indeed, come his bondage and his release.'[269]

Maharishi: See, the recognition that one is bound comes only from this absorption in Transcendental Meditation, because once one goes there, one finds 'Oh, here is Brahman.' And once one has found that here is Brahman, he has found how hidden it was. And then, when Brahman comes out with the practice, when the practice [of Transcendental Meditation] brings it out, then it gives Brahman release.

VK: (Blowing at something and making a strange sound)

MG: What is it? A mouse?

VK: No, a nasty big thing. It's all right.

Maharishi: We were talking of the release of Brahman, and it must be a big thing. (Laughter) It must be very big — the release — the unbounded is being released. (Laughter)

VK: That nasty black thing came creeping from under the book. It was being released; the unbounded was being released. (Laughter)

MG: What was it, a beetle or a fly?

(An Indian explains the species to Maharishi in Hindi)

VK: Don't know; they say it was nothing …

Maharishi: But your mind was on that release [of which the

---

269 BS 3.2.5, as provisionally translated at the time.

sūtra speaks]. And then you came upon it [the creature] and it was being released. (Laughter)

(Some amusement on the part of the Indians present at Western squeamishness about harmless creatures)

VK: But I think it should refer to the soul, Maharishi. To make bondage and freedom refer to Brahman is really very capricious.

Maharishi: But to speak of him as being hidden is equally awful. (Laughter)

VK: But he is hidden to the soul and once he is found the soul is released. But that he is bound and freed! No one ever really used 'bandha' (bondage) of Brahman — not before you came along, anyway. (Laughter)

Maharishi: We see him being bound in that field. Why [should he] come out?

VK: Yes, what you said before about him being imprisoned. You said when we were doing the Gītā — it was very beautiful — that the Self was imprisoned in the transcendental and that through meditation he would come out.

Maharishi: Be released.

VK: Well, it's much more unusual than the common interpretation.

Maharishi: See, I spoke on this for the first time in San Francisco, right back in 1959. I gave a talk on — the [gramophone] record is from that — on healing: the healing power of Transcendental Meditation. I said Transcendental Meditation heals the body, the mind, and the soul. And on healing the soul I said, 'Now it's hidden in the Transcendent, it's imprisoned; it heals, and it's out of the imprisonment.'

VK: You said it even there?

Maharishi: There, it came from that. It was the healing power of meditation.

Defect as the Basis of the Realization of Brahman

In another light and amusing conversation Maharishi points out the role of 'dosha', or defect, in the realization of Brahman. Realization of Brahman can only take place by virtue of defect, or lack of universality, in one's self. If there were no defect, no lack, there would be no need to realize Brahman. It is only because we are not at the goal that the possibility of arriving at it exists.

Like the Tahoe commentary on another sūtra containing the word 'dosha',[270] this is a beautiful example of how Maharishi transforms a seemingly negative situation into a positive one. He sees human imperfection not as an obstacle but as an opportunity for growth.

---

270 See conversation, 'Proving Brahman from Fault'.

Maharishi: 'Svapaksha-doshāch cha.'[271] 'Brahman is because of the defect on the side of the self.' See, when the defect disappears, then the self is Brahman. So it is the disappearing of the defect, disappearing of localization in time and space, which brings Brahman. So the realization of Brahman is as if due to the lack, or want of efficiency on the side of the self. Because the self lacks something, that is why he realizes Brahman. So realization of Brahman is due to the lack of efficiency, lack of universality, on the side of the self. See?

VK: If the situation were perfect, the desire wouldn't arise.

Maharishi: And the realization of Brahman would not take place. So the realization of Brahman springs from the localized conditions of the self.

VK: So rejoice in your imperfect situation.

Maharishi: (Laughing) Because without it Brahman would not be located.

MG: You know, there are people today who say, Maharishi, that without man, God could not exist.

Maharishi: It's just the same, just the same. 'Svapaksha-doshāch cha.' It is the inefficiency, it is the dosha of the self, that is, lack of universality in the self, which gives rise to Brahman. That's it. Beautiful.

VK: I knew this sūtra wouldn't remain useless for long. What

---

271 BS 2.1.10.

do they say: all is grist to the mill?

JP: Absolutely ...

Maharishi: 'Svapaksha-doshách cha.' It's brilliant, bright. No, I am admiring Vyāsa's vision. (Laughter)

VK: We know, Maharishi — we know that.

JP: We're admiring Vyāsa's vision through you, Maharishi.

VK: 'We know that [you are not admiring your own words]; you speak quite objectively. This is the marvellous thing about it. (Speaking to the others present) When Maharishi admires something, it's almost as if somebody else had said it. What he admires is not anything he himself has said. It's just because the thing is good.[272]

Maharishi: It's Vyāsa's, yes, Vyāsa's vision; it's the admiration of Vyāsa's vision. 'Svapaksha-doshāt.' On account of defect on the side of the self ...

VK: 'On one's own side', yes?

Maharishi: No, I think 'on the side of the self'.

VK: 'Sva' really means 'own', but you can use 'self'.

Maharishi: 'Self' is better, I think. Makes it more intimate — and then the commentary will be clear.

JP: Capitulation for Vernon.

---

272 See conversation, 'On Inspiration', introductory note.

Maharishi: And 'because of the defect on the side of the self'.

VK: I only take a stand where it's really necessary, to prevent the Sanskrit from being …

Maharishi: Where to blow the wind to shake the tree. (Laughter) And because of the defect on the side of the self, localized in time and space … (Maharishi proceeds to comment on the next sūtra) He wants to prove that the world is Brahman. He doesn't say the world is Brahman. He says …

VK: It's not not-Brahman.

Maharishi: Because of its non-existent nature, or some such thing. It's indirect, negative. In order to say that there is the light in the room, he says there is no darkness in the room and you can see everything. (Laughter) But this is a remarkable sūtra.

VK: This one we're doing now?

Maharishi: Yes, yes. He says, if you have derived wrong conclusions because of ill-founded reasoning, even then you are faced with the field of bondage.

VK: Well, that is not something very new: if you've drawn wrong conclusions you are faced with bondage.

JP: Even if you draw right conclusions you're faced with bondage. (Laughter)

VK: Yes, you're faced with bondage. You've only got to look round this room now.

(Maharishi, in a vain attempt to proceed with sūtra 2.1.11, begins to recite it.)

Maharishi: 'Tarkāpratishthānāt' (because of ill-founded reasoning).

JP: Who are you looking at, Vernon?

VK: Myself. (Laughter) I see the 'defect on my own side'. (Laughter)

Maharishi: (Laughing) This is Brahman.

VK: Looking in the mirror — 'svapaksha-doshāt'.

Maharishi: 'Svapaksha-doshāt'. Not 'svapyayāt',[273] not by coming to one's Self but by virtue of one's dosha, one's defect. (Laughter)

JP: What is dosha?

Maharishi: Defect. By virtue of one's defect. There was a sūtra in the previous chapter, 'on account of coming to one's Self'.

JP: I would have got to my Self long ago, if it were [to be attained] by virtue of my defects, Maharishi.

Maharishi: By virtue of the defects only, Brahman is realized, because if there were no defect, then that would be the state of Brahman, that would be the state of Brahman. The real-

---

273 'On account of coming into one's own', or 'on account of coming to one's Self', BS 1.1.9.

ization of Brahman is only from the state of non-Brahman to the state of Brahman. And the state of non-Brahman is the state of dosha, defect. So it is by virtue of the defect that one attains Brahman, that one finds that one is Brahman.

JP: Maharishi, that doesn't sound like the jet age; it sounds like going to the North Pole via the South Pole.

Maharishi: No, but the jet age makes it quick. (Laughter) This is why the journey to the North Pole is via the South Pole, through this chapter. So that means, whether you go north or you go south, you are going to arrive at Brahman. This is the universality of Brahman.

VK: Because the world is round. Wherever you are going …

Maharishi: Wherever you go, Brahman is there. (Laughing) Brahman is there.

On Inspiration

Maharishi rarely speaks directly about himself and still more rarely about his inspiration. When he does do so he is completely objective — it is almost as if he were referring to someone else. For this reason he speaks freely and joyfully about the good things that emerge during work on the commentary or on any other occasion. One can sense the difference between this and one's own elation when one has said something clever or has come out with a new idea. Then, certainly, there is the joy that something good has occurred, but there is also the pleasurable sense that *I* am responsible for it. Anything of this sort is absent with Maharishi. There is only the pure happiness that something good and beautiful is manifesting. It is more like the happiness one feels at the sight of some beautiful manifestation of nature, such as a sunset.

There follow some snatches of conversation in which Maharishi speaks spontaneously — and in the second conversation, half in jest — about the way in which his ideas arise.

On Inspiration I

The talk has been about establishing Brahman by negating the world. As so often, Maharishi looks at what must have been going on in the mind of the author, Vyāsa.

Maharishi: But his insight into a situation [during the time of dissolution] where the world is non-existent, yet Brahman is — that is beautiful. That shows in what great calmness he has written those Sūtras. Just calm. (The word 'calm' is very long drawn-out.)

VK: Without having to think of construction work,[274] or anything like that.

---

274 Maharishi was engaged, among other things, on building plans for an academy in Kashmir.

Maharishi: This morning I came to just these conclusions. When you just sit — sometimes you close your eyes and sometimes you open your eyes, and you are … I was on the introduction to these Brahma Sūtras, and then like petals they opened — this point and this point. Such an exhilarating and enjoyable situation. You are working and yet you are resting, you are there and yet you are not there. That is how, in that calm and quiet atmosphere [Vyāsa must have written his Sūtras]. This is beautiful because we can see how this Sūtra arose.

VK: We can appreciate it.

Maharishi: We can appreciate the mechanics of [it] … these flashes coming.

(Maharishi never speaks like this for long and here he returned to the translation of the Sūtras.)

On Inspiration II

On this, as on so many of the Kashmir tapes, the silences — the rests in the score — are filled by a concert of birds. This morning conversation is also pervaded by another kind of music — Maharishi's laughter. It is well known that Maharishi laughed often, but his laughter was of many different kinds. It was a language in itself. For most of the present short and not very serious conversation Maharishi is shaking with joyful laughter. The Indian student

366

who read the Sanskrit texts to Maharishi and me joined in.

Maharishi had discovered correspondences between sūtras in different chapters and sections of chapters. Thus the second sūtra of one section might correspond to the third sūtra of the next section, and so on. In this way the Brahma Sūtras seemed to have what one might call a horizontal, as well as a vertical, theme. Maharishi went through several sections to prove his point and was delighted by the whole idea.

Maharishi: Last night we did this — this is how we closed at night. The gods have been singing this whole thing [in the night] and the sun delivered it to us [new] in the morning. (Much laughter)

VK: The sun's been busy, then.

Maharishi: Yes, he is busy in the darkness of the night.

(The student says something in Hindi. I catch only the name 'Tulsidas', a famous Hindi poet and devotee of Lord Rāma, whose story he tells in his version of the Rāmāyaṇa.)

Maharishi: He was being inspired by Hanumān-ji.[275] In the night he [Hanumān] used to whisper in his [Tulsīdās's] mind about the realities of Rāma's life with which he himself was so familiar, and in the morning he [Tulsīdās] used to write. This is said of him because it's such a masterly narration of that ideal life of Bhagavān Rāma. It's not human; it's

---

275 In the Rāmāyaṇa, Hanumān — who has a monkey's body — is the loyal, courageous friend and devotee of Rāma.

divinely inspired. That's the significance of Hanumān telling Tulsīdās. (Laughter) And this is happening here, in this cowshed.[276] In the cowshed on 'Dull' Lake,[277] Vyāsa whispered the key to this. (Laughter) This is beautiful — in the cowshed. We should make it known: the Brahma Sūtras are being done in a cowshed on 'Dull' Lake. The place has been purified — because it's a cowshed.

On Inspiration III

As happened very often in Kashmir, I was so engrossed in what Maharishi was saying that I forgot to attend to the tape recorder, and the earlier part of this conversation is not recorded. I had expressed the view that Maharishi had given out the knowledge too early, before most of us were ready for it — before our experience was ripe enough to absorb it. Maharishi then enunciated a very important principle which, it seems, governs these matters.

Maharishi: But some people brought some experiences [to our attention] and we had to come out with it [that is, with the knowledge to explain the experiences].

VK: That's what I was saying. Maharishi hasn't got time; he

---

276 Cowshed — see introduction to Kashmir section.
277 Dal Lake is probably one of the most beautiful lakes in the world but — perhaps because of the summer heat — it was not felt to be inspiring in the way that Lake Tahoe was.

can't wait for us laggards, so he has to give out the teaching and it is up to us to catch up with it.

Maharishi: But it has been marvellous, year after year, year after year — very beautiful. It was such a joy. Such great appreciation.

VK: All over the world you could see that love [for Maharishi growing], and in such a short time.

Maharishi: Something very good has happened.

VK: Sometimes on the courses when you were saying something profound it was just as if the whole audience were listening as one person.

Maharishi: The whole hall.

VK: I remember when you spoke about supreme knowledge at Lago di Braies. You said 'Don't take notes', and then gave out the teaching at one fell swoop.

Maharishi: One breath.

VK: For over half an hour, with no translations. And then Nikolaus [Blücher] translated, word for word [into German] — after half an hour of your speech. It was marvellous.

Maharishi: He did very well. And all his practice of translation came out of translating me all the time.

VK: I can't understand how he did it. He says he doesn't even try to translate. He just listens and somehow it comes out.[278]

Maharishi: The steps follow.

VK: The best translator, in any language, that I've ever come across.

Maharishi: Bring out the right meaning and then apply it to the lives of the people.

VK: It's a very practical thing.

Maharishi: Bring out this truth. This is what a builder does. He builds a house and then brings some people to live in it. It is not enough to build a house and leave it. (Laughter) Someone should enjoy it.

On Devotion

We had been talking of various Indian sages when I venture to bring the conversation to a personal level. Maharishi ignores the implications of my first remark, seems to misunderstand the second, and finally capitulates to the third by talking of his love for Guru Dev. Remarkable again is the completely impersonal way in which he looks upon his teaching, unable to explain how such perfection could manifest in so imperfect a world.

Maharishi tries to channel the conversation back to the

---

278 Prince Blücher says he just listens, takes in what Maharishi says in seed form, and then recreates it.

Sūtras but somehow is not allowed to drop the subject before he has told the story of the Gopīs' (milkmaids') alleged treatment of Lord Kṛishṇa's messenger, Uddhava, when the latter tried to console their loving hearts with mere knowledge.

VK: Maharishi, you never discuss experiences with someone [with some of the other sages]?

Maharishi: It's difficult to discuss. (Laughter) Our contribution is a system.

VK: I don't know if the level of Being [that is Maharishi's] has been reached elsewhere [by other sages], but the mind certainly hasn't been equalled.

Maharishi: System ... To systematize the whole thing on the level of understanding and experience — both — that is our contribution.

VK: There must be a great refinement of the relative, in some way.

Maharishi: Great refinement of the relative — systematic evolution. Refinement of the relative. And then [pure] awareness, and [refinement of] the nervous system — on both levels.

VK: No, I mean, there must have been great refinement of [your] mind and body in order for you to have been able to give out such a teaching — there must have been, otherwise ...

Maharishi: I think my love for Guru Dev must have been the instrument — some such thing. Otherwise it's just impossible to think of such perfection in this stress-ridden world. The whole atmosphere, everywhere, is so contaminated. And from that there comes out such beautiful brilliance, such perfection of the exposition of the Absolute!

VK: I wonder just how you became realized.

Maharishi: Don't know through what, but it is there. (Laughter) It's all Guru Dev's grace, his love, his knowledge, nearness to him. Because I ... what I lived most was Guru Dev's love. Love for him was the most dominating feature in my life. So I attribute it to that. Such perfection.

VK: Because that love in itself can eliminate the self, the lower self. When something like that dominates your life so completely, *you* are not any longer.

Maharishi: No. That overtakes. Something very marvellous about the whole situation. And all that in such a natural way, without any fuss about it. (Pauses) Now, let's do this [translation].

VK: Come down to the Brahma Sūtras.

JP: Come down, Vernon?

Maharishi: (Loud laughter) Come down to the book level.

JP: Coming down to Unity? Mere Unity?

VK: Yes, I think for the bhakta (devotee) it would be; he would say 'mere Unity'.

Maharishi: Yes. The shrutis [Gopīs] said to Uddhava, 'What are you talking about, [with your] gyāna (knowledge)? We are better off.' But they were shrutis, expressions of the absolute truth on the level of the Absolute itself.[279]

VK: Shrutis — they are the Gopīs, aren't they?

Maharishi: Lord Krishna sent Uddhava — Uddhava was a great man of knowledge, a gyānī. He said to Uddhava, 'Now go to the Gopīs in Vrindāvana and console them; give them some knowledge of Unity so that they may not feel my absence so much.' And Uddhava just enjoyed the command. As he went there, the Gopīs said, 'Oh, what are you talking about? Go back.'

VK: They threw him out?

Maharishi: Very beautiful. Second section [of Chapter One]. Shall we start?

Truth in Kali Yuga

Like the conversation on 'Shruti and Smriti', which also examines the possibility of cognizing and disseminating the truth in the dark age of Kali Yuga, this conversation begins on a light-hearted note. I was objecting to

---

279 The Gopīs are traditionally identified with the shrutis, or Vedic hymns.

some translation that Maharishi had proposed and told him that he would have to compose some sūtras of his own. As in the earlier conversation Maharishi replies on quite a different level. My rather pert remark takes his thoughts to that time of freshness and purity when the Brahma Sūtras were composed, and his voice takes on a softness that perhaps reflects the character of those days long past. Maharishi's voice is a very delicate instrument. It can change the whole mood of a discussion in a second.

The glimpse into the past is swiftly transformed into a vision of the future, a vision of a better, a spiritually regenerated world. Even if the signs of the coming Age of Enlightenment were not yet definite in 1969, they were there on the horizon. Transcendental Meditation, then as now, was seen as the answer to the problems of our age. We had been speaking of the first moon landing which had just taken place. I say, 'They will go up in their capsules to meditate.' Maharishi replies, 'The whole world should. We'll make it available.'

To make this wisdom available is Maharishi's mission. When he said in an early booklet, 'The Treasury and the Market', which I helped prepare, 'My mission is to regenerate the world', I thought to myself, 'How can he say such a thing? That lone man. It's impossible.' But since those far-off days great developments have taken place: the interest of the world's youth, the research of the scientists, the formulation of the Science of Creative Intelligence, the establishment of Maharishi International University and of Maharishi European Research University, the growing accomplishment of Maharishi's World Plan in all parts of the globe, the inauguration of the Dawn of the Age of Enlightenment, the establishment of capitals of the Age of Enlightenment — one seeming impossibility after another turning into reality.

And side by side with the outward expansion of the teaching there has been the inner growth of the meditators themselves which impelled Maharishi to clarify the different states of consciousness and to bring out the TM-Sidhi[®][280] programme, through which the field of all possibilities, pure consciousness, is being enlivened on both the individual and collective level. So many ordinary people are experiencing deep silence and growing fulfilment in what has been an age of greatest stress and strife, and by their very being are raising the consciousness of those around them.

And yet Maharishi seems able to look upon his work with great objectivity. When the present conversation took place, he had already worked many years, night and day, spreading the Transcendental Meditation technique in order to relieve stress and suffering and create a better world. Yet here he is, considering the possible fate of all his work, optimistically it is true, but quite dispassionately. He speaks softly and glowingly of his vision for a better world, even as he realizes that time will consume his work as it consumes all else. And when I ask him why he should labour for what is certain to be lost,

---

280 See footnote 290 in the appendix.

he replies, 'but the *joy* that we have'. It was brought home to me again that, however close he may be to us, Maharishi also inhabits another dimension. The ways of one who single-handedly dares to take on an age of darkness in order to transform it into one of light are not our ways, nor are his thoughts our thoughts.

On 8 January 1972, Maharishi inaugurated the World Plan for the teaching of the Transcendental Meditation technique and the Science of Creative Intelligence. It was not long afterwards, I think, that something to do with the World Plan caused him to go into peal upon peal of laughter. I commented that he must be the only originator of a world plan ever to have laughed about it. I certainly could not see any world conquerors of the past, temporal or spiritual, doing likewise. 'Because we are at a distance from it', was the reply. But it is not a cold distance. Maharishi's is a passionate dispassion, for there is always 'the joy that we have'.

Maharishi: Instead of just saying 'no', we could understand the sūtra in an affirmative, positive way.

VK: You will have to compose some sūtras of your own, won't you, Maharishi?

Maharishi: No, we don't have to. I think Vyāsa did these sūtras when the whole atmosphere was so serene and pure, and there was no stress in the world. It is not possible to frame the sūtras now — so much [stress]. It is enough that we can reach near

to the comprehensive meaning of it. That itself is enough of
an achievement today. It is very, very difficult to really cognize
the whole truth in these days. A few generations — parents
and parents and parents, and their systems becoming purer
and purer ...

VK: And perhaps by that time the truth will be lost. Purity
will be found and the truth will be lost. (Laughter)

Maharishi: And then Kali Yuga will continue.

VK: That's going to be the result of your labours. Labour for
the sake of loss.

Maharishi: No, but the joy that we have.

VK: Is it probable that people will become purer and in the
process of becoming purer they will lose the truth?

Maharishi: No, not in the process of becoming purer can the
truth be lost, because increasing purity means increasing truth.
Perhaps by the time many, many generations have passed, the
simplicity, the naturalness of it may be lost, and once it's lost,
it's lost. But if one generation could be created pure, it [the
truth] will continue for thousands of generations.

VK: But won't it be?

Maharishi: It can be.

VK: But in this age where there is so much stress and tension?

Maharishi: For one thing, there could be a national policy to have an hour's silence morning and evening. An hour of silence. All the buses, all the trains, everything stops. No movement. Aeroplanes don't take off. And then a national calm hour, morning and evening, for the whole country.

VK: What about the people who look after the electricity and water supply?

Maharishi: It could be put on an automatic basis — some automatic timing device. Everything should be purposely put off, everything stopped. And then the workers don't go to the factory at seven o'clock — only at nine o'clock, ten o'clock. They should have some life at home — in the freshness of the mornings.

VK: An ideal society, but all the people wouldn't meditate anyway.

Maharishi: All don't have to meditate. Just some small percentage in society will be enough.[281] (Maharishi tries to return to the translation) 'Itara-parāmarshāt sa ... '.[282]

---

281 This was borne out at the end of 1974 when it was found that in cities where the number of meditators had reached one per cent the crime rate decreased significantly.
282 BS 1.3.18.

APPENDIX

The Introduction in this volume reviews the teachings of His Holiness Maharishi Mahesh Yogi from 1957 to 1976, to give a context for the conversations published here. To complete the overview of Maharishi's work in the world, following is a brief summary of the highlights of his teaching from 1957 until 2008. A fuller year-by-year summary is on the website www. globalgoodnews.com. A detailed introduction to Maharishi's teaching can be found in the Foreword to *Science of Being and Art of Living* (new edition, Plume, 2001). These two sources were consulted in preparing the summary below.

Maharishi's Teaching, 1957–2008
A Glimpse of Fifty-One Years Around the World

1957 Maharishi's Year of Transcendental Meditation: Maharishi inaugurates the Spiritual Regeneration Movement on 31 December in Madras, India, to spiritually regenerate the world.

1958 Maharishi's Year of Spiritual Regeneration Movement: Maharishi formally inaugurates the worldwide Spiritual Regeneration Movement on 1 January 1958. • In the first three months of 1958, 25 centres are established throughout India and thousands of people learn Transcendental Meditation. • On 27 April Maharishi begins his first world tour.

1959 Maharishi's Year of Global Awakening: Maharishi establishes teaching of Transcendental Meditation in the United States and England.

1960 Maharishi's Year of Cosmic Consciousness: Maharishi explains the development of Cosmic Consciousness rising through the daily practice of Transcendental Meditation. • In London at

379

Caxton Hall, Maharishi inaugurates his Three-Year Plan (1960–1962).

1961 Maharishi's Year of Teacher Training: Maharishi begins to 'multiply himself' by conducting the first International Transcendental Meditation Teacher Training Course in Raam Nagar, Rishikesh, India. (Over 20,000 teachers have now been trained.)

1962 Maharishi's Year of Theory of the Absolute: Maharishi unfolds to scientists in New York his 'Theory of the Absolute' to enrich all fields of relative existence, and continues to train teachers of Transcendental Meditation in different countries, using audio technology.

1963 Maharishi's Year of the *Science of Being and Art of Living*: Maharishi's first book, *Science of Being and Art of Living*, is published.

1964 Maharishi's Year of God Consciousness: In response to growing experiences of higher states of consciousness, Maharishi explains experiences of Transcendental Meditation in terms of Transcendental Consciousness, Cosmic Consciousness, and God Consciousness.

1965 Maharishi's Year of Bhagavad-Gītā: Maharishi explains experiences of Transcendental Meditation in terms of the Vedic Principle of Action — Yogasthaḥ kuru karmāṇi: Established in Being, perform action — and continues his commentary on the first six chapters of the Bhagavad-Gītā.[283]

1966 Maharishi's Year of Academy of Meditation: Maharishi inaugurates the first International Academy of Meditation in Shankarāchārya Nagar, Rishikesh, India.

1967 Maharishi's Year of Unity Consciousness: Maharishi explains the nature of Unity Consciousness, the pinnacle of human

---

283 The final phases of the commentary were completed in Oslo, Norway, in 1966.

evolution, and inaugurates the first European Meditation Academy in Bremen, Germany.

1968 Maharishi's Year of Students: The Students International Meditation Society is founded in many countries, and for the first time video technology is used to record a course taught by Maharishi — a one-month course in Squaw Valley, U.S.A. • Maharishi begins his translation of and commentary on the Brahma Sūtra at Lake Tahoe, California, U.S.A.[284]

1969 Maharishi's Year of Supreme Knowledge: Maharishi continues his work on the Brahma Sūtra, the textbook of Vedānta.[285]

1970 Maharishi's Year of Scientific Research: The first scientific research on Transcendental Meditation is published. (More than 600 scientific research studies have now been conducted at over 250 universities and research institutes in 33 countries.)

1971 Maharishi's Year of Science of Creative Intelligence: Maharishi formulates the Science of Creative Intelligence (SCI)[286] and, in a series of international symposia, works with leading thinkers — including Buckminster Fuller, Nobel Laureate Melvin Calvin (chemistry), and U.S. General Franklin M. Davis — to develop connections between SCI and other disciplines. • Maharishi works with educators to bring 'education for enlightenment' to higher education, starting with the founding of Maharishi International University (now Maharishi University of Management) in the U.S.[287]

1972 Maharishi's Year of the World Plan: To give a practical

---

284 In the summer of 1968, Maharishi invited Vernon to Lake Tahoe, California, to assist with translation of and commentary on the Brahma Sūtra. The first conversations in this volume date from this time.

285 The second set of conversations in this volume took place in summer, 1969, in Kashmir, India.

286 See Introduction, section, 'The Unfoldment of Maharishi's Teaching'.

287 See conversation 'Time Will Catch this Wisdom'.

organizational basis for the teaching of Transcendental Meditation, Maharishi inaugurates the World Plan to bring knowledge of consciousness to people everywhere.

1973 Maharishi's Year of Action for the World Plan: Maharishi trains over 2,000 teachers of Transcendental Meditation in La Antilla, Spain, and establishes 2,000 World Plan Centres to offer courses in Transcendental Meditation and the Science of Creative Intelligence.

1974 Maharishi's Year of Achievement of the World Plan:[288] The Maharishi Effect is discovered: one per cent of the population of a city practising Transcendental Meditation results in an increase of positive trends in society.[289]

1975 Maharishi's Year of the Dawn of the Age of Enlightenment: • On the basis of the first Maharishi Effect studies, Maharishi inaugurates the Dawn of the Age of Enlightenment: *'Through the window of science, we see the Dawn of the Age of Enlightenment.'* • Maharishi holds six-month Age of Enlightenment Courses to deepen experiences of higher states of consciousness and establishes MERU — Maharishi European Research University — to conduct research on these experiences. • Maharishi School of the Age of Enlightenment is established in Fairfield, Iowa, U.S.A., to bring Consciousness-Based[SM] education to elementary and secondary school students.

1976 Maharishi's Year of Government: To accelerate evolution of the individual to enlightenment and purify world consciousness, Maharishi introduces the Transcendental Meditation-Sidhi

---

288 During 1974 and 1975, Maharishi commented on the original manuscript for this volume, read to him by Vernon. These comments are included as additional explanations, postscripts, or footnotes.

289 This 1974 study, the first experimental evidence of Maharishi's teaching about collective consciousness, was the first of over 50 studies on the Maharishi Effect, many of which have been published in leading journals.

programme including Yogic Flying, based on the Yoga Sūtra of Maharishi Patanjali.[290] • Maharishi inaugurates the World Government of the Age of Enlightenment with sovereignty in the domain of consciousness.

1977 Maharishi's Year of Ideal Society: In his Ideal Society Campaign Maharishi sends groups of Yogic Flyers to 108 countries to create an effect of coherence in collective consciousness.

1978 Maharishi's Year of Invincibility to Every Nation: Scientists discover the Extended Maharishi Effect: the square root of one per cent of a population practising Maharishi's Transcendental Meditation-Sidhi programme including Yogic Flying is sufficient to create coherence in collective consciousness. Maharishi sends groups of Yogic Flyers to bring the benefit of this effect to international trouble spots.

1979 Maharishi's Year of All Possibilities: Maharishi develops practical programmes to create coherence in collective consciousness: the Global Super Radiance programme, to maximize the influence of sattwa (coherence) in the world, and the first World Peace Assembly, with several thousand participants, in Amherst, U.S.A.

1980 Maharishi's Year of Pure Knowledge, the Veda: Maharishi

---

290 The Yoga Sūtra, like the Brahma Sūtra, is the text of one of the six classical systems of Indian philosophy, also known as Darshana — see Introduction, section, 'The Brahma Sūtra'. Whereas the Transcendental Meditation technique allows the mind to dive inward to experience the settled, silent state of pure consciousness, the Transcendental Meditation-Sidhi programme, including Yogic Flying, develops the ability to think and act from this settled state. Inner silence is thus integrated with activity — even the dynamic activity of Yogic Flying, in which the body lifts off the ground in a series of 'hops'. This practice maximizes coherent brain functioning and mind-body coordination, producing waves of inner bliss and exhilaration. Ancient texts describe the ability to fly and move through the air at will as a result of perfection on the Yogic Flying technique.

brings to light his Apaurusheya Bhāshya (uncreated commentary) of Ṛk Veda, and extends his teaching into the area of preventative health care by revitalizing the ancient science of Āyur-Veda[291] — knowledge of life. • During the First International Vedic Science Course in New Delhi, with 4,000 participants, Maharishi works with Vedic Experts — including Brihaspati Dev Triguna, president of the All-India Āyurvedic Congress — to unfold understanding and experience of the structure and applications of Veda and Vedic Literature.

1981 Maharishi's Year of Vedic Science: In his Vedic Science and Technology, Maharishi organizes the centuries-old scattered Vedic Literature as a complete science of consciousness, identifying the sequential sounds of Veda and the Vedic Literature as impulses of self-referral consciousness, the fundamental structure of natural law.

1982 Maharishi's Year of Natural Law: Maharishi establishes Vedic principles and programmes for bringing life in accord with natural law.

1983 Maharishi's Year of the Unified Field: Working with physicists, Maharishi relates the self-referral field of Transcendental Consciousness to unified field theories of physics. • Inspired by Maharishi, the 'Taste of Utopia' assembly is held at Maharishi International University, Fairfield, Iowa, U.S.A. — the first assembly of 7,000 Yogic Flyers, creating the Global Maharishi Effect.

1984 Maharishi's Year of Unified Field Based Civilization: Maharishi plans large World Peace Assemblies around the world.

1985 Maharishi's Year of Unified Field Based Education: Maharishi formulates a system of Vedic Education based on development of consciousness, and begins to structure courses on

---

291 Āyur-Veda — one of the four Upaveda (subordinate Veda) in the Vedic Literature.

Vedic Science and Technology, including Yoga, Yagya,[292] Jyotish,[293] and Āyur-Veda.

1986 Maharishi's Year of Perfect Health: Maharishi implements his World Plan for Perfect Health to create a disease-free society and bring self-sufficiency in health care to every nation through the Vedic approach to health.

1987 Maharishi's Year of World Peace: In the first public demonstration of Transcendental Meditation-Sidhi Yogic Flying, in Washington, D.C., U.S.A., Maharishi presents his programme to Create World Peace to the public and the media. • Maharishi inaugurates a Global Festival of Music for World Peace, presenting Maharishi Gandharva Veda®,[294] the melodies of nature, for balance in the individual and society.

1988 Maharishi's Year of Achieving World Peace: In his Master Plan to Create Heaven on Earth, Maharishi unfolds programmes for outer reconstruction of villages, towns, and cities, to complement inner development of consciousness. This includes rural development and urban renewal, through construction of stress-free, pollution-free communities, based on Maharishi Sthāpatya Veda®,[295] the Vedic science of architecture and design.

1989 Maharishi's Year of Heaven on Earth: Maharishi implements his Master Plan to Create Heaven on Earth.

---

292 Yagya refers to ancient Vedic procedures to restore balance in nature.

293 Jyotish is the Vedic science of astrology, one of the six Vedanga (limbs of the Veda) in the Vedic Literature.

294 and 295 Maharishi Gandharva Veda and Maharishi Sthāpatya Veda are two of the four Upaveda (subordinate Veda) of the Vedic Literature, which also include Āyur-Veda for the field of health (see 1980). The fourth Upaveda is Dhanur-Veda, the science and art of defence. Maharishi worked with Vedic experts to revitalize each branch of the Vedic Literature in its completeness, in light of full development of consciousness.

1990 Maharishi's Year of Alliance with Nature's Government: Maharishi offers his knowledge and programmes to government, and develops courses applying natural law for perfection in every profession.

1991 Maharishi's Year of Support of Nature's Government: Maharishi invites governments to implement programmes for growth of individual and collective consciousness, to gain support of nature for national administration.

1992 Maharishi's Year of the Constitution of the Universe: Maharishi brings to light Ṛk Veda as the Constitution of the Universe, the totality of nature's intelligence in every grain of creation. • In 1991–2, two hundred Maharishi Vidyā Mandir Schools, with nearly 100,000 students, are established in India.

1993 Maharishi's Year of Administration through Natural Law — Raam Raj: Maharishi starts a programme for natural law-based administration to bring a nourishing influence to every government. • Four thousand Yogic Flyers from 64 countries create coherence in Washington, D.C., U.S.A. — the crime rate decreases 24 per cent.

1994 Maharishi's Year of Discovery of Veda in Human Physiology: Maharishi works with Professor Tony Nader, M.D., Ph.D., to locate the 40 branches of Veda and Vedic Literature in the structure and function of human physiology. • Maharishi focuses on implementing his programmes in the military, through a 'Prevention Wing' — groups of Yogic Flyers — to prevent birth of an enemy. • Maharishi's book *Maharishi Vedic University: An Introduction* is published — the first of a series of books published over the next four years.

1995 Maharishi's Year of Silence: Maharishi continues to develop educational programmes for India and other countries with the founding of Maharishi Vedic University — Maharishi Mahesh Yogi Vedic Vishwa-Vidyālaya — in the state of Madhya

Pradesh, India, and Maharishi University of Management in the United States, Japan, Holland, and Russia.

1996 Maharishi's Year of Awakening: All Maharishi Universities teach one basic subject — Ātmā, the Self, the field of Total Knowledge.

1997 Maharishi's Year of Global Administration through Natural Law: Maharishi establishes Global Administration through Natural Law with 12 Time-Zone Capitals, to implement knowledge of problem-free administration.

1998 Maharishi's Second Year of Global Administration through Natural Law: Maharishi establishes a network of eight satellites, broadcasting in 18 languages through Maharishi Channel, Maharishi Veda Vision, and Maharishi Open University.[296]

1999 Maharishi's Third Year of Global Administration through Natural Law: Maharishi designs the Perfect Man Course to raise the individual to higher levels of evolution, on the basis of practical knowledge of his own Self.

2000 Maharishi's Fourth Year of Global Administration through Natural Law: • Maharishi applies knowledge of Vedic Organic Agriculture to establish his programme to Eliminate Poverty through development of unused agricultural lands. • Maharishi inaugurates his Global Country of World Peace, to create an influence of non-violence in world consciousness, and inspires formation of the World Federation of Traditional Kings to awaken the parental role of leaders of traditional cultures to maintain peace in their areas.

2001 Maharishi's Year of Global Country of World Peace: Maharishi launches a global initiative for permanent world peace

---

296 See the conversation 'Shruti and Smṛiti', in which Maharishi refers to the possibilities offered for spreading knowledge quickly using modern means of communication.

in response to the outburst of terrorism in the U.S. • Programmes are designed to create a permanent influence of peace from India through performance of Yoga and Yagya by thousands of Vedic Paṇḍits.

2002 Maharishi's Year of Raam Mudrā: As part of his programme to alleviate poverty, Maharishi designs the global development currency Raam Mudrā. • Maharishi conducts one-month Enlightenment Conferences to hasten experiences of enlightenment, and begins a five-year series of weekly global press conferences, broadcast live via satellite and webcast.

2003 Maharishi's Year of Ideal Government — Raam Rāj: Maharishi establishes the largest group of Vedic Paṇḍits in India, to create world peace through Vedic recitation and Vedic Yagya, on the basis of their group practice of the Transcendental Meditation and TM-Sidhi programme. • Maharishi plans to train administrators of every government to engage the intelligence and energy of natural law, for 'Automation in Administration'.

2004 Maharishi's Year of Peace Palaces: Maharishi guides plans for construction of Peace Palaces worldwide. • Maharishi addresses conferences in the U.S. on Consciousness-Based education for developing total brain functioning for the enlightenment of every student. • Maharishi establishes the Parliament of World Peace, and begins training Raam Rāj Administrators to administer from the level of enlightenment.

2005 Maharishi's Year of Golden Jubilee: This year celebrates the fiftieth anniversary of Maharishi leaving the Valley of the Saints in Uttar-Kāshī, India, to bring the light of the Himālayas to the world. • Maharishi inaugurates the Dawn of Sat-Yuga,[297] in

---

297 In the traditional Indian cycles of time, Sat-Yuga is the era of greatest freshness of the laws of nature — see the conversation 'Shruti and Smṛiti', in which Maharishi comments on the possibility of 'the sunshine coming through the clouds of Kali Yuga' (Kali Yuga is the era of least freshness and vitality of the laws of nature).

MERU, Holland 21-25 July, and inspires builders to reconstruct the world applying principles of Maharishi Sthāpatya Veda architecture and design. • Maharishi inaugurates a programme to establish Maharishi Vedic Universities, Colleges, and Schools in 3,000 cities, and completes the first two Raam Rāj Administrator Training Courses.

2006 Maharishi's Year of Reconstruction for the Whole World to Be Heaven on Earth — First Year of Sat-Yuga: The World Capital of Peace is inaugurated in the Brahmasthān (centre) of India, where Maharishi plans to create a permanent group of 8,000 peace-creating experts, with further groups across India where Peace Colonies — each to be called Brahmanand Saraswati Nagar — will be established. • Maharishi conducts a World Peace Assembly in Holland, with 400 practitioners of Yogic Flying, as a model for similar groups worldwide, and inaugurates and guides the Invincible America Assembly at Maharishi University of Management, Fairfield, Iowa, and in Washington, D.C., U.S.A. • Maharishi launches an initiative to establish 'Invincibility Schools' in thirty countries, and guides development of the Vedic Medicine curriculum.

2007 Maharishi's Year of Capital of Global Raam Rāj: Maharishi focuses on establishing a group of 16,000 Vedic Paṇḍits at the Brahmasthān of India. • In inaugurating Administration through Silence, Maharishi states that the goals of his Spiritual Regeneration Movement are fulfilled, and expresses his desire to fully unfold gyan shakti (the power of Total Knowledge) to support kriyā shakti (the power of action).

2008 Maharishi's Year of Invincibility — Global Raam Rāj: • Maharishi inspires construction of Towers of Invincibility in 192 countries, as permanent homes of Maharishi's Vedic wisdom. • Maharishi founds the Brahmanand Saraswati Trust, to perpetually support groups of peace-creating Vedic Paṇḍits throughout India and around the world. *'Express my delight for all the millennia* *to come that the world is going to be a happy world. All Glory to Guru Dev. Brahmanand Saraswati Trust is going to take the lighted lamp every morning and every night that is going to come. The future of the world is bright, and that is my delight. Jai Guru Dev.'* — Maharishi, 11 January 2008.

Bibliography

Blakney, Raymond (trans.). *Meister Eckhart*, Harper and Row, New York, 1941.

Eliot, T. S. 'Burnt Norton', *Four Quartets*, Faber and Faber, London, 1950.

Gokhale, Dinkar Vishnu (ed.). *The Bhagavad-Gītā with the Commentary of Sri Sankarācārya*, second revised edition, Poona Oriental Series No. 1, Oriental Book Agency, Poona, 1950.

Hagelin, John. *Manual for a Perfect Government*, Maharishi University of Management Press, U.SA., 1998.

Heimann, Betty. *Studien zur Eigenart Indischen Denkens*, Mohr Siebeck,Tübingen, 1930.

Heimann, Betty. *Facets of Indian Thought*, London, Allen and Unwin, 1964.

Inauguration of the Dawn of the Age of Enlightenment, West Germany, MIU Press, 1975.

Katz, Vernon. 'Some Basic Insights of the Present Revival', *Creative Intelligence*, 1, London, SRM Foundation of Great Britain, 1972.

Maharishi Mahesh Yogi. *Science of Being and Art of Living*, International SRM Publications, 1966.

Maharishi Mahesh Yogi. *Maharishi Mahesh Yogi on the Bhagavad-Gita: A New Translation and Commentary with Sanskrit Text, Chapters 1 to 6*, Penguin Books, 1969.

Maharishi Mahesh Yogi. *Maharishi Vedic University: Introduction*, Holland, Maharishi Vedic University Press, 1994.

Maharishi Mahesh Yogi. *Celebrating Perfection in Education: Dawn of Total Knowledge*, Holland, Maharishi Vedic University Press, 1997.

Maharishi International University, Science of Creative Intelligence Teacher Training Course, Lesson 23, 'The Seven States of Consciousness', 1972.

Maharishi International University Catalogue, 1974/75, Los Angeles, Maharishi International University Press, 1974.

Maslow, Abraham. *The Psychology of Science*, Chicago, Gateway Edition, 1969.

Monier-Williams, Monier. *A Sanskrit-English Dictionary*, Oxford University Press, 1899.

Mukerji, P. N. (trans.). *Yoga Philosophy of Patañjali, containing his Yoga Aphorisms with the commentary of Vyāsa in original Sanskrit, and annotations thereon with copious hints on the practice of Yoga*, by Swami Hariharānanda Āraṇya, rendered into English by P. N. Mukerji, University of Calcutta, 1963.

Nader, Tony. *Human Physiology: Expression of Veda and the Vedic Literature* (4th ed.), Holland, Maharishi Vedic University Press, 1994.

Orme-Johnson, David W., and John T. Farrow (eds). *Scientific Research on the Transcendental Meditation Program: Collected Papers, Volume One*, West Germany, MERU Press, 1976.*

Sastracarya, Bhargav Sastri (ed.). *Brahma Sūtra Sankara Bhāsya, with commentaries of Bhamati, Kalpataru and Parimala, edited with notes, etc., by Anantkrisna Sastri*, re-edited by Bhargav Sastri Sastracarya, Bombay, Pandurang Jawaji, 1938.

Selye, Hans. *The Stress of Life*, New York, McGraw-Hill, 1956.

---

*At the time of publication of this book, five volumes of *Scientific Research on the Transcendental Meditation Program: Collected Papers* are available, with volumes six and seven in preparation.

About the Author

Vernon Katz is a trustee and a visiting professor at Maharishi University of Management, Fairfield, Iowa, U.S.A. He earned a first class honours degree and a doctorate in philosophy from Oxford University. His thesis on Indian philosophy was supervised by Dr. Sarvepalli Radhakrishnan, the eminent philosopher who became India's second president. In the early 1960s Vernon assisted Maharishi Mahesh Yogi with his translation of and commentary on the Bhagavad-Gita, which has sold over one million copies. He is currently working on another volume of conversations with Maharishi and on a translation of the Upanishads.